Additional praise for *Dream Travelers:*

"Roger Lohmann's *Dream Travelers* is a highly promising book with strong potential to attract readers in cultural anthropology and related fields. The collection is well-organized, with first-rate contributors and a clear sense of other research in the general arena of dreams and anthropology. Particularly significant is the focus on the theme of journeys, movement, and travelling. I think Lohmann is onto something here, and other scholars in psychology, religious studies, and anthropology will be interested in what he and his collaborators have to say."

—Kelly Bulkeley, The Graduate Theological Union

"My lasting impression following reading this fine collection of anthropological essays is of the dream as an alternative mode of cognition—as an important means of apprehending the world and engaging with others. Based on original fieldwork, each essay contributes rich ethnographic data to reveal the interaction between the apparently private inner realm of dreams, and shared, cultural phantasy systems. Lived culture emerges from this dynamic interplay. For all those with a serious interest in dreams, this book is a 'must.' Furthermore, if there still remain any social or cultural anthropologists who feel that dreaming is a topic better left to the psychoanalyst, or dismissed entirely, this important collection will surely convince them otherwise."

—Michele Stephen, Associate Professor of History,
La Trobe University, Australia

"*Dream Travelers* represents the best kind of collaborative anthropology: Detailed ethnography by experts in particular societies brought together to create a large and impressive theoretical vision. An important read for scholars who work outside as well as in Oceania, this volume will provide a much needed push forward for anthropological thinking about dreams."

—Susan Sered, Center for the Study
of World Religions, Harvard University

"Returning to one of the foundational problems in anthropology, the authors of *Dream Travelers* explore the cultural significance of dreaming in a fascinating journey through Melanesia, aboriginal Australia, and Indonesia. Powerfully evocative, the chapters are a pleasure to read in their own right while the collection as a whole propels our understanding of dreams in important new directions. *Dream Travelers* makes significant contributions to comparative ethnography, the anthropology of religion, and the psychology of dreaming."

—John Barker, Associate Professor of Anthropology,
University of British Columbia

Dream Travelers

Sleep Experiences and Culture
in the Western Pacific

Roger Ivar Lohmann

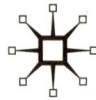

DREAM TRAVELERS
Copyright © Roger Ivar Lohmann, 2003.
All rights reserved. No part of this book may be used or reproduced in any manner whatsoever without written permission except in the case of brief quotations embodied in critical articles or reviews.

First published 2003 by
PALGRAVE MACMILLAN™
175 Fifth Avenue, New York, N.Y. 10010 and
Houndmills, Basingstoke, Hampshire, England RG21 6XS.
Companies and representatives throughout the world.

PALGRAVE MACMILLAN is the global academic imprint of the Palgrave Macmillan division of St. Martin's Press, LLC and of Palgrave Macmillan Ltd. Macmillan® is a registered trademark in the United States, United Kingdom and other countries. Palgrave is a registered trademark in the European Union and other countries.

ISBN 1-4039-6322-3 hardback
ISBN 1-4039-6330-4 paperback

Library of Congress Cataloging-in-Publication Data
Dream travelers : sleep experiences and culture in the western Pacific / edited by Roger Ivar Lohmann ; contributors, Jane Goodale . . . [et al.] ; afterword by Waud Kracke.
    p. cm.
  "Result of sessions at two meetings of the Association for Social Anthropology in Oceania"—Pref.
  Includes bibliographical references and index.
  ISBN 1-4039-6322-3—ISBN 1-4039-6330-4 (pbk.)
  1. Dreams—Melanesia—Cross-cultural studies. 2. Dreams—Australia—Cross-cultural studies. 3. Dream interpretation—Cross-cultural studies. 4. Ethnology—Melanesia. 5. Australian aborigines—Social life and customs. I. Lohmann, Roger Ivar, 1962- II. Goodale, Jane C. (Jane Carter), 1926- III. Association for Social Anthropology in Oceania. Meetings.

GN668.D74 2003
154.6'3'099—dc21

                                                                        2003041436

A catalogue record for this book is available from the British Library.

Design by Letra Libre, Inc.

First edition: September 2003
10 9 8 7 6 5 4 3 2 1

Printed in the United States of America.

Contents

List of Illustrations		vii
Preface		ix
1	Introduction Dream Travels and Anthropology *Roger Ivar Lohmann*	1
2	Dreaming and the Defeat of Charisma: Disconnecting Dreams from Leadership among the Urapmin of Papua New Guinea *Joel Robbins*	19
3	Dreaming and Ghosts among the Hagen and Duna of the Southern Highlands, Papua New Guinea *Pamela J. Stewart and Andrew J. Strathern*	43
4	Dreamscapes: Transcending the Local in Initiation Rites among the Ngaing of Papua New Guinea *Wolfgang Kempf and Elfriede Hermann*	61
5	Ambrymese Dreams and the Mardu Dreaming *Robert Tonkinson*	87
6	"This Is Good Country. We Are Good Dreamers": Dreams and Dreaming in the Australian Western Desert *Sylvie Poirier*	107
7	Dreams, Agency, and Traditional Authority in Northeast Arnhem Land *Ian Keen*	127
8	Tiwi Island Dreams *Jane C. Goodale*	149
9	The Cultural and Intersubjective Context of Dream Remembrance and Reporting: Dreams, Aging, and the Anthropological Encounter in Toraja, Indonesia *Douglas Hollan*	169

| 10 | Supernatural Encounters of the Asabano in Two Traditions and Three States of Consciousness
Roger Ivar Lohmann | 189 |
| 11 | *Afterword*
Beyond the Mythologies:
A Shape of Dreaming
Waud Kracke | 211 |

About the Contributors   237
Index   241

List of Illustrations

Cover Dowasi, an Asabano man, crossing the Om River. Photo: Roger Lohmann

Map The Western Pacific Peoples Discussed in this Volume. Map drawn by Roger Lohmann ... 7

Plates

1. Urapmin often report dreams in church services such as this one. Photo: Joel Robbins. ... 18
2. Aluni, 1998. In a space (*kene kulu kama*, "dead cordyline garden") within a sweet potato garden, men and boys thatch the cover for the new grave of an old man who has recently died. Other graves stand nearby. After a death has occurred, women's mourning songs are intended to guide the spirit (*tini*) of the deceased person to mountain caves where it will join the other dead spirits. The dead may still appear to their living kin in dreams with warnings or advice about the future. Photo: Pamela J. Stewart and Andrew Strathern. ... 42
3. "Now it was like I was a child of the Whites." Photo: Elfriede Hermann, 1989. ... 60
4. Members of the local Presbyterian evangelical "team" sing as villagers enter church in the village of Ulei for a team service aimed at the elimination of sorcery and magic from Southeast Ambrym. Photo: Robert Tonkinson, 1973. ... 86
5. Two Mardu *Maparn* with a novice, attempting to diagnose his sickness. Photo: Robert Tonkinson. ... 100
6. Budja Budja Napangarti during a women's ceremony. Photo: Sylvie Poirier. ... 106

7	Dancing "Morning Star," at Milingimbi, 1975. Photo: Ian Keen.	126
8	Rachel Puruntatamer, chief mourner at grave/memorial ritual, painted to disguise herself from the ghost of the deceased. Photo: Jane Goodale.	148
9	The construction of an effigy of the dead called a tau tau, associated with nene' spirits, who often visit people in their dreams. Photo: Douglas Hollan.	168
10	Adiabo and Jim Alosi, some of whose supernatural encounters are described here, and Robert, a boy knowledgeable in traditional myths. Photo: Roger Lohmann.	188

Preface

Out-of-body experiences are not rare occurrences that happen only to a select few. They are the nightly adventures of virtually every person, and while some regard dreams as fantasies, ethnological research has shown that members of most societies consider them to literally be soul-journeys. The dreamscapes upon which dream-selves leave dream-footprints are visited as real places in a universe that anthropologists recognize to be imagined in accordance with cultural ideals. Dreamlands are even more refined to match the imagination than the physical earth perceived in waking life, to which people also add cultural constructs. Though they are often experienced as uncannily real, dream travels lead to murky corners inside of minds which have been culturally informed. This collection of essays documents variations on this theme—the standard human explanation for dream perceptions, found in societies that are culturally very different from one another. Each of the authors offers ethnographic and theoretical contributions on the implications of this ubiquitous understanding of dreaming, including the political, cosmological, and psychological uses of the belief that dreams represent actual travels.

The chapters collected here are the result of sessions at two meetings of the Association for Social Anthropology in Oceania. At the first, a working session held in Hilo, Hawai'i in February 1999, Florence Brunois, Jane Goodale, Doug Hollan, Ian Keen, Roger Lohmann, Jeannette Mageo, Sylvie Poirier, Joel Robbins, Pamela Stewart and Andrew Strathern, Jolene Stritecky, and Bob Tonkinson presented pre-circulated papers. Our ensuing discussions covered a vast range of perspectives, from dreams as a casual topic of conversation to dreams as divine revelations. We discussed the need to distinguish between the experience of the dream and the sharing of dream narratives. In considering the experience, we agreed that one must examine the range of dream forms: how dream images are perceived, interpreted and remembered. At the level of dream sharing, questions of circumstance and motivation come into play. One must ask when, why, and with whom people share their dreams. Local theories of what dreams are and how to interpret their imagery are variable from one society to the next. Some traditions consider dreams to be random, meaningless thoughts. However, there is a widespread tendency to perceive dreams as at least significant, and at most as experiences of equal or greater validity to those of waking life. Agency issues are also important—local theories vary from understanding dreams as happening to passive dreamers to dreams as something that dreamers actively do. After reflecting on these topics, those participants wishing to continue with the project developed and revised their papers for a second meeting the following year.

In February 2000, in Vancouver, British Columbia, Jane Goodale, Doug Hollan, Wolfgang Kempf and Elfriede Hermann, Roger Lohmann, Sylvie Poirier, Joel Robbins, and Bob Tonkinson shared revised papers, as well as those by Ian Keen and Pamela Stewart and Andrew Strathern, who were unable to attend. At this symposium, our conversations turned to dreams' role in transforming, transcending, and traveling. We also focused more on the political uses of dreams to reflect, limit, and extend power. We considered the relationship between ethnographer and informant, which influences what sorts of dream narratives are produced.

Those who stayed with the project commented on each others' papers, and revised their own again to appear as contributions to this volume. We are fortunate to include an afterword by Waud Kracke. I discussed the book project with him at the 1999 meeting of the American Anthropological Association in Chicago. He graciously agreed to read the chapters and offer his comments.

Many people have aided this work through their enthusiasm and support, including the contributors, participants in the first session who are pursuing other venues, and others who contributed to our discussions at the meetings, including Ann Chowning, Maurice Godelier, and Maria Lepowsky. In preparing this manuscript, I had the benefit of an anonymous reviewer's comments and many editorial suggestions from Heather M.-L. Miller.

—*Roger Ivar Lohmann*

Chapter 1
Introduction

Dream Travels and Anthropology

Roger Ivar Lohmann

Sleep is a doorway, and dreams are roads and destinations. In dreams, people visit other places, change the shape of reality, and gain insight into causes and connections secreted beneath the cosmos of waking life. In spite of the diversity of ways culture influences and extracts meanings from dreams, everywhere we see that at least some dreams are understood to be a means of actually traveling across spatial, temporal, and spiritual dimensions. This ubiquitous belief is apparently owed to the common dream experience of the self in motion, being and doing what it cannot in alert consciousness. In this volume, we consider the significance of dreams as an experience of transportation for eleven peoples in Melanesia, Aboriginal Australia, and Indonesia.

Dream experiences of movement seem more profound than waking travel because of the potential for sudden shifts in scenarios, personal identities, and places within which these seem to be occurring. These characteristics are not learned, but reflect the electrochemical foundation of dreaming, and biological research indicates that "the illusion of movement is common to all dreams" (Hobson 1999:40). How the culturally informed mind shapes and interprets this roller-coaster ride is of great interest to ethnologists (Jedrej and Shaw 1992a; Shulman and Stroumsa 1999; Tedlock 1987b; von Grunebaum and Callois 1966). The increased mobility experienced in dreams has encouraged many peoples to develop and pass on the idea that dream traveling is superior to many waking travels and experiences. For in dreams people everywhere experience phenomena like flight, teleportation, and transformation of familiar places and people, all while surrounded by a mist of emotional significance and an uncritical acceptance of bizarre dream situations. This makes dreams appear to depict scenes of external reality and have meanings that require decipherment. Sleep travels stir imaginations to develop means of using dreaming as a vehicle to satisfy human desires.

The Anthropology of Dream Travel

In this introduction I will discuss anthropological wrangling with perceived travel in dreaming. Tedlock (1987a; 1991; 1994), Bourguignon (1972), D'Andrade (1961), Jedrej and Shaw (1992b), Kennedy and Langness (1981), and Kilborne (1981) provide helpful reviews of the anthropology of dreaming in general, and Bulkeley (2001) samples articles from a variety of disciplinary perspectives.

Dreaming has interested anthropologists since the field's inception, and awareness of the centrality of perceived travel in dreams goes back to the earliest and most famous anthropological theory involving dreaming. Tylor (1877 [1871]) saw dreaming as pivotal in the origin of the idea of spirits because in dreams we can see the dead living again, we can interact with people whom we know to be far away, and we can move about while the body remains immobile. While the absolute origin of spirit beliefs cannot of course be known, ethnographers do repeatedly find that many peoples understand what they see on dream travels as evidence for the existence of spirits (e.g., Lohmann 2000; Stephen 1979; Stewart 1997; Tuzin 1989). Others emphasize that dreaming is central to religious practice, as in many Native North American traditions (e.g., Irwin 1994). These religious uses of dreams depend on the notion that real travel takes place in dreams, either of the soul to the spirits, or of the spirits to the soul.

An empirical report of this kind regarding Polynesia is found in one of Firth's earlier articles (1934). He reports that Tikopia Islanders understand dreams to be the movements of the wandering soul, which after death can also appear in the dreams of others. Sixty-six years later, in Firth's last full article (2001:17), he describes a man who dreamed of his son who was working on another island, and because of this became convinced that the young man had died. Two days later, word arrived that he had. In this case, the dream image was interpreted as the result of a journey not of the dreamer's ego, but of the dream alter, traversing the sea to take leave of his father.

In Melanesia, Codrington (1891:208–209) reported shamans in what is now Vanuatu who used dreaming to travel in order to converse with the spirits in their own realms. Upon receiving payment, they slept so that their souls might go where their patients fell ill or to the land of the dead to persuade the spirit who was supposed to have caused the sickness to relent. Elsewhere I review reports of similar shamanic dream journeys in Papua New Guinea (Lohmann in press). Dreaming enables us to experience what appear to be travels to supernatural worlds and is certainly implicated in the ubiquity of religion (see this volume, Kracke Chapter 12).

The influx of ideas developed in psychology, most obviously those of Freud (1965 [1900]), influenced and encouraged anthropological investigations of dreams (Paul 1989). Rivers (1923), whose work spanned both fields, devoted sustained attention to the topic consequent to his experience treating psychological patients in Britain and conducting a field survey in Melanesia. He wrote in critical reaction against the universality of Freud's wish fulfillment theory, giving dreams' apparent problem-solving function greater notice. His colleague Seligman (1923) participated in the expedition to Melanesia and issued a call for more ethnological research on dreaming.

Seligman's student, Lincoln, wrote the first anthropological volume on the significance of dreams in societies around the world, with a focus on Native North America. Lincoln (1935:27) observes that peoples holding the widespread notion that dreams represent soul wanderings do not necessarily develop it as a theory. Rather, it follows straightforwardly from the experience of movement in dreams. Williams (1936:30) similarly found that while many Papuan peoples explained dreaming as the departure of one's spirit, others appeared not to have developed an explicit theory of dreaming, but nevertheless mentioned that spirits can visit dreamers, implying an implicit theory of dreaming as spirit travel.

The title of this volume is inspired by Malinowski's (1984 [1922]) classic *Argonauts of the Western Pacific*. The *kula* traders described in that work journeyed over sea and land with hope and anticipation in a quest for valuables, adventure, and fame. Likewise, the dream travelers we describe here ply the dimensions of possibility, experiencing adventures and accomplishments. As the *kula* traders attach profound value to shell jewelry, many Pacific dream travelers consider what they experience in dreams to be deeply significant and useful, and sometimes return to waking life with culturally valuable new knowledge and power. In the mainly egalitarian societies that we describe, power acquired in dream travels is often used to benefit the entire community's relationship with the spiritual world. Though we see variation in the ways in which the fruits of dream journeys are distributed, in every single society we describe, dream travels may be conducted in a quest for real valuables. As Eggan (1952) observed, dream scenarios reflect the dreamer's culture. Likewise, the dream worlds of these peoples impinge upon all elements of life, including their political, religious, ecological, and kin relationships.

The waking journeys of peoples in the Western Pacific are often inspired and justified by reconnaissance dreams that seem to predict or postdict the future. Malinowski begins a discussion of Trobrianders' dreams by noting that they gave dreams little thought (1951 [1927]:92). However, on the very next page he mentions that those undertaking *kula* expeditions ideally have dreams of successful voyages in order to have confidence in their undertaking. As their own successful dream travels indicate productive waking journeys, magicians cast a spell to induce dreams in trading partners or potential lovers, causing them to desire the wished-for exchange.

It would seem that rather than being insignificant, dreams had so great a supernatural power for Trobrianders of Malinowski's day that they may have downplayed their significance to protect themselves. This occurred in Stephen's (1995) masterful study of dreaming among the Mekeo of the Papuan Coast. Her inquiries about dreams were initially rebuked because it is in dreams that people send their "hidden selves" out of their bodies to enact sorcery, erotic adventures, and other secret activities that underlie a veneer of orderly society. And, as Lattas (1993:64–65) observes, the bush Kaliai of New Britain believe that dream flight enables people to learn about hidden truths—and Kaliai dream travels appeared to reveal that whites were cannibalizing blacks! In some societies, dream travels guide the actions and motives of waking life as much as waking life influences dreams (this volume, Lohmann Chapter 10).

Many have pointed out that anthropologists have access to others' dreams only through narratives (e.g., Charsley 1992:153). Whatever we say about dream experiences is based on indirect knowledge, filtered through multiple interpretations and reformulations by the dreamer, translated into a linguistic performance presented for a specific reason to a particular audience, and subsequently heard and evaluated by hearers, including the researcher. Narratives are heavily filtered by perceptual and cultural biases, and shaped into conventions of storytelling. Tedlock (1991:161) points out that while dreaming itself is private and has never been recorded as it occurs, dream sharing is public and necessarily happens after the dream is over. However, not all peoples feel secure in the privacy of dream travels, believing that they are interacting with others (this volume, Poirier Chapter 6).

The image-perception of dream travel not only supports the ubiquitous belief in a separable, immortal soul, but also the recurrent notion that dreams can predict the future (Basso 1987; Brown 1987; Kracke 1993; Wallace 1958). Scenarios explored in dream travels do appear to reflect the current concerns and preoccupations of dreamers (Domhoff 1993). So, simply being apparently enabled to go in a dream where something relevant to one's future is taking place makes dream travel a means of "prediction" that is like visiting next door and overhearing a neighbor's plans for the following day.

While traditions like those considered in this volume consider dream travels the experiences of the soul in an ontologically real world (see Gregor 1981), others, like psychoanalytic theory, hold that dreams are imaginary escapades revealing deep internal wishes. Both implicate dream travels as a source of information—about external reality in the dreams-are-real position (Curley 1992; Shaw 1992; this volume, Tonkinson Chapter 5), and about internal reality, in the psychoanalytic position (Róheim 1952). Moreover, from the biological perspective, the universality of the enhanced if chaotic movement and change in dreams reveals information about how the brain-mind functions (Hobson 1999). The ethnographic record shows that people gather information in dreams either by simple observation of the dream scenario, or by seeing dream events as symbols that must be interpreted. Dream journeys offer opportunities for collecting many kinds of rewards, which accounts for their fascination.

Among the most common of souvenirs sought in dream travels is communication with spirits (this volume, Goodale Chapter 8; Merrill 1988; this volume, Stewart and Strathern Chapter 3; Weiner 1986). As Levy, Mageo, and Howard (1996:13) observe, while "spirits enter the human world in possession; shamans enter the spirit world in trance and dream." For those holding the widespread belief that spirits present disguised messages in dreams, the return from dream travels in a puzzled awakening motivates and provides imagery for rich semiotic systems and religious beliefs (Brightman 1993; this volume, Lohmann Chapter 10; Mannheim 1987). Searching for meanings ranging from straightforward to obscure enables feelings to be articulated and relationships to be deepened, regardless of whether the dreamer regards the nocturnal trek as real or imaginary (Bulkeley 1999; Herdt 1987; Kohn 1995; Kracke 1999; LeVine 1981). Dream travels as experienced and reflected upon allow people to confront their fears, anxieties, and sorrows, wherever these may reside (Epstein 1998; Herr 1981; Hollan 1995; Kracke 1981; Leavitt 1995; Tuzin 1975; Wolowitz and Anderson 1989).

Finally, dream journeys allow people to follow up on the new things they hear about in waking life by means of a visit. Several Asabano people told me that they doubted that Christian missionaries were telling them the truth until they saw heaven for themselves via a dream visit (Lohmann 2000:75; see also Stephen 1982:112; 1996; Tuzin 1989). Lattas (1998:88) writes that a shaman in New Britain, curious about Europeans, dreamt "he had traveled to the land of whites, and there he had seen deceased Kaliai villagers who now had lighter skins."

Early anthropologists relied on traveler's tales to describe distant societies, and contemporary anthropologists interested in the experience of dreaming remain bound to this approach. Rather than journey as participant-observers along with our hosts' night wanderings, all we can do is sit in armchairs or on verandahs and collect the stories with which our informants describe their nightly adventures. The ethnographer cannot get inside the head of informants and directly observe or participate in the mental events in which we are interested.

One cannot conduct fieldwork in another person's dream—though some of our informants and even some anthropologists might disagree (e.g., George 1995). Nevertheless, anthropologists' dreams sometimes change to match the cultural surroundings in which we find ourselves, and this is a source of insight into local understandings (see, e.g., Lohmann 2000:97–98; Luhrmann 1989:80; Seremetakis 1991:232). We can also participate in foreign dream worlds by discussing with hosts our own and others' dream narratives, and by exploring lucidity, or active awareness and purposeful direction in dreaming—a technique that is likely widely used to further the apparent link between waking and dreaming "realities" (Goulet 1994; Tedlock 1999). There is great potential to deepen one's understanding of a foreign culture by studying the dreams and dream beliefs of its members, and much to be learned about the brain-mind by observing what characteristics of dreaming are pan-human and why. The essays in this volume on dream traveling allow us to approach both of these goals.

The Chapters

The ethnology of dreaming seeks to discover how members of various cultures elaborate, explain, react to, and use the mental experiences made possible by dreaming. In this volume we explore the experience and consequences of travel, transformation, and transcendence in the dreams of Western Pacific peoples.

The chapters are arranged to take us on a circular journey, ending close to where we started, just as all dream wanderings ultimately lead back to the place where dreamers fell asleep, the dreamer perhaps slightly changed for the experience. Beginning among the Urapmin in New Guinea's mountainous center, we travel east over jagged, forest-covered mountains, rushing rivers, and grassy valleys to visit the Duna and Mount Hagen areas of Papua New Guinea's Central Highlands. Continuing across New Guinea to the northeast, we begin our descent toward the sea to call on the Ngaing, inland of the Rai coast. Crossing the Solomon and Coral Seas, we visit the inhabitants of the volcanic island of Ambrym in Vanuatu. Swinging about to the southwest, crossing the Great Barrier Reef and the verdant Queensland coast of Australia, we continue across the arid interior to meet peoples of the Western Australian desert, including the Mardu and the Kukatja. Resuming our travel to the north and east, we approach the great peninsula of Arnhem Land to see the Yolngu, before crossing the Clarence Strait to visit the Tiwi

Map The Western Pacific Peoples Discussed in this Volume. Map drawn by Roger Lohmann

on Bathurst and Melville Islands. From here, we continue to the northwest, crossing the Timor and Banda Seas in the Indonesian archipelago before alighting in the highlands of Sulawesi for a stay among the Toraja. Finally, turning eastward we cross the western Indonesian islands and return to New Guinea. Traversing the swamps and central mountains of West Papua, near the center of the island we cross the Papua New Guinea border and walk again in forested mountains, this time among the Asabano, just a few valleys away from the Urapmin.

Contributors retell accounts of dreams experienced by members of these groups, and describe what their informants believe dreams are, what dreams make possible, and how dreaming influences their waking lives through narrative and action. Through these people's stories of their inner lives, we have the opportunity to step for a moment into other ways of living in the world, and have a chance to enrich our own by further developing anthropological theories on the relationship between dreaming and culture.

It is remarkable that in every society considered in this volume, people believe dreams to enable real and increased freedom to travel for some part of the self, with fantastic spiritual destinations and disembodied jaunts around the local settlement equally possible. This universally human experiential potential of dreams informs and undergirds the cosmologies and religious worldviews in each of these societies.

In Chapter 2, "Dreaming and the Defeat of Charisma: Disconnecting Dreams from Leadership among the Urapmin of Papua New Guinea," Joel Robbins considers a political use of dreams among a recently Christianized group. The Urapmin explain dreaming as one's soul leaving the body and contacting the spirits of other people, of nature, and of the dead. As the dreamer's soul travels it can see, or spirits can show it, things hidden in waking life. While revelatory dreams are a well-known source of religious leaders' charismatic power, Robbins shows that they can also be used in egalitarian societies to diffuse charisma and prevent powerful leaders from rising. In one case, a dream report was used to bring down the budding career of a would-be charismatic leader by predicting that he would be killed if he did not step back. Preexisting political ideologies direct the religious power of dreams, be they for aggrandizing leaders or for distributing power or knowledge.

Dreams allow many peoples to experience the continued participation of ancestors in their daily lives—this too influences decision-making. In Chapter 3, "Dreaming and Ghosts among the Hagen and Duna of the Southern Highlands, Papua New Guinea," Pamela J. Stewart and Andrew Strathern offer a vivid look at the phenomenology of dreams in two Melanesian societies. They discuss in particular dreams in which the dead come to visit the living. The dead may warn of future problems or attack. Though dream images can be unclear and in need of interpretation, this does not negate the Highlanders' understanding that one is looking upon external reality in dream journeys. After all, in waking life, too, one may catch only a glimpse of a scene, and the decontextualized fragment can be misleading and need explanation. And, like the living, spirits can purposefully mislead.

In Chapter 4, "Dreamscapes: Transcending the Local in Initiation Rites among the Ngaing of Papua New Guinea," Wolfgang Kempf and Elfriede Hermann describe dreams associated with male and female initiations among the Ngaing, who believe their personal spirits separate from the body and wander in dreams. Dreamers journey to the land of the whites/ancestors in Western cities, revealing that these places are not only one and the same, but also that they coexist in their own territory. Ngaing dreaming transforms landscapes and allows connection and travel to distant sources of power for dreamers and listeners to dream narratives.

In Chapter 5, "Ambrymese Dreams and the Mardu Dreaming," Robert Tonkinson compares the sociocultural significance of dreaming for an insular Melanesian community in Vanuatu and the Australian Aboriginal Mardu. Both peoples use dreams as sources of information for divination and healing; however, their attitudes regarding the relationship between dreaming and cosmology differ dramatically. For the Mardu, dreaming is deeply religious—one's dream-spirit can fly about and directly know spiritual powers of The Dreaming—the mythological creative period when ancestral beings molded landscapes and nature, and when norms and morals were established. In spite of long-term missionization, their Dreaming-based worldview persists strongly, and individuals continue to communicate with the creative powers through dreams. By contrast, the long-Christian Southeast Ambrymese have a relatively easygoing attitude towards religious dreams, which are seen as potentially useful for immediate concerns but are not generally regarded as revelatory of deeper religious truths.

In Chapter 6, "'This Is Good Country. We Are Good Dreamers:' Dreams and Dreaming in the Australian Western Desert," Sylvie Poirier describes the sleep world of the Kukatja and their neighbors. She observes that while the Aboriginal notion of The Dreaming (or Dreamtime) is widely discussed as the mythological foundation of society, how dreams themselves are socialized is a relatively neglected topic. While dreams and The Dreaming are closely related, they are clearly distinguished in Aboriginal thought. Poirier eloquently shows how the study of dreams can open a window on worldviews that are delightfully and radically at variance with Western notions.

Poirier writes that the Kukatja explain dreams as the removal from the body of the personal spirit, associated with thought, emotion, volition, and power. It departs from its seat in the abdomen to commune with other spirits and learn new things. The abdominal spirit that travels in dreams is also the source of power used by healers, showing that the Kukatja make a tight link between dreaming and spiritual strength.

In Chapter 7, "Dreams, Agency, and Traditional Authority in Northeast Arnhem Land," Ian Keen analyzes how dreams enable seamless change in the ostensibly unchangeable Dreamtime by examining a variety of Yolngu dream or reverie in which people acquire religious knowledge. In such dreams, young men can receive a previously unknown ancestral revelation of their group's sacra and, upon telling the dream, a male elder can verify the revelation as having been true all along. The Yolngu downplay the creative role of the individual. While Yolngu recognize individual style in apprehending ancestral knowledge through dreams and other means, the source of religious traditions and symbols is understood to be the thought of remote ancestors. Yolngu say that the dead or the Christian god can literally visit one in a dream and teach religious songs or explain the meanings behind religious symbols.

In Chapter 8, "Tiwi Island Dreams," Jane C. Goodale writes that, like Aboriginal people of mainland Australia, the Tiwi have a notion glossed as "dreaming," which connects ancestry, territory, and obligations. Their notion is, however, distinctive from that of other Australian Aboriginal dreamings. Tiwi believe that in sleep their spirits can walk about and see other spirits, especially the recently deceased. Subsequent as well as past generations are also encountered and brought into the world as fathers beget children through dream hunts on their country. The spirit self that witnesses dreams is equated with a shadow, reflection, photograph, or film—all types of images, not objects, showing that Tiwi understand the dream-self to be a picture of the physical self.

In Chapter 9, "The Cultural and Intersubjective Context of Dream Remembrance and Reporting: Dreams, Aging, and the Anthropological Encounter in Toraja, Indonesia," Douglas Hollan retells dream narratives collected from a respected elder and analyzes them to show how dreams and their remembrance bolster self-image through the aging process. He points out that which dreams are remembered and reported, and how they are interpreted, depends on both the concerns current at the time that the dream occurs and those significant at the time in the near or distant future when the dream is recalled and reported. Hollan shows the importance of lifecycle stage, of relationships between ethnographer and informant, and of post-dream interpretation in line with personal needs and cultural expectations in shaping dream remembrance and reporting. The Toraja understand some dreams to be soul wanderings in which one can encounter the souls of other sleepers or spirits. Spirits may attack in dreams, but nightmarish images may in fact portend a bright future.

In Chapter 10, "Supernatural Encounters of the Asabano in Two Traditions and Three States of Consciousness," I present a series of first-person spirit encounter narratives. The Asabano understand dreams to allow travel in a spiritual dimension, such that a personal soul can leave the body and contact other spirits. The Asabano spiritual world is rich in indigenous tradition but also reflects the rapid cultural change they have seen in recent decades. The accounts are arranged so as to provide a phenomenological comparison along two lines—how religious experiences felt different depending on the state of consciousness and on the religious idiom in which they occurred. Experiences occurring in different states of consciousness are all used to inform people in building a complete system of perception, interpretation, and knowledge. I introduce the term "night residues" to refer to dream memories that become schemas and influence future perceptions. Night residues of dreamed spiritual encounters predispose people to perceive spirit beings in waking life, and are likely a significant cause of religious convictions.

Anthropologists often provide an outsider's view of social life, and while our descriptions lack native familiarity, they make up for this by their fresh perspective. Our own formulations may also benefit when described via a visiting anthropologist's pen. To that end, Waud Kracke, a South Americanist who has worked among the Brazilian Kagwahiv for many years, responds and adds to the chapters in his rich Afterword, Chapter 11, "Beyond the Mythologies: A Shape of Dreaming." Kracke has written extensively on dreams, guided by a psychoanalytic approach (e.g., 1979; 1981; 1987a; 1987b; 1987c; 1993; 1999). His commentary, coming from an anthropologist who is a senior dream researcher, but not an Oceanist, puts the contributions assembled here into a broader context. Dreams, he observes, are not unique in being unobservable to the outside researcher—all experience is directly witnessed only by the experiencer. His point reinforces a recurrent theme in this volume: dreaming is not so exotic and mystical as it first appears, but is rather a profoundly ordinary and ubiquitous form of human experience.

The anthropological study of dream travels makes it clear that the dynamics of culture are actively pulsing in sleep experiences as well as in waking ones. Regardless of whether one believes dreams to be soul journeys, fantasies of minds, random neural noise, or logical lines of thought, they constitute a vital part of human lives and traditions.

References Cited

Basso, Ellen B.
1987   The Implications of a Progressive Theory of Dreaming. *In* Dreaming: Anthropological and Psychological Interpretations. B. Tedlock, ed. Pp. 86–104. Cambridge: Cambridge University Press.

Bourguignon, Erika
1972   Dreams and Altered States of Consciousness in Anthropological Research. *In* Psychological Anthropology. F. L. K. Hsu, ed. Pp. 403–434. Cambridge: Schenkman.

Brightman, Robert
1993   Grateful Prey: Rock Cree Human-Animal Relationships. Berkeley: University of California Press.

Brown, Michael F.
1987   Ropes of Sand: Order and Imagery in Aguaruna Dreams. *In* Dreaming: Anthropological and Psychological Interpretations. B. Tedlock, ed. Pp. 154–170. Cambridge: Cambridge University Press.

Bulkeley, Kelly
1999   Visions of the Night. Albany: State University of New York Press.

Bulkeley, Kelly, ed.
2001   Dreams: A Reader on Religious, Cultural, and Psychological Dimensions of Dreaming. New York: Palgrave.

Charsley, Simon
1992   Dreams in African Churches. *In* Dreaming, Religion and Society in Africa. M. C. Jedrej and R. Shaw, eds. Pp. 153–176. Leiden: E. J. Brill.

Codrington, R. H.
1891   The Melanesians: Studies in their Anthropology and Folk Lore. Oxford: The Clarendon Press.

Curley, Richard T.
1992   Private Dreams and Public Knowledge in a Camerounian Independent Church. *In* Dreaming, Religion and Society in Africa. M. C. Jedrej and R. Shaw, eds. Pp. 135–152. Leiden: E. J. Brill.

D'Andrade, Roy G.
1961   Anthropological Studies of Dreams. *In* Psychological Anthropology: Approaches to Culture and Personality. F. L. K. Hsu, ed. Pp. 296–332. Homewood: The Dorsey Press.

Domhoff, G. William
1993   The Repetition of Dreams and Dream Elements: A Possible Clue to a Function of Dreams. *In* The Functions of Dreaming. A. Moffitt, M. Kramer, and R. Hoffmann, eds. Pp. 293–320. Albany: State University of New York Press.

Eggan, Dorothy
1952   The Manifest Content of Dreams: A Challenge to Social Science. American Anthropologist 54(4):469–485.

Epstein, A. L.
1998   Strange Encounters: Dreams and Nightmares of High School Students in Papua New Guinea. Oceania 68(3):200–212.

Firth, Raymond
1934   The Meaning of Dreams in Tikopia. *In* Essays Presented to C. G. Seligman. E. E. Evans-Pritchard, R. Firth, B. Malinowski, and I. Schapera, eds. London: Kegan Paul.
2001   Tikopia Dreams: Personal Images of Social Reality. The Journal of the Polynesian Society 110(1):7–29.

Freud, Sigmund
1965   [1900] The Interpretation of Dreams. New York: Avon Books.

George, Marianne
1995   Dreams, Reality, and the Desire and Intent of Dreamers as Experienced by a Fieldworker. Anthropology of Consciousness 6(3):17–33.

Goulet, Jean-Guy
1994   Dreams and Visions in Other Lifeworlds. *In* Being Changed by Cross-Cultural Encounters: The Anthropology of Extraordinary Experience. Peterborough: Broadview Press. D. E. Young and J. Goulet, eds. Pp. 16–38.

Gregor, Thomas A.
1981   "Far, Far Away My Shadow Wandered . . .": The Dream Theories of the Mehinanku Indians of Brazil. American Ethnologist 8(4):709–720.

Herdt, Gilbert
1987   Selfhood and Discourse in Sambia Dream Sharing. *In* Dreaming: Anthropological and Psychological Interpretations. B. Tedlock, ed. Pp. 55–85. Cambridge: Cambridge University Press.

Herr, Barbara
1981   The Expressive Character of Fijian Dream and Nightmare Experiences. Ethos 9(4):331–352.

Hobson, J. Allan
1999   Dreaming as Delirium: How the Brain Goes Out of Its Mind. Cambridge: Massachusetts Institute of Technology Press.

Hollan, Douglas
1995   To the Afterworld and Back: Mourning and Dreams of the Dead among the Toraja. Ethos 23(4):424–436.

Irwin, Lee
1994   The Dream Seekers: Native American Visionary Traditions of the Great Plains. Norman: University of Oklahoma Press.

Jedrej, M. C., and Rosalind Shaw, eds.
1992a   Dreaming, Religion and Society in Africa. Leiden: E. J. Brill.

Jedrej, M. C., and Rosalind Shaw
1992b   Introduction: Dreaming, Religion and Society in Africa. *In* Dreaming, Religion and Society in Africa. M. C. Jedrej and R. Shaw, eds. Pp. 1–20. Leiden: E. J. Brill.

Kennedy, John G., and L. L. Langness
1981   Introduction. Ethos 9(4):249–257.

Kilborne, Benjamin
1981 Pattern, Structure, and Style in Anthropological Studies of Dreams. Ethos 9(2):165–185.

Kohn, Tamara
1995 She Came Out of the Field and Into My Home: Reflections, Dreams and a Search for Consciousness in Anthropological Method. *In* Questions of Consciousness. A. P. Cohen and N. Rapport, eds. Pp. 41–59. London: Routledge.

Kracke, Waud
1979 Dreaming in Kagwahiv: Dream Beliefs and their Psychic Uses in an Amazonian Indian Culture. Psychoanalytic Study of Society 8:119–171.
1981 Kagwahiv Mourning: Dreams of a Bereaved Father. Ethos 9(4):258–275.
1987a Encounter with Other Cultures: Psychological and Epistemological Aspects. Ethos 15(1):56–79.
1987b Myths in Dreams, Thought in Images: An Amazonian Contribution to the Psychoanalytic Theory of Primary Process. *In* Dreaming: Anthropological and Psychological Interpretations. B. Tedlock, ed. Pp. 31–54. Cambridge: Cambridge University Press.
1987c "Everyone Who Dreams Has a Bit of Shaman": Cultural and Personal Meanings of Dreams—Evidence from the Amazon. Psychiatric Journal of the University of Ottawa 12:65–71.
1993 Reasons for Oneiromancy: Some Psychological Functions of Conventional Dream Interpretation. *In* The Functions of Dreaming. A. Moffitt, M. Kramer, and R. Hoffmann, eds. Pp. 477–487. Albany: State University of New York Press.
1999 A Language of Dreaming: Dreams of an Amazonian Insomniac. The International Journal of Psychoanalysis 80:257–271.

Lattas, Andrew
1993 Sorcery and Colonialism: Illness, Dreams and Death as Political Languages in West New Britain. Man, new series 28(1):51–77.
1998 Cultures of Secrecy: Reinventing Race in Bush Kaliai Cargo Cults. Madison: University of Wisconsin Press.

Leavitt, Stephen C.
1995 Seeking Gifts from the Dead: Long-Term Mourning in a Bumbita Arapesh Cargo Narrative. Ethos 23(4):453–473.

LeVine, Sarah
1981 Dreams of the Informant About the Researcher: Some Difficulties Inherent in the Research Relationships. Ethos 9(4):276–293.

Levy, Robert I., Jeannette Marie Mageo, and Alan Howard
1996 Gods, Spirits, and History: A Theoretical Perspective. *In* Spirits in Culture, History, and Mind. J. M. Mageo and A. Howard, eds., Pp.11–27. New York: Routledge.

Lincoln, Jackson Steward
1935 The Dream in Primitive Cultures. Baltimore: Williams & Wilkins.

Lohmann, Roger Ivar
  2000   The Role of Dreams in Religious Enculturation among the Asabano of Papua New Guinea. Ethos 28(1):75–102.
  in press   Dreams and Shamanism—Papua New Guinea. *In* Shamanism: An Encyclopedia of World Beliefs, Practices and Culture. M. N. Walter and E. J. N. Fridman, eds. Santa Barbara: ABC-CLIO.
Luhrmann, T. M.
  1989   Persuasions of the Witch's Craft: Ritual Magic in Contemporary England. Cambridge: Harvard University Press.
Malinowski, Bronislaw
  1951   [1927] Sex and Repression in Savage Society. New York: The Humanities Press.
  1984   [1922] Argonauts of the Western Pacific. Prospect Heights: Waveland.
Mannheim, Bruce
  1987   A Semiotic of Andean Dreams. *In* Dreaming: Anthropological and Psychological Interpretations. B. Tedlock, ed. Pp. 132–153. Cambridge: Cambridge University Press.
Merrill, William L.
  1988   Rarámuri Souls: Knowledge and Social Processes in Northern Mexico. Washington: Smithsonian Institution Press.
Paul, Robert A.
  1989   Psychoanalytic Anthropology. Annual Review of Anthropology 18:177–202.
Rivers, W. H. R.
  1923   Conflict and Dream. New York: Harcourt, Brace & Company.
Róheim, Géza
  1952   The Gates of the Dream. New York: International Universities Press, Inc.
Seligman, C. G.
  1923   Note on Dreams. Man 23:186–188.
Seremetakis, C. Nadia
  1991   The Last Word: Women, Death, and Divination in Inner Mani. Chicago: University of Chicago Press.
Shaw, Rosalind
  1992   Dreaming as Accomplishment: Power, the Individual and Temne Divination. *In* Dreaming, Religion and Society in Africa. M. C. Jedrej and R. Shaw, eds. Pp. 36–54. Leiden: E. J. Brill.
Shulman, David, and Guy G. Stroumsa, eds.
  1999   Dream Cultures: Explorations in the Comparative History of Dreaming. Oxford: Oxford University Press.
Stephen, Michele
  1979   Dreams of Change: The Innovative Role of Altered States of Consciousness in Traditional Melanesian Religion. Oceania 50:3–22.
  1982   "Dreaming is Another Power!": The Social Significance of Dreams among the Mekeo of Papua New Guinea. Oceania 53:106–122.

1995   A'aisa's Gifts: A Study of Magic and the Self. Berkeley: University of California Press.

1996   Dreams and Self-Knowledge among the Mekeo of Papua New Guinea. Ethos 24(3):465–490.

Stewart, Charles

1997   Fields in Dreams: Anxiety, Experience, and the Limits of Social Constructionism in Modern Greek Dream Narratives. American Ethnologist 24(4):877–894.

Tedlock, Barbara

1987a   Dreaming and Dream Research. *In* Dreaming: Anthropological and Psychological Interpretations. B. Tedlock, ed. Pp. 1–30. Cambridge: Cambridge University Press.

Tedlock, Barbara, ed.

1987b   Dreaming: Anthropological and Psychological Interpretations. Cambridge: Cambridge University Press.

Tedlock, Barbara

1991   The New Anthropology of Dreaming. Dreaming 1(2):161–178.

1994   The Evidence from Dreams. *In* Psychological Anthropology. P. K. Bock, ed. Pp. 279–296. Westport: Praeger.

1999   Sharing and Interpreting Dreams in Amerindian Nations. *In* Dream Cultures: Explorations in the Comparative History of Dreaming. D. Shulman and G. G. Stroumsa, eds. Pp. 87–103.

Tuzin, Donald

1975   The Breath of a Ghost: Dreams and the Fear of the Dead. Ethos 3:555–578.

1989   Visions, Prophesies, and the Rise of Christian Consciousness. *In* The Religious Imagination in New Guinea. M. Stephen and G. Herdt, eds. Pp. 187–208. New Brunswick: Rutgers University Press.

Tylor, Edward B.

1877   [1871]Primitive Culture: Researches into the Development of Mythology, Philosophy, Religion, Language, Art and Custom. 2 vols. New York: Henry Holt and Company.

von Grunebaum, G. E., and Roger Callois, eds.

1966   The Dream and Human Societies. Berkeley: University of California Press.

Wallace, Anthony F. C.

1958   Dreams and the Wishes of the Soul: A Type of Psychoanalytic Theory Among Seventeenth Century Iroquois. American Anthropologist 60:234–248.

Weiner, James

1986   Men, Ghosts and Dreams among the Foi: Literal and Figurative Modes of Interpretation. Oceania 57:114–127.

Williams, F. E.

1936   Papuan Dream Interpretations. Mankind 2(2):29–39.

Wolowitz, Howard, and Timothy Anderson
1989　　Contributions to Psychohistory: XV. Structural Characteristics as an Index of Mental Health in Freud's, His Patients' and Colleagues' Manifest Dreams. Perceptual and Motor Skills 68:811–819.

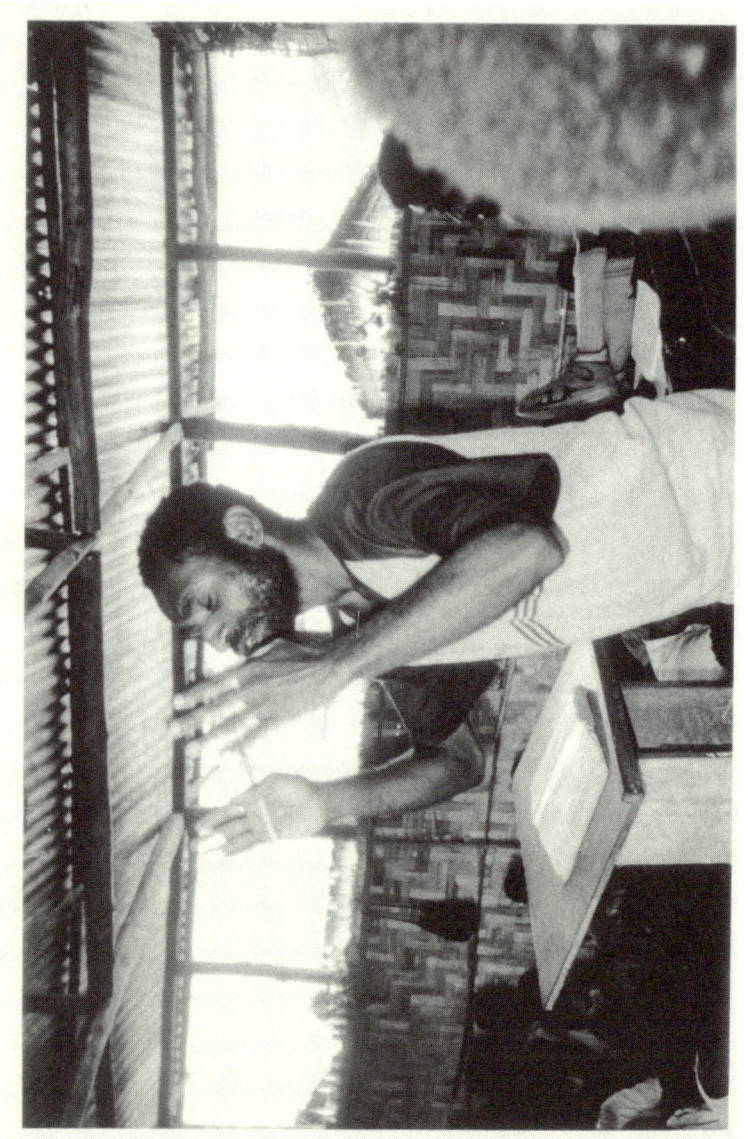
1 Urapmin often report dreams in church services such as this one. Photo: Joel Robbins.

Chapter 2

Dreaming and the Defeat of Charisma

Disconnecting Dreams from Leadership among the Urapmin of Papua New Guinea

Joel Robbins

The Melanesianist literature provides many accounts of, or at least passing references to, the importance of dreams for Melanesian people (e.g., Stephen 1979, 1982; Lohmann 2000). The literature also tells us that Melanesians often publicly report their dreams. Anthropologists studying dreams in Melanesia, however, most frequently focus not on the process of dream reporting itself, but rather on the ways that dream symbolism is interpreted to reveal the meaning of dreams. In doing so, they often neglect to consider how dream reports figure in the political life of Melanesians. Given that many Melanesians consider dreams to be bearers of significant information that is difficult to acquire via other channels, we might assume that people's reports of them do play an important role in local political processes. If this is so, the anthropological neglect of this topic would constitute a serious lacuna in our understanding not only of Melanesian dreaming, but also of Melanesian social life more generally. In this chapter I argue that in many parts of Melanesia, dream reports do have political influence. Yet I will also argue that what is perhaps most interesting about this influence is its extremely limited character.

Looking in detail at the case of the Urapmin of Sandaun Province, Papua New Guinea, I show that while dreams do play some role in the political process, local beliefs about dreams and dream reporting work to keep that role relatively contained. In demonstrating this, I embed my account within a larger argument about the way Urapmin culture systematically works to prevent the development of charismatic leadership. This broader argument aims to make this chapter's consideration of dreaming part of a theoretically motivated discussion of the nature of politics in Urapmin and other parts of Melanesia more generally.

Turning briefly to the literature on cargo cults allows us to make an initial link between dream reporting and issues of charismatic leadership. On the one hand, the one place where anthropologists have given some consideration to the social effects of dream reports in Melanesia has been in the study of cargo cults (e.g., Lawrence 1971 [1964], Burridge 1995 [1960]). On the other, the cargo cult literature also contains an extended debate about the role of charisma in Melanesian politics. Melanesianists have as far as I know completely ignored this debate, which took place between scholars who had not themselves carried out significant fieldwork in the region, but the central theme of the debate bears in significant ways on the themes of this chapter. Thus I take the debate up here as a way into my core argument about dreaming and the status of charisma in Melanesia.

In the introduction to the second edition of *The Trumpet Shall Sound*, Peter Worsley undertakes a careful Marxist critique of the Weberian concept of charisma (1968:ix-xxiff). At the heart of Worsley's argument are two claims. The first of these is not particularly foreign to Max Weber himself but is often lost in popular and even some academic accounts of his theory. It is that charisma is based not so much on a quality of the charismatic leader as it is on the willingness of followers to recognize a leader as possessing such a quality. Because charisma only exists when it is "accepted" (Worsley's term) as legitimate by a group of followers, it must be seen not as a personal attribute but rather as a social relation (1968:xiii; Weber 1978:242). Worsley's second claim makes more of a departure from Weber. He argues that people accord charisma to leaders when those leaders speak to their "unsatisfied wants" and offer some promise of the "eventual fulfillment" of those wants (1968:xiv). Later in the introduction, these unsatisfied wants are defined as "social" ones, and in addressing them the leader's function becomes one of converting "latent solidarities into active ritual and political action" (1968:xvii, xviii). Given that charisma was for Weber an irrational force, the air of realpolitik that Worsley lends it is foreign to the meaning that Weber initially gave it. Indeed, through his redefinition Worsley succeeds in shifting the concept onto territory claimed not by Weberians but by Marxists.

In a small book on, as its subtitle has it, "The Primitive Origins of Charisma," Bryan Wilson (1975) attempts to rescue a specifically Weberian notion of charisma from the popular corruptions it has undergone and the academic critiques it has sustained. On the academic side, Worsley's critique is foremost among those to which Wilson attends. Despite the fact that he recognizes that Worsley's critique is largely motivated by his desire to extend the reach of Marxist theory, Wilson chooses to counter it not theoretically but rather empirically. That is to say, he attacks Worsley's argument by making a claim about the Melanesian societies Worsley examines in his book. "In Melanesian cultural conditions," Wilson writes, "social movements and upsurges might be explained without the use of the concept of charisma" (1975:16). This may be so, he suggests, because "extraordinary social power was not claimed by reference to the divine, perhaps because power differentials between individuals were not sufficiently great to warrant appeal to exceptional sources" (1975:16). Furthermore, the Melanesians are "materialists" who are "preoccupied with trade goods" and with making exchanges and thus their "cultural preoccupations come close . . . to economic determinist expectations about social organization" (1975:16–17). Thus, Wilson implies, Worsley has found in Melanesia a set of cultures that fits his theoretical leanings exceptionally well by virtue of having similar leanings of their own. But in any case, Wilson writes, whether or not these explanations for the lack of charisma in Melanesia are correct, the conclusion he wants his readers to reach is that its absence there "does not in itself establish a case against the utility of the concept of charisma in other cultural times and places" (1975:16).

Perhaps the two ships passing in the night quality of this debate—Worsley's unabashedly theoretical reconstruction too large in scale to pay heed to Wilson's very locally phrased and empirically based attempt to make of it a matter of secondary ethnocentrism—has rendered it largely invisible even within the by now well picked-over cargo cult literature. Or perhaps its invisibility has followed from the fact that Wilson's critique, for all that it is carried out in empirical terms, is as fully motivated as is Worsley's by theoretical concerns that float above the Melanesian data. Or finally, perhaps it has been little noticed because as far as Melanesia is concerned both authors arrive at a similar conclusion and this is a negative one: charismatic leadership, they both assert, does not seem to be a particularly prevalent phenomenon in Melanesia. Having answered the sirens but arrived to find that the house was not actually on fire, Worsley and Wilson would seem to have given us scant reason to return to the scene of their discussion. But perhaps we should not be so quick to turn away from the issue they raise. If one could find a society or group of societies that allowed little or no scope for charismatic leadership, this would surely be worthy of investigation on its own terms, rather than as part of a debate between Marxist and Weberian theory (cf. Glassman 1986). Furthermore, in more regionally specific terms, a careful analysis of how charismatic leadership is prevented from flourishing in Melanesia would also help us to understand in more positive terms how leadership is constructed there.

But is it true that charismatic leadership as Weber conceived of it is unimportant in Melanesia? At the very least, it is true that charisma is not a concept that scholars of Melanesia have used in discussing social realities in the region. And in registering that fact, we need to at least entertain the possibility that this is so because, as Wilson contends and Worsley implies, there is little or no charismatic leadership strictly defined operating in the region. The literature on big men is a case in point here. Given the widely agreed upon fact that this status is one that men in most societies achieve by virtue of their own skills and efforts—and given that, as Andrew Strathern (1993) has recently reminded us, even big men often derive some of their power from ritual sources—one might expect that this form of leadership would be ripe for analysis in terms of charisma. But it is a rather stunning fact that nowhere in the voluminous literature on big men has there been a sustained effort to examine big men in terms of Weber's analysis of the bases of legitimate authority. In a later section of this chapter, I will argue that the authority of at least some Melanesian big men is not grounded primarily in charisma. For the moment, however, I want to suggest only that we take the literature's silence on this matter as an indication that in fact there really is little charismatic leadership in Melanesia, at least on the part of big men.

As interesting as the absence of charismatic authority in Melanesia is when stated as a simple fact, it must strike us as even more worthy of remark when we recognize that the beliefs that make charisma possible are everywhere in place in the cultures of the region. To demonstrate that such beliefs are in place, we first require a clear definition of charisma. Following Weber, we can define charisma as "a certain quality of an individual personality by virtue of which he is considered extraordinary and treated as endowed with supernatural, superhuman, or at least specifically exceptional powers or qualities" (Weber 1978:241). The sociological nature of this definition is somewhat hidden by the passive construction of the English "by virtue of which he is considered." What this hides is that it is the fact that followers consider leaders to have special qualities, not the fact that they actually have them, that makes them charismatic leaders. As noted above when discussing Worsley's use of the notion of charisma, charismatic leadership must be understood from the point of view of those who assent to it. What makes a case of leadership charismatic is that followers are willing in that case to accede to a relationship framed in unequal terms because they believe that the person to whom they are relating has access to knowledge and/or power given by a divine source.

Throughout Melanesia, people are regularly thought to have contact with supernatural beings, and in the eyes of those around them these contacts endow them, at least momentarily, with exceptional powers to foretell the future, heal others, and so on. Why, then, is charismatic leadership so rare? It is possible, of course, that the very regularity of these contacts with the supernatural could itself act to dampen the force of charisma. Where contact with the supernatural is so common, one might argue, it cannot provide the basis for legitimate authority. Where there is little distinction between the "supernatural" and the "natural" and where experience of the former is an everyday occurrence, to call upon well-worn claims about Melanesian religion (e.g., Schieffelin 1976, Lawrence 1971 [1964]), how can such experience underwrite charismatic power? This line of argument is not, however, sufficient to account for the absence of charismatic leadership in many parts of Melanesia. For, as this chapter will show in detail in the Urapmin case, and as it has been shown elsewhere (e.g., this volume, Tonkinson Chapter 5, Strathern 1993, see also the cargo cult literature cited above), many Melanesians do attribute some authority to supernaturally given knowledge and to those who acquire it. The real question then is not why is such authority absent, but rather how do people set limits upon authority that prevent it from becoming charismatic leadership? Looked at in light of this question, the absence of charismatic leadership in Melanesia becomes not a simple fact to be registered but rather a social accomplishment to be explained. How is it that the impact of charismatic authority is undermined and contained in Melanesia?

This is where dreams come in. For it is in dreams that Melanesians most regularly come into contact with supernaturals and with supernaturally given knowledge that may afford them extraordinary powers (Lohmann 2000). In two widely cited pieces, Stephen has argued for the importance of dreams in Melanesian societies (1979, 1982). In many of these societies, she writes, "dreams are seen as a direct means of communication with the spirits of the dead and other supernatural beings, [and thus] they enable men to participate in the spirits' realm of superior knowledge and power" (1979:6). Often, the authority vested in dream knowledge is so great that it allows dreamers to take the lead in situations of social change (Stephen 1982, see also Bourguignon 1973). Having discussed Mekeo dreamers in these terms, Stephen argues that "any of the dreamers described here might have become (and indeed may yet become) prophets of a new order" (Stephen 1982:120). What is fascinating, however, is how few of these dreamers ever do become prophets in many of the societies of Melanesia. Outside of the classic areas of cargo cult activity, one rarely hears of charismatic prophets, and there are many societies where all of the beliefs about dreams that Stephen describes are in place, yet dreams consistently fail to underwrite any tradition of charismatic leadership. Given that dreams quite easily could underwrite such leadership but often demonstrably fail to do so, they provide an appropriate focus for a study of how Melanesian societies limit the success of charismatic leadership.

This chapter takes up the question of how Melanesians defeat charisma by looking at how the Urapmin at once acknowledge the power of dreaming and seek to prevent that power from becoming a basis for charismatic leadership. The absence of charismatic leadership in Urapmin is quite apparent at the moment, for their current situation almost seems to demand it. The Urapmin are a group of 375 swidden horticulturists. Since participating in a Christian revival that began in their area in 1977, they have formed a completely Christian community (Robbins 1998b). Their current social life (in the early 1990s, which forms the ethnographic present of this chapter) is dominated by their belief in the imminence of the second coming. It oscillates between periods of everyday millennialism, dominated by talk about Jesus's return, and those of a heightened millennialism, in which people leave behind their quotidian concerns to concentrate on Christian worship and preparation for the end of the world (Robbins 1997a). These periods of heightened millennialism look very much like other millennial movements, but they noticeably lack leaders. As Talmon (1966) has noted, leadership of such movements is often charismatic. And with dreams and visions coming to people at a rapid clip during periods of heightened millennialism, the raw material of such leadership seems always to be present. Yet a charismatic leader never emerges. Thus in the Urapmin case we encounter in ethnographically specific terms the core problem of this chapter: how it is that charisma is prevented from arising when conditions appear to be so favorable for its appearance.

I seek to answer this question here by looking at how dreams and dreaming are understood in Urapmin culture and by looking at how dream reports are regulated. I then go on to consider two cases in which dreams might have provided, but in the end failed to provide, the basis of charismatic leadership. The second of these cases is particularly telling, for it turns the power of the dream against the potential leader. Having examined *how* charisma is defeated in Urapmin culture, in a final section I offer some speculations as to *why* it is so defeated by looking in Weberian terms at the character of leadership in the community.

Dreaming and the Politics of Dream Reporting in Urapmin

As do other Melanesians, the Urapmin believe that dreams (*lumti*[1]) are potentially a very important source of information that is not available through other channels. This information concerns both things that will happen in the future and things that are currently happening but are hidden from those relying on everyday means of perception. Urapmin dream theory, which is currently a complex melange of traditional and Christian ideas, holds that dreams convey this information in several ways. When a person dreams (*lumti dulamin*), his or her spirit[2] (*sinik*) leaves the body and has contact with spirits of other people and also with nature spirits (*motobil*), spirits of the dead (*sakbal*), evil spirits (*sinik mafak*), and the Christian God or the Holy Spirit. Sometimes a person's spirit simply sees (*tamamin*) things in its travels, and this can be a source of knowledge about current happenings, such as extramarital affairs, that are hidden. More often, though, the Urapmin say that one of the various "supernatural" entities mentioned above "gives" or "shows" a dream to a dreamer. In these dreams that are given by supernaturals, the dreamer may gain knowledge of the future. Often, the supernatural who gives the dream will also appear in the dream and offer an interpretation of the meaning of what the dreamer is seeing.

The epistemological approach the Urapmin take toward dreams is, like the one they take to most things, highly cautious. A member of the Min group of cultures, the Urapmin, like their neighbors, tend toward skepticism when it comes to evaluating the validity of most knowledge (Barth 1975; Jorgensen 1981). Any particular dream, they often assert, may or may not "go straight" in its prediction of the future. Dreams, and visions (*tiin begelmin*) as well, do benefit from the generally favorable evaluation of information gained visually as compared to that gained aurally (Robbins 1997b). However, because dreams may be sent by evil spirits or by nature sprits that are not particularly friendly to people, there is always the chance that they will be deceptive. Dreams sent by God or the Holy Spirit are of course veridical, or at least warn of something that will occur in the future unless people actively work to prevent it from happening. However, one can never be sure that an evil spirit has not tricked one into thinking that a dream that it has sent was instead sent by God, and hence all dreams are at least potentially suspect (this volume, Stewart and Strathern Chapter 3). Yet it remains true that dreams do in some cases provide information that cannot be gained in any other way. Thus, in spite of the fact that they may contain false information, most dreams that people report are accorded at least some attention.

For the purposes of this chapter, it is useful to sort dreams into categories by the kind of information they provide. This division is not one that is made explicit by the Urapmin, yet the distinctions between categories are clear enough in their practice. These distinctions thus form the basis for a set of latent categories, ones that while unconscious still shape people's behavior. In Urapmin, the way a dreamer responds to a dream, and the way the community takes it up if the dreamer reports it, are both very much influenced by the latent category to which it belongs.

A first, very common kind of dream is one in which a person dreams about hunting and finding game. These dreams are given either by the spirits of deceased relatives, or by one of the nature spirits that are the leaders of certain game animals, or, most often in recent years, by God or the Holy Spirit. In the dream, these figures often lead the dreamer (or her husband or brother if it is a woman who has had the dream) to places where he will hunt successfully. People rarely report these dreams, except to those with whom they will hunt, until after they have used the information that the dreams provide; to tell the dream to others would allow them to beat the dreamer to the hunting spot that the dream recommends. The one exception to this is cases where one is given a dream about hunting wild pigs. Wild pigs are hunted collectively, and people use dreams of this type to rally a group to undertake such a hunt.

A second kind of dream is one in which the dreamer sees or is shown information about hidden things going on in contemporary life. These hidden things are usually understood in Christian terms as sins, and in my experience they usually involve sexual relations (as opposed to other sins such as theft). In some cases, however, they may also reveal hidden anger that is currently causing sickness and in this way they may initiate a healing process. Urapmin work very explicitly to control reports of this kind of dream. It is not uncommon for a younger person to report a dream of this kind publicly, often in church. Yet whenever this happens older people are quick to point out that these dreams should be reported privately and only to the people whom the dream involves. The dreamer should tell the person that he or she has seen that person's sin, and should hold (*kutalfugumin*) the sinner and pray (<u>beten</u>) with him or her that God will forgive him or her. Information about sin is too socially disruptive to be made public, especially when there is a chance that it may not be true. Generally, young people who have been chastised for publicly reporting dreams that reveal the sins of others do cease under community pressure from making further reports of this kind.

A third category of dreams consists of those that foretell the future. This is a large category and can usefully be divided into two subsections. One subsection of dreams of the future is made up of those dreams that can be interpreted as providing information about the coming of the last days and about the readiness of the Urapmin community to face Jesus's return. These dreams, of which I present examples elsewhere (Robbins 1998a), are the type most commonly reported. Anyone who has such a dream may report it. The response to these dreams varies in relation to both the time in which they are told and the person who tells them. During times of heightened millennialism, such dreams are often widely discussed and interpreted, while during quieter periods they are usually discussed briefly and then forgotten. The one partial exception to this pattern is when big men (*kamok*) report such a dream. Even during quiet periods, the community attends carefully to big men's reports of eschatological dreams. It should be noted, however, that big men do not often report such dreams, and their rarity is quite possibly one condition of the attention they receive. During periods of heightened millennialism, those who are not big men will often repeat their reports of eschatological dreams that they had reported earlier to little effect. I have heard dreams up to several years old reported in this way. When reported again, these dreams add their voice to the general millennial discourse, but they do not often receive the kind of focused attention given to eschatological dreams that are newly reported at such times.

In general, it is fair to say of eschatological dreams that they are the most "acceptable" ones for Urapmin to report publicly. That is to say, no one is upbraided for reporting such a dream and they can be reported in any company at any time. Reports of them are an important part of the ongoing conversation of Urapmin Christianity and as such they are not highly regulated. It is also true, however, that these eschatological dreams are very widely distributed. Men and women of all ages report eschatological dreams and during periods of heightened millennialism, when in a sense the whole community enters something approaching a dream state, many people may report such dreams (or related visions). Thus, by virtue of their wide distribution, eschatological dreams do not confer special authority on anyone (in the case of big men, it is the dream that borrows authority from the teller, not the other way around).

The second kind of future-oriented dream is one in which a dreamer is given detailed information about a particular person's future. Often, dreamers will see in such a dream that some harm will come to the person or people about whom they have dreamed. As is the case with dreams that reveal hidden information about other people, in these cases of dreams about future harm there is strong pressure on dreamers not to reveal publicly the information they have learned. Instead, they should find the person or people to whom the information pertains, hold them and pray with them that the dream does not come true. A similar line of action was taken in pre-Christian times, for there was also an indigenous ritual that could be used to prevent a dream from coming true.

Praying that they should not come true is a common way of handling dreams that foretell specific, undesirable futures. One of the effects of this mechanism for handling potentially prophetic dreams is that it blocks people from developing a reputation for being able to predict the future. Rather than focusing on how well a particular dreamer fares in his or her predications, the Urapmin focus on praying that his or her dreams will not come true and then on forgetting the dream. It is true that in the initial report of the dream to the person or people involved the dreamer may achieve a certain one-off political effect. For example, shortly before I was to leave Urapmin a somewhat important person with whom I was not close came to pray with me that a bad dream he had about me would not come true. In the dream, he saw that I was distributing my goods to all the Urapmin before leaving, but that when I came to him I only gave him a scrawny sweet potato. At that point in the dream, a voice told him that this was what I would do, but that then I would go home and something bad would happen to me. By telling me the dream and praying over me, the dreamer was able both to alert me to need to remember him in my final gift giving and informally to indebt me over the favor he had done by preventing me from finding the harm the dream predicted. But in telling dreams and then praying that they do not come true, people trade a quick political effect for any chance of enduring power. The dreams, often not widely publicized in the first place, are quickly forgotten by most who have heard them and thus cannot make of the future a proof of any dreamer's power.

Thus far, we have seen how the epistemology of dream knowledge, normative controls on dream reporting, and the tendency to pray that dreams do not prove prophetic all serve to dislodge dreaming from the place it might hold at the base of charismatic power. There is a final category of dreams, however, of a kind that does lead to reports that regularly enter into the social process and serve to transform it. Because of their social potency, these dreams are the ones that have the greatest effect on the workings of leadership in Urapmin.

This fourth and final category of dreams consists of those that very clearly gear into current events. Almost always future oriented, these dreams have the quality of bringing out complex aspects of the current situation and linking them to an equally complex vision of the future. I will present several of these dreams in the next section, so here I will only discuss how they enter the social process. These dreams are often told publicly and widely discussed. Reports of them tend to take on a life of their own and are changed and adapted as they are retold by those other than the original dreamer. Because they enter into many conversations and allow people a forum for talking about the reigning state of affairs in the community, these dreams have the greatest social impact. For this reason, they are also the dreams that could best serve to underwrite charismatic leadership. In the following section, I look at two cases in which people reported dreams of this type. In one case, the dream was blocked from developing its charismatic potential and in the other the dreamer did deploy the dream in very charismatic terms but only to bring down a leader who had begun to develop a charismatic ability to press dreams and visions into service in his own leadership.

Dreams and Leadership: Two Case Studies

The Urapmin community, which is spread out through a number of villages, houses two church buildings. These church buildings correspond to the division of Urapmin into "Top" and "Bottom" groups (Robbins 1998a). In July of 1991, the Top Urapmin group, itself spread out through a number of villages, worked to rebuild its church in a new location. This was a major project, requiring coordination of labor on a scale that the Urapmin rarely attempt for a length of time much longer than the few days usually needed to complete the tasks of roofing houses and constructing pig fences, the two collective building projects that they regularly undertake. Carrying out this church building project smoothly would thus have been a challenge in any event. But in this particular case, matters were made worse by the fact that the location of the new church had for some time been a point of dispute.

Unlike Bottom Urapmin, where everyone in the community follows a single big man, in Top Urapmin people are split between two big men, and a significant minority follow no big man at all. The two big men of Top Urapmin each wanted the church to be built nearest to their own village. After months of struggle, it was finally agreed to build the church in an area that, while technically between the two villages, was in practical terms much closer to the village of one big man than the other. Once the initial period of work on the church had passed, it became clear that the followers of the big man who had "lost" the dispute were not going to contribute to the effort of building the church. This was a source of a good deal of anger on the part of those who were contributing their labor to the building effort.

One of the leading workers from the beginning of the construction was a man named Tambap. Tambap was at that time a mature man in his late forties who had for many years been an active and important deacon (*dikan*) in the Top Urapmin church. Since this section concerns the relations of dreaming to leadership, it is worth taking a moment to sketch the very complex social place Tambap was occupying in the early 1990s. This sketch also lays out some basic information about Urapmin big-manship that will also be relevant to the final section of this chapter.

Ideally and generally in practice each Urapmin person is a follower of one and only one big man. The nature of the big man's role and of what it means to be a follower of a big man will emerge as this discussion proceeds. An initial point to be made immediately, however, is that most of a big man's followers will live in the same village as he does, or in a village close to the big man's own in which all members are his followers. In fact, one of the main tasks a big man accomplishes is the creation of a village, for kinship and other aspects of Urapmin social structural thinking do not of their own accord produce them (Robbins 1998b). When a big man dies and no one in the village is in a position to take his place, the village in which he lived will either split, its members becoming followers of different big men, or it will remain together and everyone in it will follow a single big man who resides in another village. The one rule that applies in all cases, however, is that entire villages tend to follow only one big man.

Tambap was in 1991 living in a village whose resident big man had died in 1989. Although there was no heir apparent to its deceased big man living in the village, the village members had up to this time refused to become followers of a new big man. They were under considerable pressure from the big man who had lost the battle over the church placement to become his followers, but thus far they had not succumbed. The village thus existed in an anomalous state that left it without the support of big men when it came to organizing major projects (such as bridewealth payments).

As it happened, the location chosen for the new church was one adjacent to Tambap's anomalous village. Tambap and another deacon from the village thus ended up taking leading roles in the building effort. Because this was so, the withdrawal of labor by the losing big man and his followers, a move that was never formally announced but which was nonetheless clear in practice, weighed especially heavy on Tambap and his fellow villagers. By withholding their labor, these people not only attacked the rival big man, they also chastised Tambap and his fellow villagers for their unwillingness to follow the losing big man.

In this deteriorating situation, Tambap occupied a singular place. Not only had he been one of the most dedicated workers on the church, but he was also the one person in his village who might have be capable of assuming the now vacant role of big man. It was widely agreed within Urapmin that Tambap was the community's most diligent and successful gardener. This fact alone made him a well-known person and accorded him the kind of prestige upon which one might base an effort to become a big man. Tambap himself, however, was not eager to become a big man. Indeed, as he often told me, it was this very commitment to his gardening work that led him to shun attempts to push him into big-manship. "Being a big man simply takes too much time," Tambap said, time that he would rather spend in his gardens. Furthermore, as a very devout Christian, he shunned the aggressive behavior that is an important part of the big man role. As tensions over the building of the church began to rise, then, Tambap found himself very angry but not in a position to take on the offending big man on an equal footing of one leader to another.

To make matters worse, Tambap was angry not only that the losing big man and his followers had withdrawn their labor; as a deacon who was very much identified with the church, Tambap was also angry at the winning big man for having brought the church into an earthly political struggle that it should have remained above. But in this case, too, he had no basis on which to put his anger to work as part of a political struggle. It was a dream that Tambap had that finally provided him with a way out of the impasses he had reached with both of the big men who had been fighting over the placement of the church.

The dream itself can only be understood in the context of a very loaded remark about the situation surrounding the building of the church that Tambap made a few days prior to dreaming. Out of frustration, he announced to those building the church that the current situation was very much like the one that Noah had faced. As Tambap tells the Noah story, Noah demanded help building the ark but his fellows disobeyed him. In anger over this, Noah asked God to punish them and God sent the flood. Now too, Tambap asserted, he and other church leaders had called for help in doing God's work, but people had disregarded (spetim) their calls.

Urapmin versions of biblical stories are usually more accurate than this, and most Urapmin renditions of the Noah story are closer to the original in that Noah does not call on God to destroy those who disobeyed them. However, the Urapmin do often refer to the Noah story as one about the disastrous consequences that follow from disobedience to authority, if not that of Noah then that of God. What made Tambap's statement very potent was that it was not used to chastise general disobedience in the community, as similar references to the Noahic flood often are when people make them as part of moral harangues given in church, but was rather aimed at a very specific group of people (those who refused to work).

Tambap made his remark on Wednesday and shortly thereafter began to feel sick (anger is often thought to be a cause of sickness in Urapmin). All day Thursday, he worked despite feeling ill. On Thursday night he had the following dream.

> A man came to me [in the dream] and told me that this dream will come true. I saw a big lake. I saw Bill [the only son of the losing big man] and Jim [the younger brother of the winning big man, his closest male relative] and another man go into the water. I sat with another man, not one of us [Urapmin], on chairs on the ground. I was afraid and I was thinking, "Will this happen in the last days?" Then I looked and the water had dried up. The three men were alive and standing on the ground. Where the lake was I saw a footprint that looked like the mark made by a car tire. It was the track of a nature spirit. On the ground, the three men were standing close to the track. Then where the water had been I saw something, a machine [a machine like one Noah had used to build his ship], under a bed or table or a chair. The machine was a sign. I thought a lot about this and then I woke up and realized that I was dreaming.

After Tambap woke up he prayed, as Urapmin usually do upon awaking from a disturbing dream, and then he went back to sleep. In the morning, he went to church and reported his dream. The congregation immediately recognized the bearing of the dream on current events. It foretold that God would save only those who were working on building the church. The rest of the Urapmin, he would destroy.

The response to this dream was immediate. People felt that Tambap had, in his angry invocation of the Noah story, essentially cursed before God those who had not worked. His dream was proof that God had heard the curse and would destroy those who were not working. As talk about the dream developed over the next several days, many people insisted that Tambap must pray to God asking him to prevent this dream from coming true and entreating him to take away the trouble besetting the community. More importantly, the two big men and their followers began to talk openly about the dispute that surrounded the building of the church. This kind of frank conversation had not gone on since construction began on the church. It had long since given way to the kinds of silently aggressive withdrawals of support that I chronicled above. Now, however, it once again found a place in public discussion.

The outcome of this dream report was that people did begin to drift back to working on the church, and followers of both big men eventually came together regularly to worship there. This was able to happen largely because the two big men at the center of the dispute were able to make some kind of peace with each other through the discussions that followed in the wake of Tambap's dream.

I am sure that another outcome was that at some point Tambap did pray to God not to allow the dream to come true. But it is a mark of how quickly he retreated from the limelight that his prayer was never much talked about and did not find its way into my notes. And herein lies a crucial point. In launching his dream into the public arena, Tambap was able to have an important effect on Urapmin social life. It was an effect of the kind that mobilized labor and significantly influenced the future of social life among the Top Urapmin group, a group that had been in danger of fissioning over the church-building issue. These are the kinds of effects that would lead us to claim that Tambap had exercised leadership in this situation, perhaps even charismatic leadership, given that its legitimacy was based on his possession of supernaturally given knowledge of the future. But his leadership role was evanescent. He was forced to make a prayer that would remove the prophetic certainty of the knowledge that he had gained, and overall his role in the process of reconciliation was minor once he had reported his dream. In essence, he was able to use his fleeting charismatic authority to push established leaders to take actions that they had been avoiding, but that authority reached its limit as soon as those established powers did begin to act.

The second example of a dream that influenced current events that I want to discuss here is also one in which the fleeting charismatic authority that comes from dreaming was used to influence the actions of an established authority. This case is slightly more complex from the point of view of our theme, however, because the leader that the dreamer influenced was himself in the process of developing a charismatic style of leadership that he had not previously exercised. The dream succeeded in halting this development.

The Urapmin community as a whole elects a <u>kaunsil</u> (counselor) to represent them in the Local Government Council (LGC) that meets at the District Office at Telefomin. The kaunsil is also the District Government's representative to the Urapmin. He hears court cases and arranges the regular "kaunsil work" that Urapmin must do maintaining foot paths, building bridges and undertaking other public works. He also collects the yearly LGC tax. Although the Urapmin Kaunsil during the early 1990s was not also a big man (he was too young to have assumed this role), and was thus not among the most powerful men in the community, he was a very intelligent leader who had managed to claim as much power as his office allowed. It is fair to say, in fact, that he was the most powerful non - big man in the community.

The Kaunsil was also a very knowledgeable Christian, having received as much pastoral training outside of the community as anyone in Urapmin and having worked as a pastor in a non-Urapmin community in previous years. This made him unique among powerful secular leaders (i.e., the big men), in that the big men of the community were in their fifties and sixties and had not learned to read or to speak Tok Pisin, the language of Christian instruction. While the big men were all devout Christians, their illiteracy and lack of formal Christian training prevented them from exercising leading official roles in the church. More importantly, at present, the Urapmin in effect operate something of a diarchy. As respected as the Kaunsil is for his Christian knowledge, he cannot while holding the Kaunsil office also hold a church office such as deacon or pastor. The same is true for the big men, who even without literacy could potentially but do not in fact serve as deacons. In general, the Urapmin claim that politics—focused on the "things of this ground" and invariably entangled in the aggression and anger that lead to sin—and piety do not mix. Thus their diarchical split between secular and religious leadership, although not formally codified, rests on a frequently reiterated rationale.

While the Kaunsil has honored this arrangement by not taking a formal office in the church, his style of leadership does flirt with engaging religious power in order to develop a foothold in the realm of charismatic authority.

At church services, he often reports dreams and visions of the type we have been discussing in this section, using them to move along social processes that have been arrested by dispute. Furthermore, he frequently speaks in church and takes many opportunities to display his broad Christian knowledge. During most of the time I spent in Urapmin, these aspects of his leadership were tolerated when not welcomed, and they raised little comment.

During the Christmas season of 1992–1993, however, the Kaunsil seemed to make a move in the direction of installing himself as a leader of a millennial movement. In quick succession during that season the Urapmin held several Spirit discos (ol Spirit disko)—capitalized because it is the Holy Spirit that is involved. Spirit discos are group dances in which several participants become possessed by the Holy Spirit. Those who become possessed are cleansed of sin, and when several people become possessed it is a sign that the entire church is relatively free of sin. I have discussed the Spirit disco in detail elsewhere (Robbins 1998b) and will only emphasize here that it is rare for male leaders of the community, either secular or religious, to become possessed. The reasons for this are not entirely clear, but it is a well-established pattern. At the Spirit discos that took place at the end of 1992 and the beginning of 1993, however, the Kaunsil was regularly among the first people possessed. And before he became possessed at each dance, he noisily encouraged others in their pursuit of possession. In both of these regards, he took a leadership role within the Spirit disco and drew a good deal of attention to himself. The effect of seeing a powerful person violently possessed was indeed a riveting one, and it was clear that there was great scope here for the Kaunsil to bolster his already considerable power by adding to it a healthy measure of charismatic authority. He quickly began to eclipse the pastors and the deacons in his importance to the church.

After several nights of this, one of the pastors of the church in which these Spirit discos were being held (the Top Urapmin Church) had a dream that he reported in church. The dream is too complex to be presented in detail here, but the upshot of its message was that if the Kaunsil continued to lead the Spirit discos he would be killed. The very night after the dream was told, the church held a Spirit disco in which the Kaunsil played only a supporting role and did not become possessed. Shortly thereafter, the church stopped holding the Spirit discos on a nightly basis.

The pastor who reported this dream is not a powerful leader. He was relatively newly installed as a pastor of the Top Urapmin church, and was in any case the "number two pastor," serving under the longstanding leader of the church. Here again, then, we have a case of someone who is not a powerful leader using the charismatic authority afforded by dreaming a dream that touches on (an Urapmin metaphor) current events to influence the behavior of someone with considerably greater routine authority. In this case, the evanescent authority of the dream is furthermore put in service of setting limits to the emerging charismatic authority of an established leader. Rather than acting to establish the charismatic authority of the dreamer, who retreated even further from the public eye than usual as soon as he reported his dream, this dream worked to undo the more powerful charismatic authority of someone else. Here then is charisma as its own undoing, an extraordinary power put in service of the deflation of extraordinary power.[3] To understand why charisma should defeat itself in this way in Urapmin, we need to turn to some concluding considerations on the nature of leadership in general in the community.

Leadership and the Defeat of Charisma in Urapmin

Having looked at some of the ways in which the charisma of dreaming is both constructed and tightly controlled in Urapmin culture, it remains to ask why this and other forms of charisma are prevented from flourishing in the community. This question is best pursued through an analysis of what successful leadership looks like in Urapmin. There is no space here for a full consideration of this topic. Instead, I simply sketch the direction a more complete analysis would take.

Weber developed his well-known trichotomy of types of domination based on legitimate authority—legal, traditional, charismatic—in contrast to another type of domination based not on obedience to authority but rather on the submission that follows from an actor's calculation of the fact that such submission serves his or her own interests (Schluchter 1989:398). That is, a person can in some cases submit to domination not because it is "legitimate" but rather for what he or she understands to be utilitarian reasons. Wilson seems to imagine that the big man's domination was of this kind:

> In Melanesia, although a type of achieved status was well known and hereditary chieftainship was not the normal pattern, the status of the "self-made" man was intimately connected with the individual's abilities as a producer of foodstuffs and trade goods, as an economic organizer at the level of domestic economy, rather than as a military, political, or spiritual genius [footnote omitted]. Thus there was, even traditionally, little room for a conception of the charismatic: the "big man" of Melanesian society was too easily explained in common-sense terms to require ideas of divine afflatus (1975:15).

Badly phrased though it is, this claim is an interesting one given the themes of this paper (cf. Strathern 1993:155). It begs, however, the crucial question of how interests and "common-sense" are defined in various

Melanesian societies. Without some specification of these matters, it is difficult to evaluate Wilson's claim.

One way to achieve such specification is through an examination of the two "alternative logics" of society that have been generated by Godelier and others in the discussion of the differences between big man and great man societies in Melanesia (Godelier 1986 and Godelier and Strathern 1991). Since the basic distinctions between the two types of societies have been well summarized elsewhere (see references below), I will be very brief in laying them out here (unless otherwise referenced, these points are drawn from Godelier 1986 and 1991).

Great man societies are those in which exchange is primarily of equivalents, especially of a woman for a woman in marriage (sister exchange) and of a life for a life in warfare. The insistence on the exchange of equivalents insures that there is no opportunity to transform people into wealth and this in turn prevents the development of major intertribal trading systems such as are often found in big man societies. In the absence of such trading systems, social integration is produced primarily through initiation rituals. These rituals also serve to legitimate men's domination of women. It is also the case that in great man societies there tends to be a "*division* of leadership functions" between various kinds of great men: ritual leaders, shamans, gardeners, warriors, and so on (Liep 1991:31 emphasis in original). Power in great man societies is thus widely distributed.

In big man societies, by contrast, the most important exchanges involve non-equivalents, especially those of bridewealth for women and of compensation for homicide. Social integration is produced through the operation of extensive, competitive exchange systems that also provide the rationale by which big men dominate lesser men and women. In these systems, there is "an *addition* of functions converging on the big man" (Liep 1991:31 emphasis in original). Centered on big men, power is concentrated in big man societies.

Because they operate through the manipulation of material goods and the concatenation of chains of reciprocity, big men far more than great men appear to dominate by virtue of the utilitarian benefits their followers believe they provide. They are certainly the kind of leaders that Wilson had in mind in making the observation cited above. The great man society, with its ritual specialists, would appear to be friendlier to the development of Charismatic domination. These claims, however, need to be evaluated ethnographically.

Where, then, do the Urapmin fit into the typology of big men and great men? The answer to this question is not simple. The Min region is perhaps second only to the Angan one in terms of the closeness of fit between its most well-known societies and the great man paradigm (see Jorgensen 1991). Yet the Urapmin are not in any clear sense a great man society. True, they until recently practiced an elaborate men's cult, and they lack the major exchange systems of the highlands. But they constantly talk about their big men, of which there are only four, in terms that indicate that they see these leaders as exceptionally powerful and as very much at the center of local social life. Jorgensen (1991:257) has usefully suggested that we see big man and great man societies as operating with different understandings of the nature of differences between people. In great man societies, people are ranked on multiple scales and differences are understood to be those of kind (e.g., shaman vs. ritual leader vs. warrior). In big man societies, by contrast, people are ranked on a single scale (e.g., of prestige) and the differences involved are those of degree. It is only in big man societies that people are comfortable in pointing to specific people as the pre-eminent leaders of the community. The Urapmin clearly think of their leaders as pre-eminent in this way, and thus from this one vantage point at least they must be seen as a big man society (Urapmin views of their big men are considered in much greater detail in Robbins 1998a).

From the point of view of models grounded in logics of kinship and exchange, this meditation on how people conceive difference might be taken to be somewhat removed from the diagnostic features usually attended to in assigning a particular case to the big man or great man category. Yet even if we turn to examining these other areas, we see evidence of big man logics at work in Urapmin. For example, although they practice a version of patrilateral cross-cousin marriage, Urapmin demand the payment of bridewealth except in those rare cases in which two men exchange sisters. Young men often depend on their big man to help them acquire the shell money that they need to marry (Robbins 1999). Thus big men are centrally involved in the reproduction of the Urapmin kinship system.

Furthermore, while Urapmin big men do not engineer major exchanges beyond bridewealth, they are, as already mentioned, crucially important for their role in coordinating labor. They are able to achieve this because they are willing to violate norms against expressing anger and pushing other people to accede to one's own designs. Both of these behaviors are understood to cause illness, and big men thus take serious risks in their efforts to coordinate labor (Robbins 1998a, 1998b). But it is only through their cajoling and angry outbursts that people can be convinced to work together. Once a big man has a reputation of being able to deliver labor for various projects, he can also persuade people to work by promising them that he will deliver labor for their own projects at a later date. But a big man's willingness to use anger to bend people to his will always stands behind his ability to make people work together. In all of this, what the big man does is essentially organize the exchange of labor between households that are largely autonomous. This exchange of labor is his *moka* (cf. Strathern 1971).

In calling households largely rather than completely autonomous, I left room to point out that the two things households cannot do with their own labor is roof their houses or build pig fences. It is these major building projects that big men most often help to organize. Urapmin recognize that this is one of the most crucial services that they provide for their followers. On yet another occasion, separate from the church building incident, when Tambap's life was being made miserable by the behavior of the big man he had refused the follow (the losing big man in the church dispute), I asked him point blank why people put up with big men pushing them around. "If we didn't," he said, "how would we ever be able to get our houses roofed or pig fences built?" This is pretty strong testimony in favor of the "utilitarian" basis, as understood in local terms, of the big men's power.

This hard-headed approach to leadership goes a long way toward explaining why the Urapmin largely ignore and at times actively block the growth of the potentially significant seedlings of charismatic authority that their frequent contact with the divine regularly plants in the soil of their social life. As Wilson suggests, a model of leadership that is grounded in such mundane concerns does not lead people to look for or welcome leaders who make charismatic claims to authority. Future developments in this area are not completely clear, however. Contemporary Christian Urapmin in many ways has the look of a great man system, particularly in its enthusiasm for a diarchy that segregates Christian leadership from contemporary "secular" leadership (i.e., governmental leadership and big-manship). And there is a newly developed role of female Spirit medium (Spirit meri) that has become very important and that similarly fits within the model of divided authority that so marks great man systems. The current big men are unique for being, as the Urapmin understand it, people who achieved their success almost completely on traditional terms. They are some of the few men left who were already young men when the colonial order finally settled on Urapmin. Thus they were able to master the traditional system when all of its components were still in place. If they are not replaced, the great man system may achieve unrivaled pre-eminence in Urapmin. Were that to happen, there will probably be no shortage of dreamers ready see how far a bit of charisma might take them.

Notes

1. In this chapter, terms given in italics are from the *Urap* language. Underlined terms are from Neo-Melanesian Tok Pisin, the most widespread lingua franca in Papua New Guinea.
2. The Urapmin and the Asabano discussed by Lohmann (this volume, Chapter 10) are both members of the Min group of cultures and in many respects

their ideas about dreams are very similar. The Urapmin do not, however, share with the Asabano the notion the people have two souls.

3. This analysis obviously has some relevance for considerations of the nature of "egalitarian" societies (Robbins 1994, Clastres 1987).

References Cited

Barth, Fredrik
1975   Ritual and Knowledge among the Baktaman of New Guinea. New Haven: Yale University Press.

Bourguignon, Erika
1973   Introduction: A Framework for the Comparative Study of Altered States of Consciousness. *In* Religion, Altered States of Consciousness, and Social Change. E. Bourguignon, ed. Pp. 3–35. Columbus: Ohio State University Press.

Burridge, Kenelm
1995   [1960] Mambu: A Melanesian Millennium. Princeton: Princeton University Press.

Clastres, Pierre
1987   Society against the State. New York: Zone Books.

Glassman, Ronald M.
1986   Epilogue: Charisma and Social Structure—The Success or Failure of Charismatic Leadership. *In* Charisma, History, and Social Structure. R. M. Glassman and W. H. Swatos, Jr., eds. Pp. 179–203. New York: Greenwood Press.

Godelier, Maurice
1986   The Making of Great Men: Male Domination and Power among the New Guinea Baruya. Cambridge: Cambridge University Press.
1991   An Unfinished Attempt at Reconstructing the Social Processes which May Have Prompted the Transformation of Great-Men Societies into Big-Men Societies. *In* Big Men and Great Men: Personifications of Power in Melanesia. M. Godelier and M. Strathern, eds. Pp. 275–304. Cambridge: Cambridge University Press.

Godelier, Maurice, and Marilyn Strathern, eds.
1991   Big Men and Great Men: Personifications of Power in Melanesia. Cambridge: Cambridge University Press.

Jorgensen, Dan
1981   Taro and Arrows: Order, Entropy, and Religion among the Telefolmin. Ph.D. thesis, University of British Columbia.
1991   Big Men, Great Men and Women: Alternative Logics of Gender Difference. *In* Big Men and Great Men: Personifications of Power in Melanesia. M. Godelier and M. Strathern, eds. Pp. 256–271. Cambridge: Cambridge University Press.

Lawrence, Peter
1971   [1964] Road Belong Cargo: A Study of the Cargo Movement in the Southern Madang District, New Guinea. Atlantic Highlands: Humanities Press.

Liep, John
1991 Great Man, Big Man, Chief: A Triangulation of the Massim. *In* Big Men and Great Men: Personifications of Power in Melanesia. M. Godelier and M. Strathern, eds. Pp. 28–47. Cambridge: Cambridge University Press.

Lohmann, Roger Ivar
2000 The Role of Dreams in Religious Enculturation among the Asabano of Papua New Guinea. Ethos 28(1):75–102.

Robbins, Joel
1994 Equality as a Value: Ideology in Dumont, Melanesia and the West. Social Analysis 36:21–70.
1997a When Do You Think the World Will End? Globalization, Apocalypticism, and the Moral Perils of Fieldwork in "Last New Guinea." Anthropology and Humanism 22(1):6–30.
1997b 666, or Why Is the Millennium on the Skin? Morality, the State and the Epistemology of Apocalypticism among the Urapmin of Papua New Guinea. *In* Millennial Markers. P. Stewart and A. Strathern, eds. Pp. 35–58. Townsville: Centre for Pacific Studies, James Cook University.
1998a Becoming Sinners: Christian Transformations of Morality and Culture in a Papua New Guinea Society. Ph.D. thesis, University of Virginia.
1998b Becoming Sinners: Christianity and Desire among the Urapmin of Papua New Guinea. Ethnology 37(4):299–316.
1999 "This is Our Money:" Modernism, Regionalism, and Dual Currencies in Urapmin. *In* Money and Modernity: State and Local Currencies in Contemporary Melanesia. J. Robbins and D. Akin, eds. Pp. 82–102. Pittsburgh: University of Pittsburgh Press.

Schieffelin, Edward L.
1976 The Sorrow of the Lonely and the Burning of the Dancers. New York: St. Martin's Press.

Schluchter, Wolfgang
1989 Rationalism, Religion, and Domination: A Weberian Perspective. Berkeley: University of California Press.

Stephen, Michele
1979 Dreams of Change: The Innovative Role of Altered States of Consciousness in Traditional Melanesian Religion. Oceania 50(1):3–22.
1982 "Dreaming Is Another Power!": The Social Significance of Dreams among the Mekeo of Papua New Guinea. Oceania 53(2):106–122.

Strathern, Andrew
1971 The Rope of Moka: Big-Men and Ceremonial Exchange in Mount Hagen, New Guinea. Cambridge: Cambridge University Press.
1993 Great-Men, Leaders, Big-Men: The Link of Ritual Power. Journal de la Sociéte des Océanistes 97(2):145–158.

Talmon, Yonina
1966 Millenarian Movements. Archives Européennes de Sociologie 7(2):159–200.

Weber, Max
1978   Economy and Society: An Outline of Interpretive Sociology. Berkeley: University of California Press.
Wilson, Bryan
1975   The Noble Savages: The Primitive Origins of Charisma and its Contemporary Survival. Berkeley: University of California Press.
Worsley, Peter
1968   The Trumpet Shall Sound: A Study of "Cargo" Cults in Melanesia. New York: Schocken.

2   Aluni, 1998. In a space (*kene kulu kama*, "dead cordyline garden") within a sweet potato garden, men and boys thatch the cover for the new grave of an old man who has recently died. Other graves stand nearby. After a death has occurred, women's mourning songs are intended to guide the spirit (*tini*) of the deceased person to mountain caves where it will join the other dead spirits. The dead may still appear to their living kin in dreams with warnings or advice about the future. Photo: Pamela J. Stewart and Andrew Strathern.

Chapter 3

Dreaming and Ghosts among the Hagen and Duna of the Southern Highlands, Papua New Guinea

Pamela J. Stewart and Andrew J. Strathern

Introduction

According to many people, including Papua New Guineans, dreams allow communication with the dead, spirits, and deities. An examination of dream narratives provides a window through which to view the social life-worlds of people, perceptions of self and personhood between the genders and otherwise, and patterns of thinking. The literature on dream research and the scientific or psychological interpretation of dreaming and dreams is very extensive (see, e.g., Tedlock 1987 and Van de Castle 1994), as is work on phenomenological approaches to dreaming and to social life generally (e.g., Jackson 1996; Parman 1991; Riches 1995; Stephen 1996; Tuzin 1997). Some earlier studies of dreaming in the New Guinea Highlands include, for example, Herdt (1987); Meggitt (1962); Meigs (1983); and Wagner (1972). These studies indicate the diversity of concerns that may be revealed by or taken up in dream narratives. In all instances it is clear that dreams are treated as potentially serious, perhaps privileged, sources of information that bears on the circumstances of the dreamer. Nevertheless, people recognize that dreams may be difficult or impossible to fully interpret. Our discussion includes materials from two areas in the Highlands of Papua New Guinea, Hagen and Duna, from which we have collected ethnographic materials.

The historical timelines will be given in relation to each case. We begin our discussion with the topic of dreams and knowledge and then we show how dreaming impacts wakeful life and vice versa.

Dreams as Signs

In Mount Hagen Melpa speakers distinguish between dreams that are thought to be positive (*ur kumb,* "sleep dream") and those that are seen as negative (*mi kumb,* taboo dream). *Mi* in other contexts refers to the divinatory object, associated with the group's sacred origins, on which oaths are taken (Stewart and Strathern 2001a). The *mi* in this sense is the repository and source of "truth," used to reveal wrongdoings that have been concealed by verbal lying. *Mi* can also mean a taboo, referring to the use of material items such as tufts of grass to forbid people to enter certain garden or forest areas. In either case, the *mi* marks a boundary. Its sense in the *mi kumb* usage is that it marks the boundary between what will eventually happen and what will not. The usage sharply marks the fact that the issue of prediction is one that is important in Melpa dream exegesis as much as it is in daily wakeful negotiations between people.

In turn this issue raises the general question of access to reliable knowledge as is seen by the Melpa and their congeners and neighbors in New Guinea. In all of these cultures dreams are taken to be highly significant, owing to the widespread theory that they are the product of observations actually made by the life-spirit of the person while asleep. In Melpa people say that they "make a sleep-likeness and see something" (*ur kumb etepa köni*) when they dream. The person, through the life-spirit, sees certain things, including seeing the self interacting with others in the dream experience. The "seeing" action gives verisimilitude to the dreaming. But dream images are sometimes "turned" (*ropel rorom*) so that what is actually seen stands for something else; its meaning is cryptographic and may require the assistance of a specialist to interpret it.

Temporality is at stake. Dreams, as experienced cross-culturally, may conflate and juxtapose elements of time and space that are otherwise separated (see this volume, Kempf and Hermann Chapter 4). That they do so is in fact often taken to be a part of their message. For the New Guinea Highlanders, all of whom have traditions of the continuing involvement of dead kin in their lives, dreams are the gates through which the shades of the dead (the transformed residues of the life-spirit [*min*] among the Melpa) enter and mingle with the spirits and their living kin (see, e.g., Strauss and Tischner 1962; Hayashi 1998). This entry of the dead brings with it places in which they have lived and the dreamer's life-spirit may go there and interact with them. Indeed, in the Melpa view the *min* actually goes to the place where the spirits are and interacts with them there. Since the dead are thought to "see" more than the living and to have more power to cause events, their appearances and sayings in dreams are likely to be taken seriously. Out of ill will, however, the dead may attack their living kin or make demands of them. Sacrifices to them help to keep them on-side to help the living with knowledge and understanding of the future. In this way the dream narrative and its interpretation set up a field of social relations between people and the spirits that impinges on the conflicts and concerns of everyday life. The dead involved are almost invariably the close kin or affines of the dreamer and are endowed with the personality, history, and emotions that they had while alive. Hence dreams become one vehicle by means of which conflicts are actually expressed and dealt with, in particular those conflicts that involve aspects of relationships out of which emotions of jealousy, fear, and anger are generated between people. Whether we regard such dreams as "projective devices" or not it remains true that dream reports provide a resource in terms of which things that are hidden, and may therefore cause sickness or death if they remain unrevealed, are brought into the open.

Because the dead live in a realm that in a sense alters physical time and space, they have some knowledge of the future and can also influence future events while actively hanging on to past grievances. It is in this realm that problems of dream interpretation arise, while equally it is in this regard that the Melpa and many others are most concerned to make use of their dream experiences. Dreams are valued as omens. In today's world, as forms of Christianity more and more displace the reliance on ancestors and other spirits, the problem of correctly interpreting dream messages is altered. Some charismatic and fundamentalist Christian churches preach that the near future holds the possibility of world's end and the likelihood, at any rate, of some cataclysmic event that may profoundly alter the interaction of the living with the dead and the spirits of "evil" and messengers of God (Stewart and Strathern 1997a, 1999a, 2000). Hence there is a renewed emphasis on dreaming as a source of prophetic knowledge about one's fate in the light of these teachings. Dreams said to be given by God are highly valued by their recipients, but dreams can be deceptive and some dreams are said to be sent by Satan, "the great deceiver." Dead kin may be conflated with Satan also, but not always, since they may appear as agents of God or Jesus. The concept of the "vision" (an introduced English word used in the Melpa language and Tok Pisin) has entered Melpa discourse recently as a marker of access to prophetic truth bestowed on certain persons, including the ability to track Satan. Visions may occur during times of wakefulness, especially when fasting (see Trompf 1991 for more on visions).

The phenomenological experience of dreaming feeds into the historical processes of reformation, rejection, and transmutation of "custom" that increasingly occupy people's conscious attention in Papua New Guinea (Stewart and Strathern 1998; Strathern and Stewart 2000a, 2000b). In this chapter we take some examples of dream narratives from our field areas and look at them in the context of our remarks above, particularly with regard to prediction, morality, Christianity, and the debates about custom and "the ancestors."

Case Studies

The examples we chose are from field areas with which we have some direct acquaintance in the Hagen (Melpa speaking, in the Western Highlands Province [see, e.g., Strathern and Stewart 2000a]) and Duna (in the Southern Highlands Province [see, e.g., Stewart and Strathern 2002]) areas. It is not our aim here to differentiate and compare these areas in terms of their distinctive patterns of dream narratives and concerns, although these do exist. Rather, we use examples from both areas to illustrate common themes in the depiction of dream interactions with the dead. By presenting materials from both areas we can demonstrate themes within Highlands societies. At the most general level, also, it is not so much the theme of "access to the dead" that is at stake, though some existential issues pertain to this question; rather, it is the theme of interaction between spirits (both dead and living) in a distinctively conceptualized spirit realm. In other words, what the living and the dead share is precisely spirit. The same holds between humans and the deity in the Christian religion.

Dreams among both of these peoples can portend well or ill for people. They also vary in terms of the narrative of the phenomenological experience in the dream itself. We can construct a continuum, at one end of which the dreamer sees a scene laid out before the eyes but does not necessarily enter into; in the central section interactions of an admonitory, assisting, bestowing, or minatory kind take place, mediated by images and words; while at the other end there is spirit attack, in which a dead spirit assaults the spirit of the living dreamer, causing sickness and danger to life (in this volume, see Lohmann Chapter 10 for dreams that are "safe" and Goodale, Chapter 8 for another example of "dangerous" dreams).

Indeed, although dreams of good omen are much desired by people, there is overall a considerable concern with the idea of danger associated with vengeful or irate spirits of the dead. The dead are like the living: they acquire and hold grudges, they think they have not been given enough or appeased enough in sacrifices, they require to be named specifically in invocations otherwise they become aggrieved, they try to return to the living and claim these to take them off and share their existence in the spirit world. Proponents of Christianity point out that God can give protection against the attacks of jealous, envious, or vengeful and punitive spirits; while giving credit also to God for the benefits of well-being that these spirits were previously thought to bring.

In their original complexity ideas about spirits always show an ambiguous conjuncture of hostility and amity towards the living, a characteristic that in the African context of the Tallensi people led Meyer Fortes (1949) to regard ancestors as projections of parental figures. It is this combination of hostility and amity, aggression and intimacy, that leads to the narratives of spirit attack in dreams as well as in waking life and to rituals of appeasement or apotropaic rituals in response to such attacks. Entry of the dreamer's spirit into the world of spirits is thus hazardous (a walk on the wild side in the sense that the living enter into the unknown "virtual reality" world from which coded signals contain information that can be either beneficial or harmful). The dreamer enters a world of potentialities: the realm of arcane possibility and power, where intentions, dispositions, emotions, and imaginations mingle.

We start with ghost attacks.

Duna: The Tini *(Spirit) and Dreaming*

In the Duna case there was a sacrifice to keep the ghost of a former spouse appeased. The meat and blood from a pig were used to attract the *tini* of the dead husband into a hole on the far side of a stream, the widow being seated on the stream's opposite side. After the attacking *tini* had come to eat the pork and drink the blood, the ritual expert covered the hole with a black stone, imprisoning the troublesome and errant *tini* of the dead man, which should have stayed in its proper mountain area well above the level of human settlement. Duna rituals generally show a great concern for managing the spatial movements of the *tini* of the dead, and of the living also, in order to keep the living and the dead separate.

Duna women specialize in singing laments to send the *tini* of the dead away from the realm of the living (Stewart and Strathern 2002; Strathern and Stewart 1999). These laments evoke images of the landscape and detail the journey of the *tini* to the high mountain areas where the Female Spirit (*Payame Ima*) dwells and looks after dead souls. The birds and other animals of the forest are requested to assist in the *tini*'s transition from existing amongst the living to being with the dead. The fact that women specialize in these songs filled with the heightened pathos of both loss and longing may reflect the parallel sense of separation and loneliness that arises when women move away from their families to be in the place of their husbands at marriage. At funerals women sing out to the *tini* of the newly dead person to go to the place of the dead where they will find the *tini* of the singer's loved one(s) who previously died. The *tini* of the dead are asked to greet the incoming *tini* and help it adjust to its new place of being. An example of one of these extraordinarily eloquent laments that we collected in 1998 follows. It was sung by K. for the death of two of her young children in an epidemic of pneumonia and malaria. The places named in the lament are all limestone rock shelters where the bones of dead persons are placed in secondary burials. They are found in the high forest at the back of settlement areas.

> Mother, mother
> Child, child,
> Cockatoo bird daughter
> Cockatoo bird son
> At Yerepi the cockatoos run away
> And rest there
>
> Go and call out with the cries of the birds
> My child, my child
>
> Where are you two, the ones with the red hair?
> Where are you two, the ones with the russet hair?
> My child, my child
>
> The one with the pointed nose, and water running from it,
> Why do you not come?
>
> You stay in the limestone rocks at Yapi, at Yawepi
>
> My child, my child
> Cockatoo bird son
> Go like a bird and stay there
> Stay at Mbetana
> Go and stay with the men and women there
> Stay with your friends, are you not there?
> Where the men and the women are, over the hill,
> Where your friends are, are you not there?
> At Mbetana, Letana, Yerepi, Mbariwi
> Where the cockatoos run and hide
> Go and call out with the birds
> At Mbetana. At Letana
> At Yana, at Mbetana, where the birds circle,
> Go and sit down
> . . . .
> My children, at Mbetana, at Letana
> How could all the water have flowed
> So quickly from your bodies?

The mourner in this case thought that her two young children had been killed and eaten by witches. Dreams, witchcraft, and ideas about the dead are all integrated into the same domain of experience through the concept of the *tini*. In dreams, the *tini* of people become the agencies that perceive and experience things, which may include signs of future events. Witches operate in this same realm of the *tini*. They become themselves a kind of *tama* (a spirit being that can take the form of a creature) which attacks the *tini* of people as these wander outside of their bodies while they sleep.

Dreams are therefore a realm of danger as well as of access to knowledge.

As we have said, the place where the dead exist is also the realm of the *Payame Ima* who gives to living men the power to divine for witches. When a person lies sleeping, people say their *tini* goes outside of the house, where a witch may be waiting as a *tama* (spirit) who can abduct the person's *tini*, gaining power to make the person sick and to kill them if the *tini* is not released through a ritual sacrifice of pork (Stewart and Strathern 1999b; Strathern and Stewart 1999). The witch's own *tini* goes out and does these things, joining together with other witches that form partnerships in the hunt for *tini* in order to kill their human victims so that they can cannibalistically consume their flesh. Such a movement of the witch's *tini* may further be experienced in a dream, hence it can be risky to narrate a dream that one has had. An example follows:

In 1996 two men on a hunting expedition died in a grassland fire in the Duna area near Hagu village. Witches were said to be responsible for this. A number of women were identified as those guilty through a divination ritual (Strathern and Stewart 1999). The husband of one of these female witches had had a dream that he told to the hunting party just prior to their departure on the expedition. This man was also suspected of being a witch because his dream seemed to foretell the tragic deaths of the two men in the fire. In his dream he said that he saw a cockatoo that had been killed and he also saw a fly that had been burnt in a fire. He told this dream when the men were gathered at his house just before setting out. This was later interpreted as *yoke*, hidden talk, and the implication is that he could have warned the group that he had some premonition that two in the party were destined to be killed. The man was therefore told to pay a compensation of 200 kina (Papua New Guinea currency) in cash to the families of the dead men. Later both he and his wife left the community and took up residence in a different language area, without having paid the full total of compensation due. The witches themselves were declared to have attacked and killed the men out of jealousy over their access to money through wage labor and their "failure" to share money adequately with the witches themselves, for witches are said to be greedy and to have insatiable appetites (Stewart and Strathern 1997b, 1999b).

Hagen: Ghost Attacks in Dreams

The theme of a ghost attack caused by jealousy is prominent in Hagen also, and not limited to the context of spousal relations. Polygyny is a major locus of jealous emotions (*wölik*) in Hagen, and co-wives are thought to be jealous not only of each other but of each other's children. The case history of a woman who was the daughter of a polygynist and attributed failures in her own life to the malevolence of a dead co-wife of her father shows this pattern, revealed to her in dreams.

As a girl, L. discovered that she could not comfortably adjust to the scholastic life in a Catholic school away from her home. At a point when she found herself unable to cope she discovered a way out of her immediate difficulties by failing her end of year exams so that she was prevented from returning to the school in the next year. She attributed her failure to the actions taken by one of her father's co-wives (who had died earlier and was therefore jealous of the living) in a dream sequence the night before she was to be tested. In this dream the father's co-wife came to her and pressed her body down on top of L.'s body in a suffocating manner, making her severely ill and unable to take her tests the next day. It is significant that this was attributed to a proverbially jealous figure, the co-wife, not her actual mother's spirit.

Later as an adult L. discovered that she was infertile. She dreamt of her mother's co-wife's ghost coming and explaining that she was causing the infertility because she was *popokl*, angry with her living husband for neglecting her and thus she was cursing the daughters of her co-wives so that they could not become pregnant.

In addition to infertility angry ghosts could produce general sickness. Ru-Kundil described an example of this in July 1995:

> When one of our kinsfolk was sick, we would call on any of our dead, such as our mother, or father, brother or sister who had died. Or even the spirits of little children, we would make sacrifices to them too. We called on all of them to go in front of our faces and be "straight" there before us to make us successful. When we made these prayers we had to say the names of everyone of the dead without leaving out any names. If we left out anyone of the dead later they would come back and give us bad dreams. Then we would realize that we had not called the name and this spirit had not been able to share in the pork sacrifice. "And that is why it comes back now and gives us sickness." And so we would say, "Let us just find some very little piece of meat and sacrifice it in that one's name, and so it will be enough." The reason was the spirit was angry at being left out and sent the sickness. So when we included it everything was all right. And we would say to the spirit, "we give you this small thing," and it is all right. And therefore the sickness was over.

Dreams therefore can be an important way of accessing the feelings of the dead in order to appease them.

Hagen: The Female Spirit and Dreams

The Female Spirit (*Amb Kor*) shows to a powerful degree the element of possessiveness and jealousy that proverbially characterized spousal as well as other relations in Hagen (Strathern and Stewart 1997, 1998, 2000b). And, like all spirits, she can accordingly harm or help people, showing both an aggressive and a nurturing side.

In his autobiography, Ru-Kundil records the following:

> In 1976 . . . I received a visit from the Female Spirit. My people had not made this cult before and I was not clear about it either but the Spirit came to be with me. I dreamt and saw a woman who came to me and said, "I want to marry you." She told me this and during the night while I slept the ground shook near to my house, and in the morning when I went outside there was a lot of blood spilled on to the ground, just where the shaking and noise had been. I saw this and did not understand what it was. I was confused. The spirit thought that I could find her but I did not. Now she was angry and killed the son of my second wife, M. I was really confused. I had done no wrong, so why should my child die? I was worried. (Strathern and Stewart 2000c:121)

The account goes on to show how Ru was advised by ritual experts and set up a cult performance for the Spirit, drawing the blessings of fertility she also bestows on men who become in ritual terms "her husbands." This power to confer blessings stands in counterpoint to her jealousy, which is comparable to the jealousy of a co-wife as described above.

The Female Spirit (*Amb Kor*) is highly active and chooses the man to whom she wishes to come. She can be seen, during dreams, walking along the road to his place, in full decorations as a bride, as well as appearing in dreams and finally manifesting herself in spirit stones that become objects of the cult rituals and vessels of her "gift" of fertility to humans.

Dreaming of the *Amb Kor* therefore means that the dreamer has entered the hazardous world of experience that we may call the dream journey. The *Amb Kor* was even said to be able to kill a man's son, which may arise out of some wrongful action towards her or simply because she demands the attention of the living. In today's Christian context in Hagen, God is seen to be able to grant all kinds of blessings, yet he is seen also as punishing people for wrongdoing and may even be said to kill them. The tenor of dreams from the Christian context can be illustrated by dream narratives given by Y., a daughter of a big-man in Hagen, dating from 1997:

Hagen: Y.'s Dreams, August 1997

1. "After I had been married for three years already and had not had any children of my own I had a dream in which an old man gave me 10 kina in money and told me to get some foods, so I bought a chicken. The money in fact represented a child. In the morning I told my husband's parents and my father-in-law who is a dream interpreter said, 'Yes, you will now get a child.' And then I did become pregnant and gave birth to my first daughter. Later after I had given birth to my second daughter I asked God to give me a son. In a dream a man said, 'You will have a son.' I told this dream to older people and they said that yes I would get a son so I realized that this dream will come true." (One year after telling us this dream Y. still did not have her wish for a son, and her husband had taken a Pangia woman [from a different language area] as a second wife in his effort to produce male offspring, causing considerable conflict and violence in the family.)

2. "I am also able to interpret [*ko rui*] dreams for people: If you see yourself hitting someone with an axe in your dream that means that you yourself are hitting your own soul and your *min* [spirit] is angry with you and gives you this dream. If you see pigs tethered that means that their own souls are tethered up and nowadays we say that this represents Satan. If you see a Bird of Paradise in a dream then a big-man or important person is going to be killed."

3. "I have had dreams about my brother [who was sickly for a long time and finally died in 1995]. I had a dream in which I saw his funeral and the shoveling of earth on top of his coffin. This was when he was still living. After this dream I myself became sick. Then after he did die I had another dream in which I was shown the place where he is actually buried. I saw his body. It was enlarged and bloated but he got up and greeted me. I said, 'Your skin is bad with this sickness' and I was trying to get away from him. He said, 'You have the old man [her father] in hospital and I've come to see you.' I said to my brother, 'My mother has died and you have died, if father dies what will I do?' He said, 'It is not yet the old man's time.' And then I woke. Shortly after that dream my father became sick and was hospitalized."

4. "I had a dream also in which my dead mother came running down from the top of a mountain. She came out at a place where there was a landslide and said, 'I've got a bad sickness and I'm here.' I said to her, 'You protect us and look after us.' Then she said to me, 'I will not do anything to you but I am going to kill your brother.' And she did actually do that because he died shortly thereafter. He must have done something wrong to her and so she killed him." (He was said to

have stolen money from his mother. She died of breast cancer, a disease that attacked the breast which had fed him, and in anger she returned as a ghost and made him sick, so that he died—his sickness was from mitral valve prolapse in his heart).

Y.'s stories show a hybridization of Christian and pre-Christian themes and experiences. Dream 1 slots God in as the giver of a son where the Female Spirit or ancestors used to be. Her dream interpretations mingle old and new decodings. Dreams 3 and 4 relate to notions of family morality and maternal vengeance. The shift in the interpretation of the tethered pig is interesting. Pigs, as the older Hagen ethnography makes very clear, are the equivalent of the souls (*min*) of the dreamer, but here Y. interprets the tethering as the bonds of sin and Satan. In traditional interpretations, if someone dreams of giving a pig to an enemy group, they will stay at home the next day rather than go out, for fear of being killed (Strauss and Tischner 1962: chapter 18 section 10). Here in Y.'s parsing, Satan slots in as the great Enemy.

Hagen: Vicedom's Materials

In their early monograph based on fieldwork in the 1930s in Hagen among the Central Melpa Vicedom and Tischner (1943–1948 vol. 2:393 ff.) give examples of dream decodings that parallel those given two generations later by Y. (We have translated these from the German text):

> We have seen that the Mbowamb are worried about omens and tend to react immediately to them. It is otherwise with dreams, the people do not fear dreams but desire to have them. Dreams and omens are both harbingers of fate, through which the Mbowamb seek to make a foundation for their future. In dreams the ghosts of the dead reveal themselves. They are experiences which the soul has and draw to themselves the character of truth. "We dream, since the soul runs around outside and sets the dream in motion, the soul does what we see in the dream. In dreams one's own soul truly has dealings with the spirits of the dead, so people are not afraid of them, but wish to have them so that they can learn the future and experience success in their lives." When people wish to dream, they do not bend over water sources to drink, but take a vessel and fill it with water to drink from. They say that if they were to bend over the water their dreams could flow out into the water. . . . In bending over the water they see their images and so it could happen that the water could bear away their souls.
>
> For these people, the dream is truth. It is no different from an experience in waking life. Each dream is taken as a fact and the people adjust themselves to it accordingly. The people know, of course, that not every dream is fulfilled.

They make a distinction between *mikumb,* taboo dreams that do not fulfill themselves, and *paikumb,* dreams of wishes that do fulfill themselves.

We cannot make a systematic clarification of dream interpretations.

The authors go on, however, to give a lengthy and interesting list of examples of dream decodings (see Vicedom and Tischner 1943–1948). We give a list of these with commentaries, either by Vicedom and Tischner or by ourselves, in brackets.

Dream-meanings.

1. "When the people see in a dream that they are running around to ask for something and they receive a fish, they say 'we don't go out, because we won't get anything'" [The fish is slippery and so things will slip through their hands].
2. "When someone breaks off a red pandanus fruit, people say this means someone will die" [Pandanus fruit = person; red color = blood].
3. "When a man catches marsupials in a dream, people say that all his pigs will be stolen and killed" [marsupial = pig].
4. "If one harvests greens in a dream, it is thought that one will be given a gift of pork, since one has already collected the greens" [to be cooked with the pork].
5. "If one dreams of digging up sweet potatoes and handles many vines of the plant, people believe that they will receive a pig, since they already have the 'rope' of it" [Vine = rope by which pig is tethered, pig eats sweet potato].
6. "When a man wants to go on a visit and sees in a dream the night before that people are planting taro and have the seedlings in their hand, he says 'I can't go out, because I wouldn't get anything. I've seen people with taro'" [Taro is sticky, the goods will stick to the hands of their owners—this is our interpretation—Vicedom and Tischner say this one is unclear].
7. "When men are at war and a man dreams a pig bites him, he says he will not go out to fight the next day because the enemy would kill him" [pig = enemy].
8. "If a man has fallen in war and his widow dreams she has intercourse with another man, she will marry that man later" [The new man's spirit has come to claim her already. Vicedom and Tischner do not explain this one].
9. "If a young woman sees in a dream that she has borne a child and is giving it the breast, people say: 'this is a taboo dream [*mi kumb*]. She will not get a child'" [Opposite of wish fulfillment].

10. "If a man is lying sick and another dreams the man is dead and he himself is taking part in the funeral covered with mud and ashes, they say this also is a taboo dream. It won't happen" [Direct image is not what dream means, meanings are cryptographic, but cf. 8].

Vicedom and Tischner give in all 31 examples of dream snippets of this kind, plus their interpretations. Several of those in the series 11 through 31 recount dream interactions with the dead, largely of an admonitory kind, and often these indicate a danger of death rather than a promise of good fortune. Their own materials indicate, therefore, that dreams reflect concern or anxiety about social relations, including those with the dead, as much as trust in the goodwill of the dead. As with the living, goodwill is something that has to be maintained by good gifts. The gift theory of sacrifice rules (Mauss 1954 [1925]). The dead think and feel like the living and interactions with them mirror, as well as influence, interactions among the living. The dead and the living form a single community, and communication between them is mediated by sacrifices, omens, and dreams.

Conclusion: Like Living, Like Dead

A narrative from the early ethnography by Hermann Strauss and H. Tischner, on the Melpa, points up our conclusion (1962, chapter 21). In this story, an eldest brother refused to allocate a large pig from his sister's bridewealth as a sacrifice to their dead parents. The young woman was returning to her natal home with some pork and took refuge in a sacrificial hut to sleep. Her dead mother's brother entered, either in a dream or in a vision, and hid her in an earth oven covered with rubbish, where she saw the spirits of the dead come for a meeting.

> Now many spirits of the dead arrived for the meeting. They kept on coming until only one was missing. So one of the others went out and whistled like a bird, and at that the missing one arrived. When they were all assembled, they carved a piece of pork that they had with them and they ate it. Then they said, "A battle will take place shortly. We should decide which of our men who is still alive we will hand over to be killed by the enemy in battle." They recited a list of all the names. One spirit said that he had only three men; he was unwilling to hand over any of them, as they had to offer him sacrifices. Another spirit said that he had only two men to offer him sacrifices, and under no circumstances was he prepared to hand over one of them. All the others said the same thing. Each of them felt that if he gave one of his "sacrifice men" to the enemy in battle, then he would no longer be offered enough sacrifices. They all therefore refused to hand over any of their "sacrifice men."

The only one who remained quiet was the man whose daughter was in the cooking pit, where she could see and hear everything. But now he spoke. He said, "I have four sons. When three of these sons wanted to offer the large sacrificial animal to myself and my wife, my eldest son kept it for himself, mocking us as 'poor wretches.' So I think that he should not stay alive. What do you think, mother?" But the mother said, "I won't hand him over, under any circumstances! Do you imagine that if we did that other men would offer sacrifices to you?" She strongly opposed the idea. Then the old man said, "You are an old woman, and you don't know what you're talking about. I will not take any notice of you!" The others agreed with him. So the old woman said, "In that case, you'll have to run round imploring all these other spirits to give you a share when sacrifices are offered to them. But they're the ones who don't want to hand over one of their own 'sacrifice men' now. Well, if that's what you want, go ahead—hand your oldest son over to the enemy so that they can kill him! I'm not going to give my other three, and I hope you don't think you're going to get a share when they make sacrifices to me. I won't give you a thing, wait and see!" The old man retorted, "I'm not going to take any notice of you. You're always contradicting me. Do you think anyone is going to make a decent sacrifice for us if he's already kept the large sacrificial animal for himself and stopped his brothers from giving it to us, even though it was due to us as part of our daughter's 'bride price?' If he had not mocked us both and if he had had the decency to promise us the large sacrificial animal, then we would let him stay alive. But because he begrudged us it, I will carry him away and hand him over to the enemy in battle!" All the other spirits of the dead, whom had nothing to lose, entirely agreed with the old man. They said, "You are quite right! You have four sons, after all. We only want to take one of them away and give him over to the enemy." And this they decided to do.

The condemned man's uncle, however, secretly gave his niece a piece of the sacrificial pork which the spirits had divided up and which he had saved, and whispered to her in the cooking pit, telling her to take it to the brothers and warn the oldest one not to go into battle, because his father wanted to let him be killed. Next morning she set off very early and went to the settlement of her brothers. When she arrived, she said, "Brothers, do not enter into battle! I heard our dead mother and father saying they were going to carry off one of you [she did not specify the oldest brother for fear of hurting his feelings] and give him over to the enemy in battle. See this piece of sacrificial meat from the spirits! It proves that what I'm saying is true. Don't imagine I'm lying."

But the brothers refused to listen to her. They prepared their weapons, and when the fighting broke out, they set off. Her oldest brother was struck by the enemy's arrows and then pierced by spears. The three other brothers came back and said, "Our sister was telling the truth! If only we had listened to her! So now don't let us ever again take a sacrificial animal belonging to our father and use it for other purposes! The dead hear everything, see everything, and know everything, and they are filled with revenge anger when we do not follow their wishes. So let us honor them by offering sacrifices, and then they will 'take hold of our heads' and 'carry us around and care for us!'" (Strauss and Tischner 1962: chapter 21, our translation).

The mixture of filial piety, self-interest, meanness, generosity, waywardness, vindictiveness, sympathy, belligerence, and regret shown in this narrative of what was either a dream or a dream-like vision of the dead, heard from an earth oven as a hiding place, demonstrates clearly that dreams are like life. They involve attempts to resolve conflict, including those between the living and the dead. Dream, omen, or vision is to be followed by the sacrificial gift (Mauss 1954[1925]). Exchange maketh manners, and dreams stimulate gifts to the dead, just as they continue to make people redouble their presentations of prayers, songs, and monetary contributions to God's cause today. God, too, punishes people with sicknesses that can kill them. Night-long vigils in churches are followed by early morning dreams (cf. Tuzin 1997). In our recent field visits to Hagen our most characteristic early morning experience was to be woken at dawn by the sounds of people coming out of their houses and calling to one another, with exhortations, admonitions, suggestions, and complaints. These evidenced a rather seamless transition from the world of their dreams into the world of their waking efforts to express and resolve conflicts: both to assert their own wishes and to re-work their relationships. Although spirits in dreams and the spirits of the dead may be said in some senses to be "on the wild side" of existence, in other ways what is most striking is the intimate sense of symbiosis between the living and the dead that is portrayed in dream narratives and their consequences. Equally, dreams about the dead enter into people's conflicts, defining, explaining, resolving, or further complicating them.

References Cited

Fortes, Meyer
1949   The Web of Kinship among the Tallensi. London: Oxford University Press.
Hayashi, Isao
1998   The Topology of Dream Narratives: Narratives by Spirit Mediums among the Bedamuni, Papua New Guinea. Bulletin of the National Ethnology Museum 23(1):95–127.
Herdt, Gilbert
1987   Selfhood and Discourse in Sambia Dream Sharing. In Dreaming: Anthropological and Psychological Interpretations. B. Tedlock, ed. Pp. 55–85. Cambridge: Cambridge University Press.
Jackson, Michael, ed.
1996   Things as They Are: New Directions in Phenomenological Anthropology. Bloomington: Indiana University Press.

Mauss, Marcel
1954 [1925] The Gift. London: Cohen and West.
Meggitt, Mervyn J.
1962 Dream interpretation among the Mae Enga of New Guinea. Southwestern Journal of Anthropology 18:216–229.
Meigs, Anna S.
1983 Food, Sex, and Pollution: A New Guinea Religion. New Brunswick: Rutgers University Press.
Parman, Susan
1991 Dream and Culture. New York: Praeger.
Riches, David
1995 Dreaming in Social Process, and its Implication for Consciousness. In Questions of Consciousness. A. Cohen and N. Rapport, eds. Pp. 101–116. London: Routledge.
Stephen, Michele
1996 A'aisa's Gifts: A Study of Magic and the Self. Berkeley: University of California Press.
Stewart, Pamela J. and Andrew J. Strathern, eds.
1997a Millennial Markers. Townsville: Centre for Pacific Studies, James Cook University.
Stewart, Pamela J. and Andrew J. Strathern
1997b Sorcery and Sickness: Spatial and Temporal Movements in Papua New Guinea and Australia. Discussion Papers Series 1:1–26. Townsville: Centre for Pacific Studies, James Cook University.
1998 Money, Politics, and Persons in Papua New Guinea. Social Analysis 42(2):132–149.
1999a Time at the End: The Highlands of Papua New Guinea. In Expecting the Day of Wrath: Versions of the Millennium in Papua New Guinea. C. Kocher-Schmid, ed. Pp. 131–144. Port Moresby: National Research Institute.
1999b "Feasting on My Enemy": Images of Violence and Change in the New Guinea Highlands. Ethnohistory 46 (4):645–669.
2000 Introduction: Latencies and Realizations in Millennial Practices. In P. J. Stewart and A. J. Strathern, eds. Millennial Countdown in New Guinea, Ethnohistory (Special Issue) 47(1):3–27.
2001a Origins Versus Creative Powers: The Interplay of Movement and Fixity. In Emplaced Myth: The Spatial and Narrative Dimensions of Knowledge in Australian Aboriginal and Papua New Guinea Societies. A. Rumsey and J. Weiner, eds. Honolulu: University of Hawaii Press.
2002 Remaking the World: Myth, Mining, and Ritual Change among the Duna of Papua New Guinea. Washington: Smithsonian Institution Press.
Strathern, Andrew J. and Pamela J. Stewart
1997 The Efficacy-Entertainment Braid Revisited: From Ritual to Commerce in Papua New Guinea. Journal of Ritual Studies 11(1):61–70.

1998	Embodiment and Communication: Two frames for the Analysis of Ritual. Social Anthropology 6(2):237–251.
1999	Curing and Healing: Medical Anthropology in Global Perspective. Durham: Carolina Academic Press.
2000a	Arrow Talk: Transaction, Transition, and Contradiction in New Guinea Highlands History. Kent: Kent State University Press.
2000b	The Python's Back: Pathways of Comparison between Indonesia and Melanesia. Westport: Bergin and Garvey.
2000c	Stories, Strength, and Self-Narration: Western Highlands, Papua New Guinea. Adelaide: Crawford House Publishing.

Strauss, Hermann and Herbert Tischner
1962   Die Mi-Kultur der Hagenberg-Stämme. Hamburg: Cram, de Gruyter and Company.

Tedlock, Barbara, ed.
1987   Dreaming: Anthropological and Psychological Interpretations. Cambridge: Cambridge University Press.

Trompf, G. W.
1991   Melanesian Religion. Cambridge: Cambridge University Press.

Tuzin, Donald
1997   The Cassowary's Revenge: The Life and Death of Masculinity in a New Guinea Society. Berkeley: University of California Press.

Van de Castle, Robert L.
1994   Our Dreaming Mind. New York: Ballantine.

Vicedom, Georg F. and Herbert Tischner
1943–1948   Die Mbowamb. 3 vols. Hamburg: Friederichsen, de Gruyter and Company.

Wagner, Roy
1972   Habu: The Innovation of Meaning in Daribi Religion. Chicago: University of Chicago Press.

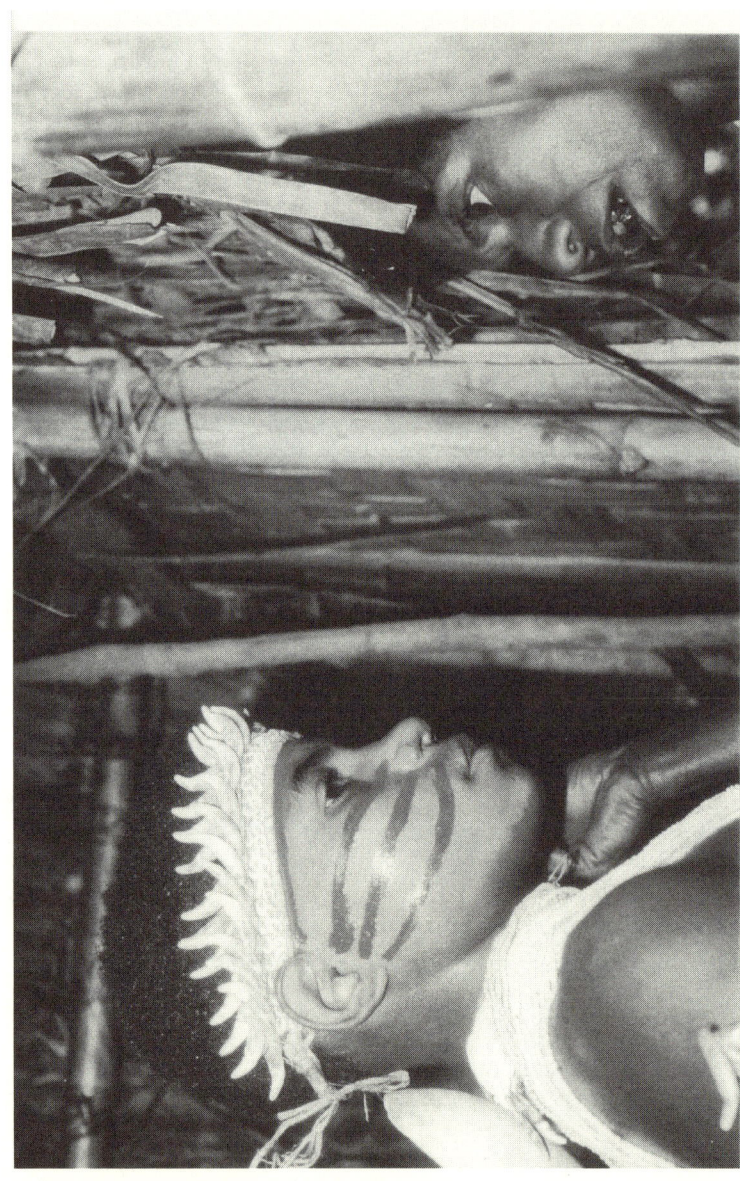

3 "Now it was like I was a child of the Whites." Photo: Elfriede Hermann, 1989.

Chapter 4

Dreamscapes

Transcending the Local in Initiation Rites among the Ngaing of Papua New Guinea

Wolfgang Kempf and Elfriede Hermann

Dreams can contribute much to elucidating how cultural conceptualizations of space are variously generated in a historically constituted terrain of power and knowledge. Our treatment focuses on dreams that deconstruct entrenched demarcations between inside and outside, between the local and the global world. Thus it focuses on dreams that elucidate space as a flexible and negotiable construction. These nexi between dream and space we will attempt to identify with particular reference to the culture of the Ngaing in Papua New Guinea, a group that has become well known through the work of Peter Lawrence (1964, 1965).

We principally intend to highlight a series of dreams that were narrated, in one case, by young men and, in another, by a girl as they underwent initiation in the neighboring Ngaing villages of Yawing and Yasaburing respectively. In the case of Yawing, it was an initiation rite for young men that combined penile foreskin superincision, imported several decades earlier, with local ritual practices. The Yasaburing initiation, on the other hand, was a rite of passage performed on a girl to mark her first menstruation.[1] Thus, in both cases, what we have are dream narratives linked to a specific segment in the life of young adults. This incorporation of specific phases of life into the analytic account of dream narratives—as is also shown by Hollan's case study on dreams in old age (this volume, Chapter 9)—can shed much light on our understanding of dreams.

In their dream interpretations, the initiates in Yawing and their female counterpart in Yasaburing made manifold references to their respective initiations; these point to the fact, *inter alia,* that the site of seclusion can exert an influence over the dream experience itself. By fixing on ritually structured environments as the immediate point of departure of our discursive analysis—and so building on the above—we are making common cause with those anthropological studies that insist on dream contextualization (e.g., Tedlock 1987; Jedrej and Shaw 1992). Apart from this immediate framework, however, our aim is also to extend contextualization to the embedding of narrated dreams in an historically molded field of hegemony and counter-hegemony, a field generated by the colonization and missionization of the Ngaing and responsible for a discontinuous history of initiation rites.

From the multifaceted repertoire of the dreams that were narrated during both initiations, we have selected those turning on a spatial transcending of the local world. The seclusion sites in question turned out to be pivotal loci, points of departure for dream events evoking an urban world of whites inhabited by ancestors and spirits. The transcending of the local during the initiation rites ushered in distinctly European dream landscapes, which to the indigenous eye represented loci of knowledge and power. Landscapes marked by Western characteristics occurred not only in the dream narratives told during the initiations, but also in tales narrated in other contexts of men and women. In both Yawing and Yasaburing, we found a well-established discourse on just such European spaces. This space-predicated discourse dispenses a complex body of knowledge to which male and female initiates could both refer in their dream interpretations. As Michele Stephen (1979, 1982) has emphasized, not only can dream experiences in Melanesia give access to knowledge and power through contacts with ancestors and spirits, they can also display a creative and innovative potential that is socially regulated.

The dreamscapes conjured up in the context of the initiation rites transcend the narrow bounds of an anthropological spatial order that would link cultures to fixed locations. Anthropological discourse committed to the territorial confinement of culturally homogeneous groups as the natural basis for cultural difference assigned people and cultures to sites of authenticity. This left little room for any incorporation of the continued implosions of the local and global world (Appadurai 1988; Gupta and Ferguson 1992; Hastrup and Olwig 1997).

Also the Ngaing, a language group of currently some 1,600 speakers whose ancestral homeland, cleft by the foothills of the Finisterre Range, is the rugged Rai Coast hinterland of Papua New Guinea's Madang Province, were exposed to hegemonic influences that brought fundamental changes to their way of life. Thus, for instance, the growing of cash crops, especially coffee and cocoa, as well as cash income from migrant workers, has recontextualized the original subsistence economy of swidden agriculture and small-scale pig husbandry. And the continuing presence of the Lutheran and Catholic mission societies has meant for the local people conversion to Christianity, with the Ngaing today mostly professing the Catholic faith.

Central to our research is the notion of the permanent changeability of cultures, seen as the result of historically arisen reticulations of the inside and outside, of local and global articulations (see Clifford 1988:14–17; Marcus and Fischer 1986:77–78). Dreamscapes and rites of initiation alike did not escape exposure to global forces; they were not conserved in some sealed-off inside that might have enabled them to avoid tectonic displacements and pervadings from the outside. When Ngaing initiates relate translocal dreams, their spatial depictions prove recalcitrant to simplifying assumptions of autonomous and clearly circumscribed sites of the authentic. Rather the communicated dream landscapes turn out to be products of a history of multiple traversings and hierarchical connections (Gupta and Ferguson 1992:16) located in the variable interstices of "here" and "there" and demonstrating the cultural constructions of local space. What the dream narratives show is that a Western-colored milieu of whiteness has become an integral part of the Ngaing's local world, which should alert us to the pivotal role dreams play in localization within a globalized terrain (cf. Lohmann 2000:78–79).

Dreams: Experiences and Narratives

Dreaming for the Ngaing is an experience of the self. This can be inferred from Ngaing statements with regard to dream experiences, interpreting these and, when necessary, using them as a springboard to action—statements that in their general formulations constitute a discourse on dreaming. This discourse bears a resemblance to cultural nexi of dreaming with experience, such as have been noted by various authors in many societies (see Tedlock 1987:5ff.; Jedrej and Shaw 1992:8; Herdt 1987:58; Stephen 1989:161; Lohmann 2000:76–77; and the authors in this volume).

Dreaming for the Ngaing means most of all experiencing an essential component of the self, which we may refer to in this specific context as the dream-self. Indeed, through the experience of the dream-self and by reflecting on it in a waking state, dreaming also becomes an experience of the self, construed as the comprehensive entity of a person.

The cultural concept of the person/self, as it is found among the Ngaing, connotes living corporeality, thinking, and feeling linked to a personal spirit being (Hermann 1995:56ff.; cf. this volume, Poirier Chapter 6). In the vernacular this spirit-being is known as *asabeiyang* or alternatively *ananuang*, which the Ngaing translate into Tok Pisin (the Papua New Guinean lingua franca) as *tewel, spirit* (both meaning "spirit") and *sol* ("soul"). Having to deal with the hegemonic discourses of the missionaries has led them to conclude that *asabeiyang* corresponds roughly to the Christian soul. The complex form of the self exists in a network of multifaceted social relationships to other persons, living and deceased, and in proximity to other powers of the local and global milieu. A pivotal component of the self, the spirit-being (*asabeiyang*) is, in the everyday situations in the waking life of a normal person, bound to that person with an intimacy that permeates, replenishes, and fortifies. In this state it is manifested as a person's shadow or mirror image. It is also characteristic of an *asabeiyang* that it possesses the ability, under certain conditions, to leave a person's body and to lead an independent existence. While explanations of how a newborn child's spirit originates vary—some hold it to be sent by a god described in Christian terms and identified by some specialists with the ultimate power of thunder—it is clear that a person's *asabeiyang* does separate from the body after death and continues to exist in its own right. In the specific context of religious practices relating to communication with the ancestors, the complex of the *tambaran*[2] (Tok Pisin), the Ngaing refer to a deceased person's spirit as *gabu*. But even during a person's lifetime, the *asabeiyang* can detach itself from the body in certain situations and move as a partial self. This can happen, for instance, when a person falls seriously ill or is sleeping deeply and dreaming (cf. this volume, Lohmann Chapter 10). Should a sick person happen to lose consciousness, this would clearly signal that his or her spirit-being had departed. Should a sleeping person fail to waken after first, cautious attempts are made to rouse him or her, this would likewise signal that the *asabeiyang* is absent. In both cases the absence of the *asabeiyang* can spell danger for the person, for without it an essential part of the latter's being has been temporarily lost (cf. this volume, Tonkinson Chapter 5). One is only part of one's former self. But while a sick person's spirit being can only be fetched back by ritual practices, in the case of sleeping persons the spirit being usually returns of its own accord.

This partial self, *asabeiyang*, or dream self, experiences everything the dreaming sleeper sees, feels, hears, and sometimes says in the first person. Often on its excursions the dream self encounters other persons (relatives, acquaintances, or strangers). Strictly speaking, as the Ngaing responded to our questions, those encountered are naturally not the persons themselves, but once again their spirit beings (cf. Stephen 1989:167). When living persons are encountered, these are their dream selves; but when they are already deceased, these are their persisting spirit beings. Dream experiences therefore constitute a way of encountering the spirit beings of the deceased, that is, the ancestors (cf. Lawrence 1965:207; this volume, Stewart and Strathern Chapter 3). Also possible are dream encounters with spirits of a different kind; these not being identified as deceased humans or ancestors, but as especially powerful beings known from narratives of myth, trance, or dream. Like the ancestors, they too are frequently associated with sites of power.

"I have dreamed" is translated into the vernacular as "*amang enatemang,*" which means literally "I have seen a dream" (Hermann 1995:83–85). This "seeing" contains in any case the experience the dream self conveys to the dreamer. For whatever experiences the *asabeiyang* has in the dream world—whether these take the form of observations, encounters, or deeds—these experiences conceal in-sights for the dreamer, who upon waking is sometimes able to recall them and reflect on their meaning, though he or she sometimes also forgets them. A crucial feature is that the dream has the potential to reveal something that is otherwise hidden (cf. this volume, Lohmann Chapter 10; Robbins Chapter 2; Keen Chapter 7): this may be knowledge of events or actions, knowledge of powerful formulae and objects, or knowledge of spaces. As a rule the Ngaing do not deliberately induce dreams in order to obtain knowledge of this kind. However, male ritual specialists in particular possess methods of deploying paraphernalia like bullroarers at specific taboo sites (*tut*) to conjure up dreams and so obtain novel insights. Dream experiences, so the Ngaing profess to know, can additionally visit consequences upon people in their everyday waking lives. Thus, for example, it may not remain without consequences if a person's *asabeiyang* consumes something in the dream world. Then too, events in a dream may contain messages such as admonishments or solutions to outstanding problems (cf. this volume, Stewart and Strathern Chapter 3). Sometimes something is even shown in the dream world that occurs in the waking world shortly afterwards. Through their knowledge of this potential contained in dreams, the Ngaing articulate a concept encountered worldwide in many societies (cf. Tedlock 1994:286; this volume, Tonkinson Chapter 5).

However, as the Ngaing emphasize, such premonitions or messages of whatever kind can be correctly interpreted only if one understands the particular logic of the dream. The specific logic of events in the dream world does not necessarily equal that of the waking world. Sometimes it shows an order of things representing the "opposite" of that of everyday life, as the Ngaing know to report from their dream experiences (cf. Stephen 1989:166). Following a law of its own, dream events may also contain indirect references to the everyday world of people, these being communicated through specific dream symbols. These symbols must be decoded if one wishes to learn the dream's meaning. Thanks to their record of successful dream interpretation over the years, experts dispose of an especially comprehensive knowledge of dream symbols, thus providing them with a discursively founded power to implement their interpretations. However, a certain set of the most frequently discussed dream symbols, along with at least some rudiments of the prevailing dream logic, are available to all members of Ngaing society. Thus each person, depending on degree of interest, is free to interpret his or her own dreams and also, if necessary, those of others.

Dreams are either interpreted by the dreamers themselves or with the help of others, enlisted if needed. Thus it is not unusual to find dreams being related to a group of trusted others and analyzed for their meaning. Should it transpire that a dream contains messages relevant to the whole collectivity, the dream may be narrated and interpreted in a larger social context, culminating even in a full village assembly (Hermann 1995:240–289). What determines whether the dream interpretation can be elicited within a more or less intimate group setting is the nature of the social context. The ritual framework of initiation, in the cases we will shortly look at more closely, offered a specific context that ensured that dream themes were exclusively handled in an intimate group at the seclusion sites themselves. The initiated young men related and interpreted their dreams in small groups, in which Wolfgang was included. The initiated girl did this more or less only in Elfriede's company. Thus it was through the narrated dream experiences that we heard the dreams of the initiates—and so these dream narratives constitute the platform on which our following remarks about "dreams" build.

Male Ritual Practices in Transition

Secret initiation rites for the young men of the Ngaing have over recent decades undergone radical changes in many places (Kempf 1994; 1996). The mission societies active in Papua New Guinea's northeast, and which in the 1920s and 1930s extended their work to Ngaing territory, made it their business to defame and destroy the existing ritual complex in the region, with its secret paraphernalia and men's meeting houses barred to women. Both Lutheran and Catholic missions routinized a Manichean discourse affirming the opposition of light and darkness, a discourse that localized the secret ritual activities of the men in the dark and menacing spaces of indigenous "heathendom." By thus constituting "dark" indigenous spaces and bodies, the mission societies justified the humanitarian need for their presence to bring light into this local world of secrecy and darkness, of sinfulness and dirtiness. Christianity was associated with purity and light, metaphorically linked to the power-knowledge and the moral supremacy of whiteness. If the officers of the colonial administrations long regarded the men's secret ritual practices among the Ngaing primarily as a positive tradition deserving preservation, this appraisal was reversed in the late 1940s after the Yali movement had crystallized (cf. Hermann 1997:93; Kempf 1996:80). At that time, the Australian administration finally saw itself as obliged to temporarily ban and so criminalize the men's ritual domain. Although the ban was relaxed later and after some years rescinded, the men's ritual complex persisted as a domain that was tolerated (even as it was policed) by the administration.

The historically multifaceted and often contradictory discourses and practices castigating the men's ritual domain as negative tradition, or alternatively protecting, tolerating, and monitoring it as a positive custom, were elements in the implementation of a hegemonic claim over indigenous space and bodies. On the indigenous side, these colonial and postcolonial pervadings were met with a broad spectrum of resistances and adaptive tactics. Particularly the constant crusade against the men's secret ritual activities spawned an indigenous discourse about tradition (*kastom* in Tok Pisin), which was directed against the diabolization and criminalization of this ritual domain and that sought to preserve its continuity. To this local counterstrategy of demanding back power over body and space also belonged, however, the importing of ritual superincision here and there.

Penile incision was first performed in Yawing at the start of the 1950s. This settlement in the heart of Ngaing territory had been selected to set up an aid post providing local medical service. A medical orderly from the Finisterre Range to the west took up residence, and soon afterward he was performing occasional penile incisions, which he considered effective prevention against venereal disease. From then on, the practice of incision expanded into a key component in the local initiation rites for young adults, a position it still maintains. The reasons for adopting penile incision are manifold. Thus, on the one hand, a hygiene discourse has established itself on the local level, one pointing to the practices of white doctors in local hospitals during the colonial era. Then too, the people of Yawing justify the need for penile incision in terms of removing maternal blood, classified as "black" and "impure," from the young man's body. Ritual incision brings "a new light" into the initiate's "black" body and transforms him into a healthy and powerful man, who now possesses a different, "shining" skin. Moreover, the frequent association of ritual incision with Jesus Christ's crucifixion suggests that the Christian notion of redemption from guilt and sin played a role here (see Kempf 1994:113).

The recent adoption of penile incision and its continued practice as a rite of passage for young men belongs to those forms of cultural appropriation and poiesis[3] that constitute local resistance within the confines of hegemonic incorporation (De Certeau 1984:xiii-xvii). The men of Yawing adopted penile incision with its references to Western preventive medicine, to luminous bodily transformation, and to Christian salvation in the hope of reconstituting their indigenous space and bodies. The performance of penile incision ranked as a key innovation and a much-needed adjunct to the men's traditional ritual complex, the *tambaran,* which was defined and practiced in this relational field as "kastom." Through this recombined ritual practice, the men of Yawing were able to establish anew their local power-knowledge, thereby authorizing a poietic capability susceptible to confirmation in dreams and dream interpretations.

Male Initiation, Dream Worlds, and Power Areas

Scheduled in Yawing for April 1989 was a ritual incision involving five candidates.[4] Selected for this ritual purpose was a secluded area: a formerly tabooed site (*tut*) associated with a mythical old woman. The large boulder that once represented this old woman's house had been destroyed much earlier by a landslide, and the old woman had herself eventually disappeared. All that now remained was a steep slope, thickly overgrown and impassable, in whose immediate environs the five candidates underwent penile incision. In this operation a razorblade was used to perform a superincision, that is, a longitudinal cut along the dorsal side of each initiate's foreskin. After the "black," "female" blood had been allowed to flow off, efforts were made to catch the ensuing "pure," "male" blood and to store it in small bamboo tubes or flasks. During seclusion, this "pure" blood was first mixed with oil and other ingredients, and then tied into a bundle with special plants, bullroarers, and each initiate's personal incision-related utensils. The substances were intended for use as "body oil" to enhance one's personal appearance and replenish one's male vigor; other very potent mixtures were designed to exert power over a woman and make her receptive to marriage. The young men were handed their bundles at the closing ritual presentation, which marked the end of the initiation ritual and their readmission to the village community. But first the five candidates had to spend the next three weeks concealed in the seclusion area, until their incision wounds were more or less healed. During this time, women, children, and other noninitiates were strictly forbidden entry to this terrain, which was difficult to reach at the best of times.

Residing in the immediate vicinity of this area was the old and highly respected ritual expert Irawa. Here he guarded his "thunder house" (*rong rumbang*) with its secret paraphernalia for wielding influence over sun, rain, wind, earthquakes, and the like. This precinct—in which the initiates after penile incision spent their seclusion, all the while observing food and washing taboos—had been carefully selected. Some time before, in connection with secret preparations for a *gabu* ceremony, three of the five initiates had built there a small hut, and this now provided housing for the five newly incised young men. One of the latter, Jethro, had this to say:

> Irawa respects this place. The area around here is a "city.". . . Here there are different sections lived in by people. And promptly—as soon as we first came

here, got the area ready [built the hut] and slept here, we dreamed of whites.... We fashioned our [*tambaran*] dancing decorations, we called on the ancestors and we followed the taboos and stayed here. White men and white women, old women came in large numbers, looked at us and spoke to us.... And we went off to the dance festival with a very strong power. For when we set off, old Yutka turned to them and called out, "Follow us!" And they followed us. (April 7, 1989)[5]

The elder Irawa had, by means of trance experiences,[6] obtained a precise knowledge of the area and its various sectors. As his respectful behavior and repeated statements underscored, here was a seat of the ancestors and the spirits, one that manifested itself as a powerful site inhabited by whites. The insights and experiences rendered in the dream narratives of the three young men revealed the area's concealed properties anew. This interplay of vistas of inside space that constituted the knowledge and truth of the area's power seems, in essence, to be what decisively influenced the choice of venue for performing ritual incision.

The "purified" condition of the newly incised, their adherence to the numerous taboos (especially those proscribing sex, food, and washing), their condition of concealment at a power-imbued site, the exclusion of female influences that was such a vital part of seclusion—all this conduced to equip the initiates with power-knowledge. The older men used the special condition of the novices to induct them ritually in a variety of ways, to strengthen them and acquaint them with secret practices and ritual domains of men's knowledge. The initiates' dreams were seen as linked to being removed from everyday life. Thus several of the newly superincised reported having secret formulae (*mana* or *baru*) dictated to them in their dreams by close relatives, so as to confer potency to ritually significant substances. Other dreams indicated future events. For instance, when a red substance was handed to the dream-self, this signaled the imminent handing over of clan-specific ritual knowledge to the initiate in waking life. Other dream symbols could reveal to the initiate and his attendants the shadows of death approaching.

And just as with the above-mentioned dream experiences during the secret preparations preceding a *tambaran* performance, so too the specific context of a ritual seclusion permitted the one initiate or the other to obtain knowledge about the invisible quality and spatial configuration of the area. Though this insight was closed off to the waking eye, the dream-self could reconnoiter the inner world of the terrain. Cliff, one of the older initiates, had dreamed of the seclusion area in the night immediately after his penile incision. He reported how, accompanied by the other four initiates, he had first visited the classroom of a school. Then he had gone alone to where he had been incised, which was also where the mythical old woman had formerly had her abode. From there he could make out, close by, a large room in which he met the ancestors of earlier times. Presided over by the old woman, meetings and advisory sessions were being held. Cliff was offered a chair. Questioned repeatedly, he insisted he had simply dropped in on a short visit. Then he went off to the right and climbed the steps of the nearby mountain, paused briefly, looked back over the meeting of the old men, and climbed even higher up the steps—and woke up.

The explanations and discussions among the initiates made clear that Cliff's dream recognizably manifested several of those sections of the inner world (along with several of its denizens, which the aged ritual specialist, Irawa, had already glimpsed in trances).

> THEO: [The old man Irawa] knows this terrain and its different sections.... Here is another section—here not far away is the [former abode of the mythical] old woman. The old woman [and] the other ancestors are normally behind there. And up there is the hospital. On the mountain there's a big hospital.
>
> CLIFF: And my dream, Wolfgang, it's about this area here, this same bit of area...
>
> TIM: That's the part where we're in the city.
>
> JETHRO: We're in the city, in a part that joins onto it.... Here it's full of whites!
>
> WOLFGANG: [laughing in surprise]
>
> CLIFF: I didn't know anything about this area either. But when I dreamed of it, I said, "That must be this woman." And the others here said, "That is the woman." And up there it was the same again.
>
> WOLFGANG: Did she appear to you in the dream as a white?
>
> CLIFF: Those were whites! All of them whites! The woman sitting there, she was a Miss. Her skin was the same as yours.... These guys here [pointing to Jethro, Mathew, and Theo], they know this area a little already. But in my case, I knew nothing. I came here and in the very [first] night I got it [and] the main thing was I was able to picture it to myself (April 7, 1989) (cf. Kempf 1996:189).

These representations by the initiates relate to how the area in question was sectioned in terms of the "city," the mythical old woman's former precinct, the female and male ancestors of ancient times, and the hospital. Cliff stressed that, despite being ignorant of Irawa's version, the terrain had been manifested with sufficient clarity in his dream. There were the old woman and the old men from the past, all of whom he had encountered as whites, as he later added. And he climbed the steps of the hill, without however reaching the hospital that was situated on top. Notwithstanding, for both him and the other novices present there was no doubting that the dream was set in this very same terrain. Although Irawa, who was later drawn in to shed light on its sectioning, exhibited much more complex insights in his account of the area (see Kempf 1996:193–199), the group of initiates readily latched on to the points of overlap with the individual sections and groups of persons. Where the elder, Irawa, differed from the initiates was that he did not explicitly speak, at least initially, about a "city." Rather, he described the section in his own words as a milieu of the Western kind, full of white people, cars, airplanes, rifles, suitcases, and a hospital where he himself had received medical treatment. For the initiates and the supervisors present, however, it was clear that Irawa's representations described nothing less than a "city" and they saw the place where they were staying as situated within this urban area.

A dream of another initiate confirmed the view, prevalent in the group of newly incised young men, that their seclusion site was located in an urban setting. Tim had dreamed that all five initiates were staying in a modest-sized urban location, as evidenced by paved roads, street lighting, and a large volume of cars. Since they wanted to get to a village, they took a car. First they drove along a great highway; this they left after a while and continued along a small road until they came to a village. This location was full of people, but also a variety of animals were present. Men, women, and small children were present in great numbers. The houses seemed brand new; there was not a single old building to be seen. The five initiates, who wore socks, shoes, and wristwatches, entered the village and were received by the inhabitants. They were conducted to a house, where a table decked with tablecloth had been spread with food and chairs were at the ready. The initiates sat down at the table and ate. It was at that point, according to Tim, that the dream ended. The discussion that followed clarified that the dream was about a village of indigenous inhabitants who dwelt in houses built from bush materials. For the participating initiates, the dream's positive significance was plain to see. Thus Jethro pointed out that they had experienced a transformation through ritual incision, as expressed in the fact that they wore shoes, socks, and wristwatches when they returned to the village. He also said, "We have been remade and they [i.e., the village inhabitants] have equipped us with power. They offered us table and chairs—so you see, they received us favorably. And that means we will be in good form again. The dream shows that [the initiation] will go well" (April 7, 1989).

Tim's dream was interpreted, within the group of initiates, as showing the way back from their initiation-imposed isolation to the everyday life of the village community. Thus when the initiates were staying in an urban setting, this corresponded to their ritual seclusion during the incision rites. Endowed with all the attributes of whites (shoes, socks, and wristwatches) that signified ritual transformation culminating in public presentation of the young men, the initiates were reintegrated into society. In the view of the interpreters, the dream was a forecast anticipating the successful conclusion of the initiation rite.

The public ritual presentation of the initiates, marking the end of their three-week long seclusion along with many of its attendant taboos, was preceded by the decoration of the young men. Local-historical developments in the context of incision being imported had caused the Yawing to discriminate two different ways of readying the newly incised for presentation. One group of ritual experts for penile incision spoke of the style of the sunrise, as represented by the initiates being traditionally decorated with red ocher, bark cloth, dog's teeth, headbands, and so on. This was opposed by the style of the sunset, where the initiates were released from seclusion mostly wearing European clothing. As it happened, the latter variant was the one finally used in the above-described presentation. The division of the various ways of presenting initiates into sunrise/east and sunset/west was not infrequently accompanied by the attribution of blackness and whiteness. The further one moved from the east to the west, the more skin color changed from deep black through multiple intermediary shades to the white skin of Europeans.

Blackness and whiteness are additionally seen as connected with outer and inner earth layers: the outer (upper) earth is considered black and changes, as one digs down into the deeper layers, from brown to red to white limestone. This discursive order, where the outer levels are black but whiteness predominates in the inner ones, is mirrored in local beliefs concerning the *sariwat* palm tree, which plays a central role in Yawing creation narratives. This tree's outer layer of black and hard wood, from which bows, arrowheads, and (especially) bullroarers are fashioned and that encloses a white inside, corresponds to the indigenous blacks, whose poietic capability is limited through their being positioned on the periphery. The palm tree's white interior, so Yawing secret knowledge would have it, is vital for its growth and in turn corresponds to the whites, who are able to produce cars, airplanes, factories, and the like. Ever since the creation of the cosmos, the primeval palm tree has existed within the earth and held it together. Indeed it is within those great elevations in the landscape classified as *tut* sites that parts of this primeval palm tree are situated, thereby giving these features the power they have.

Impurity, sinfulness, and the low standing of the local culture, so the internalized discourse in Yawing has it, are responsible for the peripheral and disadvantaged condition of blackness. Particularly social conflicts, taboo infringements, and other breaches of the rules have helped ensure indigenous exclusion from the power-knowledge associated with whiteness. Ritual practices, which together with spatial separation and observance of taboos induce a purified bodily state, can, however, according to many villagers, conduce to gaining access to the power of the inside (*buing;* or *insait* in Tok Pisin). The ritual incision of young men, when performed in an area divided into immanent, invisible sections with their diverse properties of whiteness, should be seen within this discursive order.

The dream experiences of the initiates in the context of ritual incision demonstrate through their spatial insights that just such a power world of whiteness was situated within the seclusion area. Incorporated into the local discourse, according to which outer appearances conceal a quite different interior, the dreams of the initiates—as also the trance experiences of the aged ritual expert—revealed power-imbued city spaces filled with the power-knowledge of the white ancestors and spirits. The siting of the dreams showed the initiates that whiteness was an interior aspect of blackness, thus contributing to internalization of experiences and convictions legitimizing ritual incision as a necessary male power practice.

Female Initiation: Performance of a Tradition

While in 1989 Yawing staged an initiation rite for young men, which several decades earlier had not existed in that form, in the same year the neighboring village of Yasaburing arranged a "traditional" girl's initiation in a form that had not been customary for many years.

Over the course of recent decades the Yasaburing had gradually introduced various changes in how initiation rites for girls were performed. These changes were closely related to the encounter with discourses of the Catholic mission and the Australian administration, along with those of the administrative and educational institutions of the newly independent Papua New Guinea. Tradition at one time had required, so the elders in Yasaburing recall, that when an adolescent girl had her first menstruation she was immediately placed in seclusion, where she had to remain for several months—all the while strictly observing rules of conduct. When this time had elapsed, she was ritually adorned for presentation to the village community, this time as a young woman, and simultaneously married to a man. Since the mid-1950s, women are no longer handed over to their husbands immediately after initiation, and by the 1980s Western clothing had been substituted for the ritual decorations at their presentations; also, the hard discipline during her seclusion was gradually relaxed and the perforation of the nasal septum abandoned. Bit by bit the duration of seclusion was shortened, so that by the 1980s an initiate usually spent only a week in physical isolation from society. Indeed, in the case of a girl required to attend school, her initiation was put off, in view of this necessity, until the school holidays (Hermann 1998:89ff.).

A further change concerned the spatial aspects of the seclusion. Earlier the girl spent her time in a menstrual hut, built on the fringes of a settlement or in the nearby bush. In the course of the decades, the menstrual space (*ya buluk*) moved ever nearer to the village living space. In some cases, the menstruation hut was built in the direct vicinity of the dwellings of particular families; and in other cases, a small room was set aside at one end of a dwelling. This spatial reordering notwithstanding, the cultural gender discourse even today imposes certain conditions upon the initiate—as is generally the case with menstruating women. The Yasaburing represent this practice as the continuation of their tradition. For the entire duration of her seclusion, the initiate's living space is restricted to this single room, which is usually extremely small. For the girl, moving freely around outside this room is absolutely taboo. Contacts with men of whatever age is strictly forbidden.

In conversations on female initiation, older women and men of Yasaburing reflected carefully on the historical changes. When, in February 1989, as chance would have it, a girl undergoing menarche was about to be sent into seclusion, the responsible adults warmed increasingly to the idea of her initiation being enacted as a traditional rite, the first time it had been so enacted for decades. The idea of organizing a traditional female initiation, so Yasaburing elders revealed, was not unconnected with there being an anthropologist on the scene; its enactment would serve to demonstrate the tradition not only to younger generations of villagers but to Elfriede too, thus allowing her to document it directly.

The first decisions in favor of using traditional procedures in this initiation came after Madubang, an adolescent girl of around fourteen, following the onset of menarche, was taken by her aunt to a small menstruation chamber. Situated in the dwelling of her maternal uncle, in whose family Madubang was living as an adopted daughter, this was a corner room in the rear section facing into the bush and only accessible from that side. Throughout her entire initiation, Madubang was obliged to observe a strict code of conduct with special reference to washing and eating taboos as prescribed by tradition. Then she was inducted step by step into further traditional procedures, with each step marking a different phase of seclusion. Also—and this was entirely in compliance with the cultural codes—she was ritually purified, as the end of her seclusion drew near, and strengthened in her internal capacity as a woman. At the same time, she was decked out in colored paints, grass skirts, and traditional valuables to lend her the aspect of power-imbued radiance. When the day of her presentation arrived, the performance culminated in a traditional rite, with Madubang going through a simulated marriage ceremony in the manner that had formerly been required.

As Madubang's initiation got underway, it was not clear how long she would have to stay in seclusion. To be sure, she knew from the initiations of other, slightly older girls in the village that they had spent about a week withdrawn from public view. However, with each new planning stage and implementation of successive ritual acts, all proceeding in line with the traditional codes, the duration of her seclusion became more and more drawn out. This invariably meant resigning herself to remaining incarcerated ever longer in the narrow and dark menstruation chamber, still observing the food taboos and the prohibition on washing. By the time her initiation was over, she had spent a total of four-and-a-half weeks in seclusion. For the whole of this time, the only regular visits she had were from her aunt, who brought food. On rare occasions one or other of her older female relatives called to communicate instructions on a wide range of matters; now and again a village girl of her own age stopped by; and every one or two days Elfriede was there.

Dream Space in Female Initiation

I thought I was in a city. It was a big city! Now it was like I was a child of the whites. Of the whites. Of course I was a black, but a white man adopted me and gave me medicine that turned me into a white. So I always called this man "father," and his wife I always called "mother." Both had adopted me, okay, and this country, well I thought we were in Australia. And then we went into a department store. There you could read "Australia B. V." Now although I couldn't read what this said, I asked a salesman. "Read it out for me!," and so he did just that. After he had read it out and I had heard it, he said, "You must not go in there and touch the various things on the display counter. Or you'll be put on trial!" Now I clearly heard what he said, but all the same I went and touched the things on the display counter. Then the "security" man came behind my back and seized me. And as he seized me, he said to me, "Now you're going off to prison!"

Madubang went on, in fervent tones, to tell Elfriede a dream she recently had during her seclusion.

MADUBANG: "And so I went to gaol."
ELFRIEDE: "Really?"
MADUBANG: "Yes, I went to gaol. They said, 'You will only stay three weeks.' So there I was in prison. 'Only for three weeks,' [or so they said]."
ELFRIEDE: "Oh, you poor thing!"
MADUBANG: "So there I was, but I didn't have to stay the three weeks, because soon they came and told me, 'You'll only stay a week.' And then my adopted father fetched me out of prison. My next thought was, 'now I'll be able to stay a child of the whites! Now I'll be staying here in Australia.' But nothing has come of it. I woke up in the morning thinking I was in Australia now. But then I saw this hut here, the bamboo wall. But it wasn't a permanent building," [she gives a little laugh].
ELFRIEDE: [laughing too]
MADUBANG: "And then I stood up and said to myself, 'How is it that I dream the things I do?' I sat down and thought, and then I said to myself, 'Perhaps it's like this: I went into seclusion and stayed exclusively in this house, and that is just as if I were in prison.' Three weeks in a dream were like one week, and so I said to myself, 'Now I've been here for five and a half

weeks,[7] so I dreamed the opposite: three and one, that makes three and a half weeks.' That's what I dreamed."
ELFRIEDE: "Is that true?"
MADUBANG: "But nothing came of it [as to shortening the time I spent in seclusion] and so I'm still here."
ELFRIEDE: "You know, Madubang, I find your thinking on this very interesting, the way you interpret your dream."
MADUBANG: "Hmm."
ELFRIEDE: "I really do."
MADUBANG: "And as far as me being changed into a white is concerned, what this means is: right now I'm not clean. I mean, being dirty is what's holding me back."
ELFRIEDE: "Yes, hmm. Right now you're not clean and?"
MADUBANG: "Yes."
ELFRIEDE: "So you want?"
MADUBANG: [thinks hard]
ELFRIEDE: "So as you were saying, now you dreamed the opposite?"
MADUBANG: "Yes!"
ELFRIEDE: "Hmm, that's right. And that's how you become clean and really white!"
MADUBANG: [gives a little laugh]
ELFRIEDE: [laughing too] "That's true, isn't it?"
MADUBANG: "Yes! It has to be the opposite, so that means I'm black and really unclean. Being clean and really white—that refers to me being unclean."
(March 20, 1989)

Before Madubang related this dream, she expressed the same opinion she had on previous days, namely that she was fed up with having to stay in the menstrual chamber. The room was heated on one side by the sun and there was no cross-breeze whatsoever. It was so hot that she sweated profusely during the day, so she complained. Asked what was going through her mind, she answered, "I just imagine myself going into the bush and washing myself at the river!" The stifling narrowness of the menstruation chamber, in which she had already spent three-and-a-half weeks, was hard for her to take. In view of the prohibition against leaving it, she could only move around in her imagination—going into the shadowy forest surroundings, or down to the river to freshen up and clean herself. As her associations in the wake of her dream narrative revealed, she was longing for the day when she would see the last of her seclusion room.

Many of the dreams she would have during the night transported her dream-self beyond the narrow spatial confines of her room. Just a week after commencing her seclusion, Madubang related, she had dreamed of an excursion to a nearby coastal village, where she met her natural parents. This same coastal village, however, in her dream bore a changed aspect: everywhere there were walled, solid buildings built on the sea, and in between Madubang was traveling in a fast motorboat. Also, in the same village, she went into a well-stocked store in whose deep freezers she found some fresh fish, which were then fried up and served to her. From this coastal settlement her mother then sent her to a village in the vicinity of Yasaburing, where she paid a visit as she had been instructed to do.

The dream of staying in Australia gave Madubang a further opportunity to travel outside—one might say break out of—Yasaburing. If in her earlier dreams she had seen the familiar landscapes of the neighboring region, such as the coastal settlement, as partly exhibiting the infrastructure of an industrialized state, the other space that she now penetrated was revealed to her in its most concentrated form: as the "city." In this landscape of buildings, she set out on a journey into yet more spaces: first into a sales room full of merchandise, from where she was then taken to a prison cell, from which, however, she was soon released, finally to live as a free person in "Australia."

When interpreting her dream, Madubang drew a clear linkage between the space she was dreaming of and the space she was dreaming in. Here she latched on to the self same spatiality of the dream world whose constraining rigors in the waking world she then so keenly felt, namely her "prison"—for in her seclusion room she did indeed feel "as if [she] was in prison." While these spatial conditions found a dream reflection in a metaphor analogous to waking everyday life, the fact is that confinement in the dream world was of much shorter duration than her ever-longer drawn out confinement in seclusion. This dream experience Madubang recognized in what she knew of the dream's specific logic as the "opposite" of how she experienced the waking world (which caused her so often to complain).

What Madubang did not further interpret was the other dreamspace—Australia—the country to which her dream-self journeyed from the seclusion room and where it lived after her liberation from prison. While it is clearly the case that this space, too, complied with the dream's oppositional logic—it was manifested in her dream narrative as a "large city" abstract in size—as a space that was therefore also, in comparison with the seclusion room, characterized by reversed dimensions. One could go even further: this space proved a counter-space in which Madubang hoped to be able to live freed (from vegetating in prison). Many things she knew of Australia Madubang had gleaned from her schoolbooks (she had made a point of busying herself with these during her seclusion).[8] Often too, she had heard older people telling stories about Australia, as when they related how Yali, a famous man from their village, many years before had traveled several times to that country. Thanks to these many journeys and what had befallen him during them, Yali was represented in these reports as having amassed a store of experience. That, in combination with other experiences, endowed him with a respect-compelling knowledge and power, so that once he had even headed a whole social movement (Lawrence 1964:116–139; Hermann 1995:86–199). In local discourse Australia represents a great and far-flung country of progress and power, this being mirrored in the economy and standard of living. Again we find the city featuring as the quintessence of all these things, a place where power finds concentrated expression. These symbolical readings of Australia and the city, which Madubang had in turn picked up from the local discursive world, did not fail to color how she described her dream world.

Her transformation into a white person while her dream-self was staying in the city continued to preoccupy Madubang in her dream interpretations. Spontaneously she saw her body's transformation, in line with the dream logic, as again oppositional to her present physical situation: her impurity enforced by taboos was turned into purity, which for her was symbolized by the process of being changed from a black into a white. This transformation of her outer self occurred from her body's inside, but only after she had, as she told me, taken the medicine her white adopted father had given her. The dream truth of being adopted while in the city not only referred to her situation as an adopted daughter, mirroring her own situation in her uncle's family; it also established—and this was particularly important to Madubang—a kinship link to a man of European origin and his wife. This kinship link plus the medicine she had been given turned Madubang into a "white" among "whites."

To be sure, the symbolic importance of "whiteness" was not made explicit in this conversation with Madubang. Nevertheless, it can be concluded from the cultural specifics of local dream interpretation discourses in Yasaburing that the "whites" may also stand proxy for the ancestors, associated with power as both of these are. This equivalence is in fact signaled in another of Madubang's dream narratives. About eight days after entering into her seclusion Madubang had dreamed of being visited by a girl from a neighboring village. When she related this dream to Elfriede, she explained that this girl, who had come accompanied by her sister, had died a short time before. And now the dead girl stood with her sister at the threshold of the seclusion room. Madubang insisted that both were white, that they were in fact two white girls. They had a radio with them; they wore wristwatches; they were decked out with ornaments; they had on blouses, pants, and shoes. In this dream perspective, which we shall not pursue further here, we again find deceased persons being identified with whites. As local statements imply, their material objects signify a capacity of producing that associates whiteness with comprehensive power.

Immediately after interpreting her transformation into a white girl, Madubang spoke of how her presentation to the village community was planned for the Easter Monday. This meant she would only have to spend another week confined and subjected to food and washing taboos; that she would soon be returned to public life. This step, however, had to be preceded by ritual purification and decoration. In her thoughts about the closing sequences of her initiation Madubang revealed ambiguous feelings. On the one hand, she longed for her time in seclusion to be over; on the other, she articulated misgivings at then being placed in the middle of things. To be sure, Madubang's dream narrative reported that in her dream she was already "pure and truly white." Thus the conclusion here suggests itself, based on her dream interpretation, that her dream-self had managed to vicariously anticipate the experience of being purified and adorned. By virtue of taking the medicine in her dream into her being and turning into a white, these ritual steps were already prefigured from the inside out, as it were. And in fact, a few days later, she did appear in public decked out in magnificent decorations—radiant as the Morning Star, as the local discourse had it.

Dreaming of being transformed into a European girl yielded for Madubang experiences predicated on her status as an initiate. Even if this dream, as a result of Madubang's isolation, was not negotiated in a social context, her statements with reference to being purified and transformed during initiation were anchored in local discourses. In this context, her dream experiences were important for how she experienced initiation. Although Madubang distinguished her experiences in the dream world from those in the waking world, she was still aware that her dream experiences referred to the transformation of her body and self taking place during initiation. The point we wish to emphasize is that the transformation of her dream-self was only possible through transcending local space. By granting access to a power-imbued domain, her dream enabled her to emerge from the initiation transformed—not only in her gender status, but also in how her body and self were constituted.

Dreamscapes

Our account of selected dream landscapes among the Ngaing, with special reference to those centered on recognizably Western city environments,[9] shows that dream experiences and dream narratives are indissolubly linked to the political process of spatial construction. In his observations on Ludwig Binswanger's "Dream and Existence," Foucault has drawn attention to space as a little-noted element in dream experience (Foucault 1984–1985:60ff.). Apart from his plea to focus more on the spaces experienced in dreams, of primary importance to us is Foucault's perspective of historically specific nexi pertaining between spaces and power relationships, which resists any conceptualizing of space as a passive, neutral backdrop of discursive events (Foucault 1977; 1980:70, 149; 1986:22–24). This perspective we have transferred onto our interlocutor's accounts of dream landscapes, derived as these are from experiences had by the dream-selves of the initiates.

The interplay between hegemonic pervasions and indigenous reconstitutions of body and space has fostered not only local self-awareness of an existence at once peripheral and subordinated; it has also called forth local counter-versions of the dominant discourses. Internalizing the essential inferiority of blackness was attended by the process of recognizing whiteness as the *fons et origo* of morality, knowledge, and power (Lattas 1992). Counter-hegemonic practices like the newly introduced ritual incision, dream and trance experiences, and narratives on the manifold cosmological orders of the inside/outside have certified whiteness as an integral part of blackness. Hence it is that the dream narratives related as part of the initiation rites and that tell how the dream-self had journeyed to the metropolitan habitats of (at once) the whites, the ancestors, and the spirits map the zones where (from a Western point of view) incompatible spaces coexist. These spaces can only be understood in the context of historical contacts and multiple interactions. Dreamscapes are subject to continuous change and are woven into the constitution of counter-spaces or "heterotopias" that focus attention on the instability, discontinuity, and ambiguity of spatial orders (see Foucault 1986).

Characteristic local landscapes pervaded by elements of the infrastructure of an industrial country were repeatedly described even in dreams by persons outside ritual confines. Such landscapes additionally assumed clear contours in rare trance depictions tendered by a number of gifted persons. Our tactic of selecting for closer study pertinent locations from initiates' dream narratives was prompted for two reasons. First, because the city in these cases, in the quite unconnected seclusions of the young men and the girl, occupied such a broad area; and second, because an atmosphere had been created for the duration of the initiations, fostering intensified preoccupation with questions of knowledge and power.

The European spaces depicted respectively by the young men and the girl showed pronounced traces of a powerful practice of Western medicine. Even the newly introduced penile incision of young men in Yawing was, according to local discourse, an indispensable practice recommended and performed by whites, one that purified and fortified the black body even as it was held to ward off disease. The dream experiences within the seclusion area selected as the incision site—which, the initiates were persuaded, enclosed an urban expanse—even ultimately confirmed that a European hospital was present at the site. Madubang in turn related how during her dream she had journeyed to a Western city and been given medicine that turned her into a white girl. Hence, the dreamscapes with their discursive counter-spaces of whiteness established therein included Western medical facilities, whose mighty capability for transformation extended the promise of "healing" the misery of blackness (cf. Comaroff 1985:8–9, 196–198).

The spatial enlargement enacted by dream events had the effect of making whiteness a component of the local world. The dream journeys into Western city landscapes[10] helped confirm the transformations effected during the ritual initiations. In both cases—that of the young men and that of the girl—the dreamers' narratives and interpretations pointed to the approaching ritual presentations. With the young men, an initiate's dream showed the novices being decked out with the attributes of whites, and the festive reception in a village showed the initiation being successfully concluded with a ritual presentation in public. The girl too associated her bodily transmutation into a white girl (in the course of a dream journey to Australia) with her imminent ritual presentation. During this final step after her seclusion she reappeared in public, purified and inwardly white and radiant. The dream narratives with their descriptions of dream landscapes and experiences of the dream-self during the seclusion supported the indigenous discourse of endowing the initiates with power. The spatial stories about the dream landscapes, about Western urban environments and interactions with whites, ancestors, and spirits, reveal the power-knowledge of the whites as a central aspect of the local world. The dream-self cannot be dissociated from the dream landscapes wherein it moves. The spatial experience of the dream-self contributes to an altered bodily experience during initiation and may be implicated when the initiates, after several weeks of seclusion and intensive ritual exposure, are presented to the community in a "purified" condition involving a "radiant" outer appearance.

The initiates' dream reports about their encounters with whites in a Western-colored environment doubtless were affected by the presence of us European anthropologists. At the times of the initiations a trusting relationship had long since grown up between the young men and Wolfgang, and between Madubang and Elfriede. As Tedlock (1987:23) stresses, it cannot be overlooked that we, as anthropologists, played a role in the production of dream narratives (e.g., Herdt 1987:70, 75–76). Thus it may be surmised that the dream narrators, in their dealings with us, emphasized their possibilities of gaining access to power, so that our conversations were a way of negotiating status and power, just as Hollan's analysis (this volume, Chapter 9) suggests. However, it is important to note that we were not the instigators of the initiates' dream excursions into Western worlds. The point is rather that a wider-reaching context of Western hegemony and indigenous counter-hegemony instigated them to position themselves within this power matrix.

The dreamscapes, as became clear during the two initiation rites we have described, fit into a discursive terrain of indigenous counter-strategies, which reverse hegemonic spatial configurations and use the ensuing foldings to set up alternative versions of space. It is precisely the seclusion during initiation, as a phase involving social and spatial isolation at specific locations, that is turned into a timespace transcending this confinement. The dream-self's insights (or in-sights) gained during this specific ritual context reveal the power of the whites within the local inside, even as they constitute participation in the attendant poietic capabilities. Dream experiences and narratives shape an imaginative field authorized by ritual power practices, one that constitutes counter-spaces by instigating a strategic extension of the local world. In these discursive counter-strategies lies the real power of dreamscapes.

Acknowledgments.

In the years 1985–86 and 1988–90—as well as a month in 1996—we carried out anthropological fieldwork respectively in the villages of Yawing and Yasaburing (both names are pseudonyms). We wish here to record our deepest gratitude, especially to the inhabitants of theses villages—with particular reference to the male initiates and the female initiate, who generously allowed us partake in their dream worlds. Also to various Papua New Guinean institutions for granting authorizations and otherwise extending their good offices, without which our research would have been impossible. Our thanks also go to the state of Baden-Württemberg's postgraduate program, as well as to the German Academic Exchange Service, for the generous financial support they extended to the two research projects. An earlier German version of this text appeared in *KEA-Zeitschrift für Kulturwissenschaften,* volume 13, *Träume/n,* 2000:91–118. Bruce Allen, as usual, did a wonderful job of translating the text. We wish to thank the participants of the workshop on dreams at the ASAO Conference in Vancouver, BC, in February 2000 for their helpful comments, in particular Roger Lohmann and Joel Robbins for their attentive reading and valuable suggestions. The responsibility for any remaining shortcomings rests, as ever, with us.

Notes

1. The prevalence of an approach whereby initiation is primarily associated with groups has meant all too often that individual rites for girls—that is, a separate rite for each girl—have eluded analytic attention (see Allen 1967:5–7, Keesing 1982:6). Lutkehaus and Roscoe (1995), in their essay collection on female initiation rites in Melanesia, draw attention to precisely this matter and provoke a revision of this group perspective and its viability. We follow their lead and also designate the rite of passage the Yasaburing perform to mark a girl's first menstruation as a case of initiation.
2. The term "*tambaran*" in the lingua franca signifies the men's secret ritual domain. In the Ngaing vernacular this secret ritual domain is called *gabu*—referring to ancestral spirits (see also Lawrence 1965; Kempf 1994).
3. This term is used by Michel De Certeau (1988:xii) to mean "production" or "creation."
4. The male initiates were aged between 18 and 35, that is, they were relatively old. The normal average age of initiates, however, is between 12 and 18

years. Two of the initiates who were already married and had children were exceptionally permitted to undergo the incision rite, this on the grounds that they had long been obliged to live as migrant workers elsewhere in the country (see also Kempf 1996:171–230).
5. This original quotation was translated from the Tok Pisin original, as were all following passages quoted.
6. Some Yawing experts like Irawa insisted that it was precisely their dealings with this secret ritual domain of "thunder" that had caused their own trances. However, other guardians of the "thunder house" in the Ngaing area have never fallen into a trance.
7. Madubang's estimate of how many weeks she had spent apart is certainly not to be understood in absolute terms. The three-and-a-half weeks she had spent in seclusion so far actually seemed longer to her.
8. Though Madubang's schoolbooks offered subjects for conversation with Elfriede, Madubang never questioned Elfriede about Australia or cities in general.
9. Indigenous imaginations associating Western cities with heaven or with the beyond were found in societies of the Madang region by Lawrence (1964:77–78) and in other parts of Papua New Guinea by Kulick (1992:183–185), Stephen (1982:112–113) and Lohmann, personal communication; see also Kempf (1999).
10. In very general terms, the Christian communities of the Ngaing can be seen as dwelling in a condition of traveling (see Clifford 1997:2, 36) to the "City of God" (see Dougherty 1980; Hawkins 1986) from which they derive their specific Christian identity.

References Cited

Allen, Michael R.
1967 Male Cults and Secret Initiations in Melanesia. Melbourne: Melbourne University Press.
Appadurai, Arjun
1988 Putting Hierarchy in its Place. Cultural Anthropology 3(1):36–49.
Clifford, James
1988 The Predicament of Culture: Twentieth-Century Ethnography, Literature, and Art. Cambridge: Harvard University Press.
1997 Routes: Travel and Translation in the Late Twentieth Century. Cambridge: Harvard University Press.
Comaroff, Jean
1985 Body of Power, Spirit of Resistance: The Culture and History of a South African People. Chicago: University of Chicago Press.
De Certeau, M.
1984 The Practice of Everyday Life. Berkeley: University of California Press.
Dougherty, James
1980 The Fivesquare City: The City in the Religious Imagination. Notre Dame: University of Notre Dame Press.

Foucault, Michel
1977 Discipline and Punish: The Birth of the Prison. New York: Vintage Books.
1980 Power/Knowledge: Selected Interviews and Other Writings, 1972–1977. C. Gordon, ed. New York: Pantheon Books.
1984–1985 Dream, Imagination and Existence. Review of Existential Psychology and Psychatry 19:29–78.
1986 Of Other Spaces. Diacritics 16:22–27.
Gupta, Akhil, and James Ferguson
1992 Beyond "Culture": Space, Identity, and the Politics of Difference. Cultural Anthropology 7(1):6–23
Hastrup, Kirsten, and Karen F. Olwig
1997 Introduction. In Siting Culture: The Shifting Anthropological Object. K. F. Olwig and K. Hastrup, eds. Pp. 1–14. London: Routledge.
Hawkins, Peter S., ed.
1986 Civitas: Religious Interpretations of the City. Atlanta: Scholar's Press.
Herdt, Gilbert H.
1987 Selfhood and Discourse in Sambia Dream Sharing. In Dreaming: Anthropological and Psychological Interpretations, B. Tedlock, ed. Pp. 55–85. Cambridge: Cambridge University Press.
Hermann, Elfriede
1995 Emotionen und Historizität: Der emotionale Diskurs über die Yali-Bewegung in einer Dorfgemeinschaft der Ngaing, Papua New Guinea. Berlin: Dietrich Reimer Verlag.
1997 Kastom Versus Cargo Cult: Emotional Discourse on the Yali Movement in Madang Province, Papua New Guinea. In Cultural Dynamics of Religious Change in Oceania. T. Otto and A. Borsboom, eds. Pp. 87–102. Leiden: KITLV Press.
1998 Geschlechterdiskurs und historische Differenz: Dis/kontinuitäten in den Geschlechterbeziehungen bei den Ngaing in Papua-Neuguinea. In Differenz und Geschlecht. Neue Ansätze in der ethnologischen Forschung. B. Hauser-Schäublin und B. Röttger-Rössler, eds. Pp. 78–106. Berlin: Dietrich Reimer Verlag.
Jedrej, M. Charles and Rosalind Shaw
1992 Introduction: Dreaming, Religion and Society in Africa. In Dreaming, Religion and Society in Africa. M. C. Jedrej and R. Shaw, eds. Pp. 1–20. Leiden: E. J. Brill.
Keesing, Roger M.
1982 Introduction. In Rituals of Manhood: Male Initiation in Papua New Guinea. G. H. Herdt, ed. Pp. 1–43. Berkeley: University of California Press.
Kempf, Wolfgang
1994 Ritual, Power and Colonial Domination: Male Initiation among the Ngaing of Papua New Guinea. In Syncretism/Anti-Syncretism: The Politics of Religious Synthesis. C. Stewart and R. Shaw, eds. Pp. 108–126. London and New York: Routledge.

1996   Das Innere des Äusseren: Ritual, Macht und historische Praxis bei den Ngaing in Papua Neuguinea. Berlin: Dietrich Reimer Verlag.

1999   Cosmologies, Cities and Cultural Constructions of Space: Oceanic Enlargements of the World. Pacific Studies 22:97–114.

Kulick, Don

1992   Language Shift and Cultural Reproduction: Socialization, Self, and Syncretism in a Papua New Guinean Village. Cambridge: Cambridge University Press.

Lattas, Andrew

1992   Skin, Personhood, and Redemption: The Doubled Self in West New Britain Cargo Cults. Oceania 63:27–54.

Lawrence, Peter

1964   Road Belong Cargo: A Study of the Cargo Movement in the Southern Madang District, New Guinea. Melbourne: Melbourne University Press.

1965   The Ngaing of the Rai Coast. *In* Gods, Ghosts and Men in Melanesia. P. Lawrence and M. J. Meggitt, eds. Pp. 198–123. Melbourne: Oxford University Press.

Lohmann, Roger Ivar

2000   The Role of Dreams in Religious Enculturation among the Asabano of Papua New Guinea. Ethos 28(1):75–102.

Lutkehaus, Nancy C. and Paul B. Roscoe, eds.

1995   Gender Rituals: Female Initiation in Melanesia. London: Routledge.

Marcus, George E. and Michael M. J. Fischer

1986   Anthropology as Cultural Critique: An Experimental Moment in the Human Sciences. Chicago: University of Chicago Press.

Stephen, Michele

1979   Dreams of Change: The Innovative Role of Altered States of Consciousness in Traditional Melanesian Religion. Oceania 50(1):3–22.

1982   "Dreaming Is Another Power!": The Social Significance of Dreams among the Mekeo of Papua New Guinea. Oceania 53(2):106–122.

1989   Dreaming and the Hidden Self: Mekeo Definitions of Consciousness. *In* The Religious Imagination in New Guinea. G. H. Herdt and M. Stephen, eds. Pp. 160–186. New Brunswick: Rutgers University Press.

Tedlock, Barbara

1987   Dreaming and Dream Research. *In* Dreaming: Anthropological and Psychological Interpretations. B. Tedlock, ed. Pp. 1–30. Cambridge: Cambridge University Press.

1994   The Evidence from Dreams. *In* Psychological Anthropology. P. K. Bock, ed. Pp. 279–295. Westport: Praeger.

4 Members of the local Presbyterian evangelical "team" sing as villagers enter church in the village of Ulei for a team service aimed at the elimination of sorcery and magic from Southeast Ambrym. Photo: Robert Tonkinson, 1973.

Chapter 5

Ambrymese Dreams and the Mardu Dreaming

Robert Tonkinson

> *To dream a dream and make it come true; to realize the shape of what can be seen only in the mind's eye; to feel compelled to bring about the seemingly impossible—these are the prerogatives of man.*
>
> —K. O. L. Burridge (1969:3)

Introduction

In this chapter I discuss the status of dreams and the social significance and consequences of dream experiences in two contrasting societies: Melanesian swidden horticulturalists in Southeast Ambrym, Vanuatu (henceforth SE Ambrym), and the Mardu, Aboriginal hunter-gatherers who now live in settlements in Western Australia's desert. The nexus between the dream experience, or inspiration, and its mediation in social process—its subsequent impact, if any, on human actors and the social fabric—is a challenging topic, because it entails a movement from an intensely private experience into the realm of shared understandings that is so variable as to make generalization difficult. As Hollan (this volume, Chapter 9: 169) notes, "People do not merely register or reproduce cultural meanings and beliefs in their dreams; they use, manipulate, and transform those cultural resources in personally creative and expressive ways." A major inspiration for this attempt at comparison has been the work of Ken Burridge, who, in his groundbreaking studies of millenarian movements, *Mambu* (1960) and *New Heaven, New Earth* (1969), has explored the complex interplay of real-world experiences, ideas, and desires and their expression in myths and dreams.[1] In his writings, Burridge has made patently clear that issues of status, politics, and power are inevitably implicated in the passage of dreams outwards from a reported individual experience and in their diffusion and potentially transformative impact on a given group or society. His writing on prophecy and the role of the myth-dream in communicating new knowledge and understanding about the world also underlines the great significance of dreams in many societies as catalysts in cultural transmission (cf. Lohmann 2000, who provides a convincing demonstration of this process in relation to Asabano religious beliefs).

The SE Ambrymese and the Mardu Aborigines, both of whom I have worked with since the 1960s, are alike in that the events taking place in their dreams are often believed to contain truths that have a bearing on, and consequences for, human affairs.[2] There are also important differences in the status of dreams between the two societies. SE Ambrymese dream experiences, while not unimportant in certain cultural aspects, particularly those relating to divination, sorcery, and curing, do not appear to have occupied a central place in the "traditional" cosmic order in SE Ambrym. My evidence suggests that, regardless of the far-reaching effects of prolonged contact with Europeans and the adoption of Christianity, dream experiences among the SE Ambrymese were never integral to the formation or maintenance of major cultural structures, such as the religious life. In the Aboriginal case, however, they are at the very heart of cosmology, innovation, and social reproduction, and the prominence of their status as a generative and integrative force is undeniable (cf. Stanner 1966; Burridge 1973:74). At the outset, however, I acknowledge that the SE Ambrym case may be atypical, since Burridge's superb account of the myth-dream in *Mambu* and evidence from other parts of Melanesia demonstrate clearly the important role played by dreams in many Melanesian cultures (cf. Berndt 1962; this volume, Kempf and Hermann Chapter 4; Lindstrom 1990; Lohmann 2000, this volume, Chapter 10; Meggitt 1962; this volume, Robbins Chapter 2; Stephen 1979, 1982, 1987a; Wagner 1972).

Dreaming in Southeast Ambrym

The southeastern corner of Ambrym, with fifteen villages and a resident population of between 1,500 and 2,000, forms a distinct culture area. The island's two volcanoes and the surrounding ash-plain divide it into three separate inhabited sections, with different languages and in some respects contrasting post-contact histories. For example, some of the inland villages in North Ambrym have strongly resisted Christianity to this day (cf. Patterson 1981); in the southeast, however, all were at least nominally Christian by the early 1920s (Frater 1922). Within the SE Ambrym culture area, there is a high degree of social and political homogeneity, aided in part by the dominance of a single major denomination, the Presbyterian Church, which claims over 90 percent of the inhabitants.

What the north and southeast do appear to share is an aspect of their traditional religions, namely a markedly "secular" tone (cf. Guiart 1951; Tonkinson 1966, 1982). Jean Guiart has described North Ambrymese rituals as lacking mythological validation and exhibiting a highly secular character. In SE Ambrym, too, there is little or no evidence of any fit between myths and rituals, very little correspondence among songs, dances, and rituals, and no indication of an indigenous view that the system was either well integrated or possessed something like an organic unity. Mary Patterson (personal communication), on the basis of her research in North Ambrym, concurs with these generalizations. What could be construed as further corroborative evidence comes from Lane (1965), in his overview of the religion of South Pentecost, which lies just to the north of Ambrym. Robert B. Lane concluded that order was not an explicit feature of the religious system of South Pentecost, and beliefs were neither precisely and systematically detailed nor woven into any larger cosmological scheme.[3] This looseness of fit, plus the prevalence of cultural borrowing (see below), may help explain the structural peripherality of dream experiences in SE Ambrym.

Dreams (*metuvuei*)[4] are not routinely reported among SE Ambrymese: "*moletin houlu lametuvue–letaaveteniti*" [lots of people dream (but) they don't tell them]. One conceptualization of dream experiences holds a person's spirit (*ninin*) to be the agent responsible for out-of-body travels. Yet some SE Ambrymese seemed unsure about whether seeing themselves elsewhere in dreams indicated that part of them had traveled from their body during sleep.[5] Dreams are most often invoked in particular circumstances; for example, when their reported content is used to shed light on a sudden death in which sorcery is suspected or if it is interpreted as portending some future occurrence. People who dream of others may inform them of this fact, and are generally then questioned by the person dreamed about for details regarding what they saw. As in most human societies, the amount of credence given to the content of dreams varies greatly, as does the decision of whether or not to transmit what was dreamt, and the degree of conscious fabrication on the part of the dreamer who is intent on disclosure to certain others. Certainly, not all dreams are held to be true. For example, the events depicted may be regarded as true but the *dramatis personae* involved as mistaken, or the dreamer may assess the credibility of the dream experience according to its perceived bodily or emotional impact (see this volume, Hollan Chapter 9). As in the rest of Melanesia, considerable attention is paid to reported dream experiences that constitute potential sources of explanation and evidence for events—most often of an unusual or unpredictable kind—and dreams are of major importance in both divination and sorcery (cf. Stephen 1987a:63–66; 1987b:294–295). Since the adoption of Christianity, dreaming appears to have become the altered state of consciousness most often connected to encounters with, or revelations from, the Holy Spirit. For some it is the source of very powerful conversion or faith-renewal experiences that ensue from following instructions that are part of particularly vivid dreams (cf. Lohmann 2000, who suggests that, in times of confusion and fear when people are giving up traditional beliefs and practices for Christianity, dreams can play a major role in resolving incongruities and in bolstering their commitment to the new faith).

Throughout Vanuatu, there is a connection between dreams and specialist roles of divining and curing, and the Pidgin term *kleva* (clever) is used to denote men, women, or children who are believed to possess special powers to divine and treat illness (Tonkinson 1979). Although there are several possible sources of their power and many different techniques are employed by them, these part-time specialists most commonly use dream-divination. This procedure necessitates the *kleva*'s sleeping on an item of the patient's clothing (known as *-paat paen* in SE Ambrym), or the use of leaves or other objects that have been in contact with said patient. During sleep, the *kleva* is said to dream the source of the illness, either by direct perception or by sending out a spirit-familiar to investigate the problem. Using a spirit-familiar in this way is congruent with a widespread belief that chronic illness is characteristically caused by the stealing and imprisonment of a person's spirit or soul by sorcerers or malevolent spirits. Part of this process may entail a spirit of the dead possessing the patient and thus diminishing his or her life-force. In some cases, a sick person may dream of seeing a dead person, that is, the possessing spirit, and can thus diagnose his or her own illness.

Old people say that in the past in SE Ambrym there were very few *kleva* (in the local language, *linglingtemaet* or *livaivai*) and in recent times there have been only one or two reported practitioners, both men. However, this paucity of adepts performing such a socially important role is illusory, for two reasons. One is that today church leaders are often called upon to perform a similar role, as parishioners ask them to pray for sick people or for the recovery of lost objects. The SE Ambrymese leader of the Presbyterian Church's national evangelical "team" refers to his house as the "Number Two Clinic" because he is so often visited by people seeking such help.[6] Secondly, there *are* a small number of diviners (*lele*), men and women who discover causes of illness, locate lost property, and foretell events. Their powers are acquired via secret initiation and are believed to reside in their noses. In the past, a major role they played was that of warning individuals of an impending sorcery attack. They are not usually curers, though. The use of leaf-medicines is universal, and knowledge of the recipes is distributed widely among families throughout the region. Particular families hold knowledge of the medicines for particular illnesses (e.g., the medicine for injuries sustained in falling from a breadfruit tree is different, and obtained from a different family, than that for a fall from a coconut palm), but no one individual or family claims exclusive possession of a large number of different medicines, or practices as a specialist. Today as in the past, new leaf-medicines may be revealed to people via dreams; traditionally, the transmitter of such information would have been the spirit of a dead relative (*temaet*). Near every hamlet or village was a special *tabu ples* (tabooed place) or *votut,* where the living could communicate by calling out to their dead patriline ancestors, but at the urging of Church leaders these sites have been planted over in the Christian era.

By the time of my first fieldwork in Melanesia in 1966–1967, no material vestiges and not a great deal of knowledge remained of the "traditional" religious life in SE Ambrym. In talking to the oldest people throughout the area about what they remembered of that life before Christianity arrived, I was able to glean information concerning men's cults and initiation and the "graded society" (cf. Blackwood 1981), but no one mentioned dreams as playing any part in these religious institutions. The strong impression I gained, of an extreme looseness of fit among the various major elements of SE Ambyrm religion, led me initially to attribute this lack of systematization to cultural loss and the effects of Christianity. For example, upon conversion, people in many villages burned their slit-gongs and other ritual paraphernalia and abandoned their dancing grounds (Frater 1922). However, subsequent reassessments of the early contact era indicated evidence of both a high level of cultural diffusion in the central Vanuatu islands and an openness in much of the rest of the social system (Tonkinson 1982, 1994; see also Larcom 1982; Patterson 1981).

It is thus reasonable to conclude that the various components of the traditional religious life in SE Ambrym were loosely integrated. Magical rites and communication with ancestral ghosts carried out by individuals seemed to have assumed far greater religious importance than collective rituals or appeals to mythic beings. At the level of individual religious practice, then, dream experiences may well have played a significant divinatory and explanatory or facilitatory role—no doubt basically similar to those roles described for other Melanesian societies (cf. Lohmann 2000; this volume, Chapter 10). Yet except for the fact that individual rituals were acts toward, and reactions to, concerns of wider social groups, there appears to have been no society-wide integration in any way analogous to the Aboriginal case. There was nothing akin to the "Dreaming" concept, which in "traditional" Aboriginal Australia can be fairly described as the key cultural symbol, since it underpins the entire cultural fabric (cf. Stanner 1979; this volume, Keen Chapter 7; Maddock 1984; Morphy 1988; Poirier 1996; this volume, Chapter 6).

Aboriginal Dreams and The Dreaming

The similarities between the SE Ambrym and Western Desert cases are greatest at the individual level, where there is shared conviction concerning the reality of dream experiences and the importance of dreams in explanation and in foretelling or forewarning of future events. Yet it must be stated at the outset that dream experiences play a far more significant role at all levels of Mardu society than in SE Ambrym. In the case of part-time specialism, close parallels exist between the use of dream experiences by the *kleva* in divining illness and their use by the Mardu diviner-curer (called *maparn* throughout the Western Desert region). Many *maparn* use spirit-familiars, usually birds, which are said to play major roles in both divination and curing.[7]

Whereas many of the ni-Vanuatu who today practice as *kleva* prescribe leaf-medicines in the treatment of the illnesses they diagnose, *maparn* rely almost exclusively on their own magical "operations." Their powers, like those of their spirit-familiars, derive ultimately from the creative ancestral beings of The Dreaming; as such, they are thoroughly integrated into the spiritual foundation of the Aboriginal cosmic order. In SE Ambrym, understandings about the powers of individual diviner-curers do not include any hints of connectedness akin to Aboriginal cosmological conceptions. A Mardu and a SE Ambrymese would, I believe, readily agree on the lived reality of dream experiences and on the notion that spiritual powers may be curative or harmful, but their ideas as to the sources of that power would be quite different.

Although Jigalong was a mission station when I first worked there in 1963, Christian beliefs had made little or no impact on traditional understandings and on Mardu religious life, which flourished under the very noses of the disapproving missionaries (Tonkinson 1974). The beliefs outlined below are still held today, although hand in hand with a growing—and in many respects competing—body of knowledge about the society that encapsulates them and is impinging on their lives with ever-increasing intensity. Every Mardu has a dream-spirit (*partunjarri*), which can leave the body during dreams (*kapukurri* or *jukurrpa*) and fly about. No one questions the reality of such journeys, and people sometimes complain of exhaustion after long and/or dangerous trips (cf. Stephen 1987a:52, whose account of Mekeo dream-spirit journeys and their dangers is strikingly similar to what obtains among the Mardu). Bad trips involve encounters with malevolent spirit-beings, and it is considered dangerous for women or children to "go *partunjarri*" in case they encounter objects or activities that are secret-sacred to initiated males. Since a person's spirit goes on these journeys, accidents during travel could cause the body to sicken and die, and the temporary absence of the spirit is why sleeping people should never be awakened suddenly, lest the spirit not have sufficient time to re-enter the body.

For people without the powers of the *maparn* diviner-curer, it is safer to travel in convoy, with the *maparn* riding shotgun at the front of the special "vehicles" (huge snakes, or "airplanes" made from sacred objects), on which large numbers of people sometimes ride. Such mass trips are sometimes an integral part of a particular ritual, as in the case of rainmaking, in which the dream-spirit journeys that are said to occur take people inside the major rainmaking waterholes (cf. Tonkinson 1970). Their major intent is to induce the ancestral snake-men who dwell there to send out their rainmakers and follow the travelers back to where the rain is required.

The regeneration of plant and animal species on which continued existence is believed to depend is achieved through periodic ritual performances at "increase sites" scattered far and wide through the desert (cf. Meggitt 1962:220–221). It may happen that the local "bosses" for a given site are a great distance from it when the time for the ritual is nigh (a not unusual situation, given the paucity of rainfall in this area, which at times necessitates extended absences from home territories). They must thus visit the site in dream-spirit form, flying deep inside to persuade the spirits of the plant or animal concerned to emerge into the natural world in response to their human guardians' ritual entreaties. The spirits are strongly urged to be plentiful throughout the whole of the desert region, thus bringing food and contentment to human society. This is one major sense in which such experiences are, in the Aboriginal view, essential to social reproduction (cf. Tonkinson 1988; see also Hamilton 1982). When many Mardu moved to settlements some distance from their homelands, dream-spirit journeys became very important in maintaining strong spiritual bonds to country. This purported ability to take action in dreams in order to exert a major influence on the physical world does not appear to be a feature of the Melanesian societies reported on in this volume.

Upon further examination, the connection between dream experiences and the concept of the Dreaming (*Mangunypa* or *Jukurrpa*) reveals even more clearly the fundamental importance of the *partunjarri* journey and the extent of its embeddedness in the cosmological and cultural core of Western Desert society. Aborigines throughout Australia seem to have chosen the English gloss "Dreaming" or "Dreamtime" to convey to non-Aborigines an idea of this key concept, no doubt because it is during dreams, in an altered state of consciousness, that individuals are most often able to come close to the spiritual realm of the ancestral creative beings. As Poirier (this volume, Chapter 6: 110) notes, dreams and dreaming are vital expressions of the Dreaming and share a common aesthetic; they are relationally complicit, but nevertheless "they represent two structurally distinct levels of reality." The creative beings (*jukurtani* or *mangunypa*) of the Dreaming epoch withdrew from the human realm at the end of their lives on earth and thenceforth no longer impinged directly on the affairs of the living. Nevertheless, they are believed to keep watch on the earthly doings of their human Aboriginal descendants and to release life-sustaining power into that realm in response to correct ritual performance. In addition, via the use of spirit-being intermediaries, called *jijikarrkaly,* they release new knowledge, particularly of a religious kind (songs, dances, designs, objects), to individuals, most often in sleep during the wanderings of their dream-spirit (cf. Lindstrom 1990; Wagner 1972).

Mardu men share such revelations with others, including at times women, and the outcome is sometimes a complete new ritual.[8] Those who contribute songs give credit to the ancestral beings as the source of knowledge they have gained, explaining that they were "given," or "shown," or "found," the information concerned (Tonkinson 1970). The work of Robbins (this volume, Chapter 2), concerning the Melanesian Urapmin, shows some interesting parallels with the Mardu case; for example, the describing of dream revelations as given or shown to the dreamer, and the establishment or reinforcement through dream reporting of a dominant theme (in the case of the Urapmin, it is often a millennial one). Not only dreams, but reverie, too, may prove revelatory for the Mardu, as when a man "sees" something buried in a particular spot which he visualizes. Later, he may visit the spot and unearth an object, which will then be shown to a gathering of male elders in order to have its religious significance verified and validated in communal discussion (cf. this volume, Hollan Chapter 9, who discusses the post-hoc attribution of significance).

In the genesis of ritual, two kinds of transformation occur. First, individual experience may be transmuted into collective endeavor in the creation of a new ritual; and second, dream-spirit rituals (*partunjarrijanu,* literally "dream-spirit from") enter the desert circuit and soon become, to distant recipient groups, *Mangunyjanu* (Dreaming from) rituals, believed to have their origins in the long-past creative era. They quickly lose their here-and-now quality as they are handed on, and their human composers are forgotten as their time scale expands to become immutable. Róheim (1945) suggested that the origin of Aboriginal rituals lay in dreams, but was unsure how an individual experience came to be translated into collective creative activity. During his fieldwork, he must not have witnessed the coming into being of dream-spirit rituals, for this process would have provided the answer. I am sure that Róheim is correct and that, in the Western Desert area at least, rituals have their origin in reported dream experiences, which provide the necessary inspiration for this kind of innovation.

This denial of human creativity is a means of providing legitimacy and authenticity, and helps hasten the process of conversion of dream-spirit derived rituals into the timeless and immutable "Dreaming" rituals, which become part of the chain of diffusion that characterizes the entire Western Desert area. As among the Yolngu of northeast Arnhem Land, there is a distinct downplaying of creativity in favor of the power of the original creative beings (see this volume, Keen Chapter 7, who suggests that this de-emphasis may be linked to particular concepts of mental processes). The conversion of what is specific in terms of time, space, and human actors to an unquestioned view of the ritual as immutable may take only a few years. The religious life must constantly be invigorated and recharged, and the central role played by ritual innovation reflects the immense significance of dream experiences in desert cultures.

What other kinds of altered states are evinced by the Mardu Aborigines? One important manifestation is said to occur when people dance the role of ancestral beings, particularly when men, in secret-sacred contexts, carry sacred objects and wear "powerful" body decorations. It is believed that, for the duration of the dance, they do not merely imitate or emulate the movements of the particular being depicted, but that they leave their earthly state and temporarily become one with that being, entering the spiritual realm. The great intensity of their movements and facial contortions often suggested to me a total absorption in the role, an almost trance-like state that is witnessed outside this particular context only on the part of novices undergoing very painful physical initiation, such as circumcision. The dance is meant to be a transcendent experience, one that takes the actor into contact with the ultimate powers. That it is clearly a dangerous and liminal state—the human spirit being thus freed and therefore highly vulnerable while it is out of its normal element—is indicated by the action of one or two members of the audience, who, upon completion of the dance, dash forward and touch the dancer, to bring him back into the physical world. Typically, Mardu have little to say about the meaning of such experiences to them, so the observer has to guess.

An interesting Australian parallel can be found in the impressive work of Munn (1973) on the Warlpiri of central Australia, who are in many ways culturally similar to the Mardu. From the accounts of both men and women, Munn (1973:114fn) gained the strong impression that "the dreamer felt himself to be both a kind of observer of the events of the dream and at the same time an actor in the dream, identified with the ancestors." This kind of identification accords strongly with the situation of the Mardu dancer while within the performance frame. The focus of Munn's study is Warlpiri iconography, and in her view the notion that ancestral designs originate in dream experiences is fundamental to Warlpiri thought. Munn suggests that such dreams entail the "rerunning" of daily experience under the guise of ancestral experience (1973:113). The imperative that such dream experiences be reproduced in the waking world and observed by others suggests to Munn (1973:226) the importance of binding "the inner self to the external social order."

Divining that altered states entail liminality and therefore danger is easier in the case of dream-spirit travels, because people sometimes offer vivid explanations about encounters with malevolent spirits and "near-misses," and if stricken by a spirit-missile they seek the divinatory and curative services of the *maparn*. Just how dangerous dream-spirit journeys may be depends largely upon whether one is a *maparn* or a *munta* (someone who lacks such magical powers). It is believed that *maparn* have within their bodies powerful objects which protect them, enable them to "see" what others cannot, and can be used as offensive weapons against people or malevolent spirits. Thus dream-spirit travel is safer if undertaken in the company of *maparn*, not only because of their special powers but also because they are already well known to most spirit-beings as a result of their allegedly more frequent communication with the spiritual realm. In addition, they are the only humans said to be able to see the creative ancestral beings themselves. Their journeys into the spiritual realm make them ideal curers, because a strong and recurrent theme in the dreams of Mardu involves being attacked by malevolent spirits who throw so many missiles that the dreamer is unable to dodge them all. A person thus afflicted would call in one or more *maparn*, who use their powers to locate the position of the foreign object(s), and then by manipulation magically "remove" it from the patient's body. The object, most often a wooden or stone sliver, is then shown to the greatly relieved sufferer, whose subsequent recovery is generally rapid.

Conclusion

In both Mardu and SE Ambrym societies, dreams may be sources of information, inspiration or anxiety. Depending on their credibility for the dreamer, and sometimes also for others with whom the dream experience is shared, they may act as potent motivators to or inhibitors of people's behavior. For SE Ambrym, I have very little evidence of altered states of consciousness; there, the kind of possession by spirits of the dead that occasionally occurs is evinced by illness and not by other kinds of atypical or excessive behaviors. Among the Mardu, however, both men and women report that spirit-children who have entered their mothers sometimes "push" these pregnant women into uncharacteristic and excessive acts, for which the spirit-child and not the woman is blamed (Tonkinson 1984).

At times of heightened spiritual awareness, as during an anti-sorcery evangelical campaign I witnessed in SE Ambrym in 1973, some people reported having dream experiences involving visions, inspiration, spiritual directives to action, and the presence of the Holy Spirit. As longtime Christians, the SE Ambrymese look to the Holy Spirit to fill them with beneficent power and to protect them against evil powers, such as those manipulated by sorcerers. To my knowledge, however, none of this manifested itself in trance, possession or great bursts of prophecy as it has elsewhere in Melanesia. (I should note here that SE Ambrym appears never to have been the locus of millenarian activities, nor have I ever detected anything in people's discourse that could be construed as reflecting a millenarian or "cargoist" mindset.)

Certainly, the evangelical campaign engendered a great deal of religious fervor, much more than their normal Presbyterian worship would have generated, and there was palpable euphoria in SE Ambrym as a result of the apparent defeat of the forces of evil (Tonkinson 1981:249–254). However, as orthodox Christians not given to glossolalia or other manifestations of the spirit in individuals, the SE Ambrymese tended to perceive the Holy Spirit's presence as a general manifestation, affecting everyone in a consciousness-raising way rather than inducing radically altered individual states.

At the level of the individual, parallels are discernible between SE Ambrym and desert Aboriginal divinatory uses of dream experiences by part-time specialist curers. Yet divination is much more of an acquired skill among SE Ambrymese practitioners than Mardu *maparn,* whose powers are most often inherited and connect back into the Dreaming itself, as their purported ultimate origin. Aboriginal understandings about dream experiences and curing powers reveal these phenomena as embedded within an integrated cosmic order. In the creation of new rituals, and the annual summoning of plants and animals essential to human survival, dream experiences play a crucial generative and reproductive role, while at the individual level they are both a major cause of dis-ease (manifesting the perils of approaching too close to the vast powers of the spiritual realm) and of its cure (through *maparn,* whose special powers make entry into that realm much less dangerous). In SE Ambrym, however, the dream experiences of the diviner-curer are not similarly integrated into any over-arching cosmological framework. In the sense that they are not held to relate to spiritual powers, and probably never were, it would thus be possible to conclude that they are not "religious."

As noted above, it would be unwise to generalize for the Melanesian region as a whole from the SE Ambrymese case, since there is such enormous cultural variation, even over quite small distances. As Chowning's (1977:2) oft-quoted statement warns, "it is literally impossible to make more than a handful of generalizations that will apply to even the majority of the societies in Melanesia." Furthermore, some of the cosmological systems described for Melanesian peoples display strong correspondences with aspects of the Aboriginal cosmic order as already outlined (see, for example, Lawrence's accounts of the Ngaing and the Garia of the Rai Coast; 1964, 1965, 1984, 1987). Also, as I have remarked, there are Melanesian societies in which dream experiences *are* much more integral to the culture taken as a whole. On the broadest comparative level, however, and in view of the major contrasts that can be identified between Melanesian and Aboriginal modes of adaptation, it is not difficult to posit strong reasons why my conclusions may have wider applicability. Chowning's admonition aside, the Melanesian cultural milieu can be accurately characterized as much more competitive, materialistic and exchange-oriented than that of hunter-gatherer Aboriginal Australia.[9]

It is therefore more likely that Melanesian diviner-curers will employ their skills and powers in ways calculated to enhance the practitioner's personal prestige, power and, possibly, material wealth than in the promotion of broader, society-wide concerns of the kinds discussed in Robbins (this volume, Chapter 2). In the case of the Western Desert Aborigines, there would perhaps be prestige value in the exercise by the *maparn* of his curative and divinatory skills, but such a consideration would be overshadowed by the strongly held Mardu conviction that his skills are given to him for the benefit of all. (This, however, is not to deny the more positive aspects of Melanesian sorcery directed at social control or protection/offense against enemies; cf. Stephen 1987b.) Also, much of his role entails cooperation with his fellow *maparn* in activities aimed at the protection of the local "residential" group or community at large, with services freely given. In view of the centrality of the concept of the Dreaming in Aboriginal cultures, and in the desert a strongly inclusivist ethos that defines "society" in the widest geographical and social terms (seen most clearly in regional interdependence concerning the maintenance of animal and plant fertility via "increase rituals"), it is predictable that the major significance of dream experiences would lie in their generative and reproductive roles (cf. Tonkinson 1987).

The antisocial and destructive face of the diviner-curer role, so prevalent in Melanesian societies, is present in the suspicions of many Aboriginal groups concerning their practitioners, but is nowhere held to be the predominant characteristic of this social role. It is noteworthy, however, that sorcery in Melanesia as a whole is often associated with high status positions, such as the big-man or chief (cf. Zelenietz 1971; Tonkinson 1981), and is an integral part of what Lawrence (1987) would describe as a unified cosmic order. Along with dream experiences and states of altered consciousness, it thus may have high epistemological value (Stephen 1987b:294). In other words, the SE Ambrym case may be exceptional in the apparent disconnectedness of the diviner-curer role from the cosmological realm, past and present.

If there is a common denominator, something that makes sense of both these quite contrasting situations, it has to be related to the apprehension and exercise of power, whether or not the origin of this power is clearly spiritual, or inherent in objects themselves (as in the SE Ambrym sorcery and divination-curing cases). The powers exercised by the SE Ambrymese *kleva* or sorcerer or *lele* are not integrated into a wider moral system but stem from a "democratic" view of what is available somewhere "out there," and are therefore potentially manipulable by anyone mature enough to possess the necessary performative skills. To this must be added an abiding and seemingly universal Melanesian conviction: that an individual's power is inherently variable and therefore, like a reservoir, can accrete or be depleted by human ritual action of an essentially individual and often, but not necessarily, antisocial kind (see, e.g., Kelly 1976).

For the Mardu, there is the same concern about power, but its source is clearly defined, as are the lines of access, and it is not "democratically available." Differential access defines the grosser inequalities of sex and age, with older males the principal vehicles for—and facilitators of—the outpouring of power from the spiritual realm and into human affairs. The pervasiveness of the Dreaming renders it much more morally charged and structured than in the SE Ambrym case, and less amenable to individual, antisocial manipulation (though this occurs). If, as Ken Burridge (1973:159) has suggested, "There is no culture from whose activities and categories of understanding it is not possible to infer an instruction to break free of moral constraints and soar, like a hawk, beyond and above the laocoon coils of given social relations," then the SE Ambrymese individual seems far better poised to succeed in such a liberating leap than his or her Mardu counterpart. Despite the much greater constraints, notably those exercised by the web of kinship and by an abiding ethos of "assent to life's terms," to quote the apt phrase of Stanner (1965), the desert Aborigines have greater opportunity to convert dream experiences, initially highly individual, into cultural structures of great importance. This potential contrasts markedly with the SE Ambrym case, where there is in a sense nowhere far that a people, even a *kleva* or a *lele* diviner, can take their dreams as "marketable commodities"; the *kleva* is curing individuals, not society. The desert Mardu, on the other hand, while certainly not "breaking free from moral restraints," always has the possibility that oaks of ritual will grow from his acorn of dream experience. The existence of this possibility relates to the status of human actors as culturally divorced from innovation, so that individual Mardu strongly see themselves as acting merely as vehicles or intermediaries for communication between omnipotent spiritual forces and the human cultural realm. Though it must be

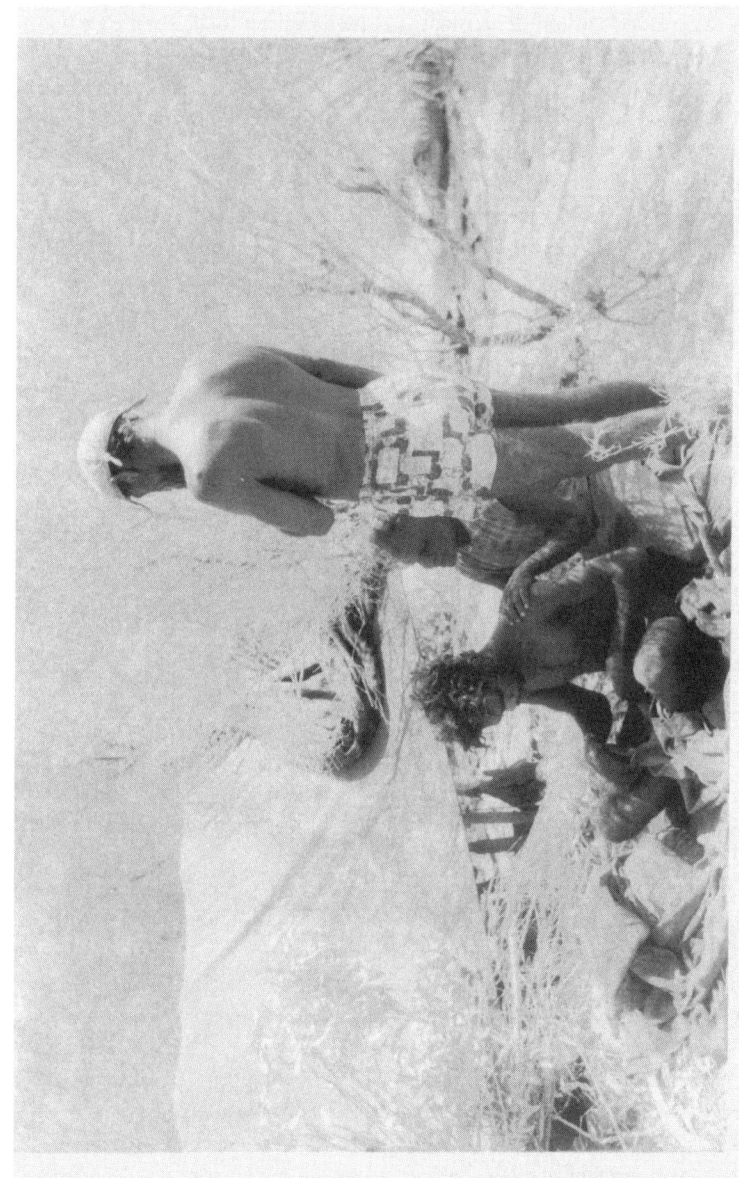

5 Two Mardu *Maparn* with a novice, attempting to diagnose his sickness. Photo: Robert Tonkinson.

said that SE Ambrymese are not given to possession by the Holy Spirit, so the probability of empowering visions is not great, no such severe limits are placed on the individual to prevent the conversion of inspiration and innovation into social capital and concomitant prestige. The limits of, and on, power appear to be very different, but as Ken Burridge suggests in the quote with which I began this chapter, the prerogatives are shared. The potential for manipulation, for individual or in-group gain, is no doubt always present in all societies, and in this volume both Keen (Chapter 7) and Robbins (Chapter 2) explore, for an Aboriginal and a Melanesian society respectively, relationships between dreams as a mode of revelation and structures of authority. In both cases, they show, as have I, a range of largely inhibiting factors that stand between the creative individual dreamer and the achievement of a socio-economically gainful realization of that vision.

Notes

1. I did my Ph.D. at the University of British Columbia, under Ken Burridge's tutelage, and it was the fact that he has contributed significantly to our understanding of both Melanesian and Australian Aboriginal cultures which prompted me to attempt a comparison involving both these areas.
2. Cf. Stephen (1982:107), although in a subsequent article, in discussing the role of the sorcery adept in Melanesia, she suggests that "dreams and similar states represent to him a different reality underlying mere surface appearances" (1987b:295).
3. Scholars as far back as Codrington (1891) suggested that there was a lack of systematization in the worldviews of Melanesians and a willingness to borrow cultural elements. More recently, Brunton (1980), for example, argued that Melanesians religions are weakly integrated and characterized by a high degree of individual variation, as well as high rates of innovation and obsolescence.
4. The noun is *metuvueien;* the verb is *-metuvueini;* for example, *nametuvueini* = I dream. There is no separate word for "nightmare," which translates as *metuvueien misa* or bad dream.
5. As with most matters concerning the pre-Christian past in SE Ambrym, people express uncertainty about the nature and power of such phenomena, and their responses are generally hedged about with qualifiers, such as "the old people never explained these things properly to us, so we aren't sure." Most people I asked thought that the power of the *linglingtemaet* was acquired rather than inborn, most probably from being given a special leaf-medicine to drink, or, according to one informant, from encountering and being instructed in the art by a *titamol* (a small, hairy trickster who lives in banyan trees and sometimes interferes mischievously in human affairs) in the form of a small boy.
6. For biographical information about this remarkable leader, Jimmy Anson, and his pivotal role in the growth of Church power in SE Ambrym, see

Tonkinson (1981:249–54). Anson's recommitment to a Christian life stemmed from a sudden collapse, "as if shot by a .22," and the voice of Jesus Christ telling him to return immediately to his home island, where "work is there for you" (J. Anson, personal communication, May 1999).
7. There is an extensive literature on Aboriginal "men of high degree," as they have been dubbed by Elkin (1977) in a major work on the subject. See also Reid 1983; Tonkinson 1991:128–132; M. Tonkinson 1982).
8. Within the realm of Mardu women's secret-sacred activity, however, I cannot comment on whether or not in similar fashion dreams form the basis for ritual creation, but good evidence exists for the Warlpiri desert people (see Munn 1973 and Dussart 2000 on Warlpiri women's creativity and ritual politics).
9. For example, neither Chowning, nor (more surprisingly) Trompf in his overview of Melanesian religion (1991), has much to say about basic concepts of power and causation, which appear to show much consistency throughout this region. In my view, there is sufficient similarity in Melanesian modes of adaptation, political structures, worldviews and value systems to allow a certain level of generalization, especially when the region of contrast is Aboriginal Australia (cf. Tonkinson n.d.).

References Cited

Berndt, R. M.
1962   Excess and Restraint: Social Control among a New Guinea Mountain People. Chicago: University of Chicago Press.
Blackwood, Peter
1981   Rank, Exchange and Leadership in Four Vanuatu Societies. *In* Vanuatu: Politics, Economics and Ritual in Island Melanesia. M. Allen, ed. Pp. 35–84. Sydney: Academic Press.
Brunton, Ron
1980   Misconstrued Order in Melanesian Religion. Man (NS) 15 (1):112–128.
Burridge, Kenelm O. L.
1960   Mambu: A Study of Melanesian Cargo Cults and their Social and Ideological Background. New York: Harper and Row.
1969   New Heaven, New Earth: A Study of Millenarian Activities. Oxford: Basil Blackwell.
1973   Encountering Aborigines, a Case Study: Anthropology and the Australian Aboriginal. New York: Pergamon.
Chowning, Ann
1977   An Introduction to the Peoples and Cultures of Melanesia, 2^d edition. Menlo Park: Cummings.
Dussart, Françoise
2000   The Politics of Ritual in an Aboriginal Settlement: Kinship, Gender, and the Currency of Knowledge. Washington: Smithsonian Institution Press.
Elkin, Adolphus P.
1974   Aboriginal Men of High Degree, 2^d edition. Brisbane: University of Queensland Press.

Frater, Maurice
1922   Midst Volcanic Fires. London: James Clarke and Company.

Guiart, Jean
1951   Sociétés, rituels et mythes du Nord-Ambrym (Nouvelles Hébrides). Journal de la Société des Océanistes 7:5–103.

Hamilton, Annette
1982   The Unity of Hunting-Gathering Societies: Reflections on Economic Forms and Resource Management. *In* Resource Managers: North American and Australian Hunter-Gatherers. N. M. Williams and E. S. Hunn, eds. Pp. 229–247. Boulder: Westview Press.

Kelly, Ray
1976   Witchcraft and Sexual Relations: An Exploration in the Social and Semantic Implications of the Structure of Belief. *In* Man and Woman in the New Guinea Highlands. P. Brown and G. Buchbinder, eds. Pp. 36–53. Washington: American Anthropological Association.

Lane, Robert B.
1965   The Melanesians of South Pentecost, New Hebrides. *In* Gods, Ghosts and Men in Melanesia. P. Lawrence and M. J. Meggitt, eds. Pp. 250–279. Melbourne: Oxford University Press.

Larcom, Joan
1982   The Invention of Convention. *In* Reinventing Traditional Culture: The Politics of Kastom in Island Melanesia. R. M. Keesing and R. Tonkinson, eds. Mankind (Special Issue) 13(4):330–37.

Lawrence, Peter
1964   Road Belong Cargo: A Study of the Cargo Movement in the Southern Madang District, New Guinea. Manchester: Manchester University Press.
1965   The Ngaing of the Rai Coast. *In* Gods, Ghosts and Men in Melanesia. P. Lawrence and M. J. Meggitt, eds. Pp. 198–223. Melbourne: Oxford University Press.
1984   The Garia: An Ethnography of a Traditional Cosmic System in Papua New Guinea. Melbourne: Melbourne University Press.
1987   De Rerum Natura: The Garia View of Sorcery. *In* Sorcerer and Witch in Melanesia. M. Stephen, ed. Pp. 17–40. Melbourne: Melbourne University Press.

Lindstrom, Lamont
1990   Knowledge and Power in a South Pacific Society. Washington: Smithsonian Institution Press.

Lohmann, Roger Ivar
2000   The Role of Dreams in Religious Enculturation among the Asabano of Papua New Guinea. Ethos 28(1):75–102.

Maddock, Kenneth
1984   The World Creative Powers. *In* Religion in Aboriginal Australia: An Anthology. M. Charlesworth, H. Morphy, D. Bell, and K. Maddock, eds. Pp. 85–103. Brisbane: University of Queensland Press.

Meggitt, Mervyn J.
1962   Desert People. Sydney: Angus and Robertson.

1965 The Mae Enga of the Western Highlands. *In* Gods, Ghosts and Men in Melanesia. P. Lawrence and M. J. Meggitt, eds. Pp. 105–131. Melbourne: Melbourne University Press.

Morphy, Howard
1988 The Resurrection of the Hydra: Twenty-Five Years of Research on Aboriginal Religion. *In* Social Anthropology and Australian Aboriginal Studies: A Contemporary Overview. R. M. Berndt and R. Tonkinson, eds. Pp. 239–266. Canberra: Aboriginal Studies Press.

Munn, Nancy D.
1973 Walbiri Iconography: Graphic Representation and Cultural Symbolism in a Central Australian Society. Ithaca: Cornell University Press.

Patterson, Mary
1981 Slings and Arrows: Rituals of Status Acquisition in North Ambrym. *In* Vanuatu: Politics, Economics and Ritual in Island Melanesia. M. Allen, ed. Pp. 189–236. New York: Academic Press.

Poirier, Sylvie
1996 Les jardins du nomade: Cosmologie, territoire et personne dans le désert occidantal australien. Münster: Lit.

Reid, Janice
1983 Sorcerers and Healing Spirits. Canberra: Australian National University Press.

Róheim, Géza
1945 The Eternal Ones of the Dream. New York: International Universities Press.

Stanner, William E. H.
1965 Religion, Totemism and Symbolism. *In* Aboriginal Man in Australia. R. M. and C. H. Berndt, eds. Pp. 207–237. Sydney: Angus and Robertson.
1966 On Aboriginal Religion. Sydney: Sydney University.
1979 White Man Got No Dreaming: Essays 1938–1973. Canberra: Australian National University Press.

Stephen, Michele
1979 Dreams of Change: The Innovative Role of Altered States of Consciousness in Traditional Melanesian Religion. Oceania 50(1):3–22.
1982 "Dreaming Is Another Power!": The Social Significance of Dreams among the Mekeo of Papua New Guinea. Oceania 53(2):106–122.
1987a Master of Souls: The Mekeo Sorcerer. *In* Sorcerer and Witch in Melanesia. M. Stephen, ed. Pp. 41–80. Melbourne: Melbourne University Press.
1987b Sorcery and Witchcraft in Melanesia: An Overview. *In* Sorcerer and Witch in Melanesia. M. Stephen, ed. Pp. 249–304. Melbourne: Melbourne University Press.

Tonkinson, Myrna
1982 The Mabarn and the Hospital: The Selection of Treatment in a Remote Aboriginal Community. *In* Body, Land and Spirit: Health and Healing in Aboriginal Society. J. Reid, ed. Pp. 225–241. Brisbane: University of Queensland Press.

Tonkinson, Robert
1966 Maat Village, Efate: A Relocated Community in the New Hebrides. Eugene: University of Oregon Press.
1970 Aboriginal Dream-Spirit Beliefs in a Contact Situation. *In* Australian Aboriginal Anthropology. R. M. Berndt, ed. Pp. 277–291. Perth: University of Western Australia Press.
1974 The Jigalong Mob: Victors of the Desert Crusade. Menlo Park: Benjamin/Cummings.
1979 Divination, Replication and Reversal in Two New Hebridean Societies. Canberra Anthropology 2(2):57–74.
1981 Church and Kastom in Southeast Ambrym. *In* Vanuatu: Politics, Economics and Ritual in Island Melanesia. M. Allen, ed. Pp. 237–267. New York: Academic Press.
1982 Vanuatu Values: A Changing Symbiosis. *In* Melanesia: Beyond Diversity. Vol. 1. R. J. May and H. Nelson, eds. Pp. 73–90. Canberra: Research School of Pacific Studies, Australian National University.
1984 Semen Versus Spirit-child in a Western Desert Culture. *In* Religion in Aboriginal Australia: An Anthology. M. Charlesworth, H. Morphy, D. Bell, and K. Maddock, eds. Pp. 107–123. Brisbane: University of Queensland Press.
1988 "Ideology and Domination" in Aboriginal Australia: A Western Desert Test Case. *In* Hunters and Gatherers: Property, Power and Ideology. Vol. 2. T. Ingold, D. Riches, and J. Woodburn, eds. Pp. 170–184. Cambridge: Berg.
1991 The Mardu Aborigines: Living the Dream in Australia's Desert, 2^d edition. Fort Worth: Holt, Rinehart, and Winston.
1994 Melanesia: Culture, Technology and "Tradition" Before and After Western Impacts. *In* Traditional Technological Structures and Cultures of the Pacific. R. A. Stephenson, ed. Pp. 32–66. Micronesian Area Research Center, University of Guam.
n.d. Millenarianism and the Permeability of Indigenous Domains: A Melanesian-Australian Comparison. Manuscript.
Trompf, G. W.
1991 Melanesian Religion. Cambridge: Cambridge University Press.
Wagner, Roy
1972 Habu: The Innovation of Meaning in Daribi Religion. Chicago: University of Chicago Press.
Zelenietz, Marty
1981 Sorcery and Social Change: An Introduction. *In* Sorcery and Social Change in Melanesia. M. Zelenietz and S. Lindenbaum, eds. Social Analysis (Special Issue) 8:3–14.

6 Budja Budja Napangarti during a women's ceremony. Photo: Sylvie Poirier.

Chapter 6

"This Is Good Country. We Are Good Dreamers"

Dreams and Dreaming in the Australian Western Desert

Sylvie Poirier

In Australian Aboriginal studies, much emphasis has been placed on the Dreaming (or Dreamtime) as a cosmological order or Ancestral Law—in other words, as an all-encompassing field having a hierarchically superior value. Yet, as a field of anthropological investigation, the cultural systems of dreams in Australian Aboriginal societies, in terms of their epistemological and ontological principles and the semantic and pragmatic dimensions of dreams and dreaming, have somehow remained neglected. Indeed, we know very little about the representations and the enactment of dreams in terms of local dream theories, modes of dream sharing, or dream interpretations.[1] These are some of the gaps that this chapter will begin to fill in, with a particular focus on Western Desert societies. I will, at first, share a few thoughts about what I consider some of the difficulties inherent in promoting an anthropological approach to dreams and dreaming. This approach is concerned with achieving a fuller understanding of the social and cultural dimensions of dreams, and of the complexity and diversity of cultural systems of dreams.

E. B. Tylor (1871) was the first to propose, although within the premises and the paradigms of his time, an anthropological conceptualization of dreams and dreaming. In many respects, however, his initial efforts were brushed aside with the dismissal of the classical theory of social evolutionism. Since the turn of the twentieth century, the study of dreams in our society, in which dreaming is viewed solely as a private experience, has been taken over by psychology and psychoanalysis in particular, and it is no wonder that anthropologists investigating dreams in other cultures have, aside from a few exceptions, borrowed from these sciences. It seems as if, since Tylor, the discipline has had a lack of inspiration (or imagination), at least in that domain. If the focus is on the social process of representing and enacting dreams (Tedlock 1987), or performing dreams (Graham 1995), rather than on dreams solely as objects or products (of the mind), then dreams and dreaming are likely to become a field of inquiry worthy of fuller consideration by anthropologists. To the extent that dreams are capable of informing us about local notions of the person, local theories of human and non-human action, the cultural construction of experience, and the status of the imaginary—in short, about specific modes of being-in-the-world, dreams are of interest to anthropology. I think then that dreams and dreaming can be approached as a "royal road," not, as Freud would have it, to the unconscious, but to cultural ontology and epistemology, including those dominant in Western cultures.

Obviously, then, one of the first steps in such an approach would be to perform a critical and reflexive evaluation of the dominant theories and discourses regarding dreams and dreaming in Western societies. We know that since medieval times in Europe, owing to the role played by the church as censor of the imaginary, dreams and dreaming, which had been so prized during antiquity, were gradually banished from the public sphere, their social uses denied. According to the French historian Jacques Le Goff, after the Middle Ages we witnessed the emergence of a society "whose dreams are blocked, a society which, in the realm of dreaming, has become disoriented" (Le Goff 1985:292).[2] The notion of the person as composite and separable so that one's soul or spirit can temporarily leave the body for dream wanderings, which was still prevalent in the Middle Ages, came to be considered heretical and, later on, irrational. In his *Traité de l'homme,* which he started writing in 1633, Descartes proposed a theory that quickly became official in the West and endures to this day. He suggested that dreams are products of the mind and fully psychic events, and that the mind or spirit is bound to the body (Fabre 1996). As anthropologists, most of us are heirs to this Cartesian tradition, which makes it rather difficult for us, not only to understand other traditions, representations, and practices with respect to dreams and dreaming, but also to consider these seriously and at face value.

The Freudian approach has further contributed in reinforcing the focus on the psychic and solely private dimension of dreams and dreaming and in denying their social values. In this view, dreams only concerned the dreamer (and his or her individual [hi]story) and are considered, in the words of Freud, as being "completely asocial." While Freud did, in fact, give social relationships a predominant place in his mode of dream interpretation, he nevertheless wrote that the dream "has nothing to communicate to anyone else; . . . it remains unintelligible to the subject himself and is for that reason totally uninteresting to other people" (Hunt 1989:12). Undoubtedly, such an outlook would be looked on as incomprehensible for Australian Aborigines. For them, dream experiences and dream narratives have not only a deeply embedded social dimension (in their entertaining and aesthetic values, among others), they are a means to connect (in reality and not metaphorically) to one's social, cosmological and physical surroundings.

As a general rule, in Western societies dreams are viewed as private and inner experiences that are rarely shared. Furthermore, given the solid anchoring of an individualistic ideology within dominant dream theories, in combination with the absolute division between mind and body deriving from Cartesian dualism, it is unthinkable, on the basis of Western objectivity, that dreams might well be addressed to another person, or that while dreaming, one's spirit might penetrate someone else's dream. And yet, such permeability and communication between dreamers are meaningful notions in other cultural settings; the anthropological literature is quite eloquent on this topic.[3] For anthropologists, the question then arises as to how we are to account for traditions where dreams and dreaming are expressed within a cosmocentric worldview rather that an anthropocentric one; where they are valued as acts of communication and exchange, and as a barometer of the state of the relationships between humans and their sociocosmic environment.

As far as methodology is concerned, when studying a cultural system of dreams and dreaming, I think it relevant to consider five aspects of the process of dream socialization: (1) local dream theories, and whatever they might reveal about the local notion of the person (either dualistic or composite, individual or "dividual"[4]), and about local theories of human (and non-human) action within the world, local ontology, and epistemology; (2) dream narratives as a process of translating, structuring, and communicating a dream experience, a process in which the embodied social, cultural, and symbolic components as well as contextual and personal variables come into play from the moment a dream is simply remembered and thereafter communicated.[5] It might be added that, in some societies, dream stories may also be considered as "narrative events" (Bauman 1986), by no means a minor consideration, considering their social and political, but also entertaining and aesthetic dimensions; (3) modes of dream sharing—that is, where, when, why, how, and with whom one shares dreams; in this connection, Gilbert Herdt (1987) has identified public, private, and secret spheres to dream sharing in one Melanesian society; (4) local modes of dream interpretations, or, wherever present, local dream typologies, both of which are undoubtedly a rich source of information as long as their truth value is not undermined in favor of more hegemonic grids in the anthropologist's society; and (5) the mediating, revealing, and often creative and innovative role ascribed to dreams in a number of societies throughout the world, including in Aboriginal Australia. Given the scope of this chapter, with its focus on Australian Aboriginal societies and particular emphasis on the Western Desert, I can, of course, deal only briefly with each one of these aspects.

I might add also that recent tendencies in the study of hunting-and-gathering worlds, that are more concerned in investigating their ontological and epistemological principles, bring new and refreshing insight to our understanding of their respective and distinctive sociality. I think here particularly of Tim Ingold's "ontology of dwelling"[6] and Nurit Bird-David's "relational epistemology," where the notions of the person and sentient agents are not limited to humans only and where "maintaining relationships with . . . other local beings is critical to maintaining . . . personhood" (Bird-David 1999:S73). Both authors stress also in such ontology the absence of any absolute division between nature and culture, or between mind and body. While these authors do not deal specifically with dreams and dreaming, their respective contributions certainly open up interesting avenues for the study of dreams. I wish particularly to emphasize what I call the "relational" role of dreams and highlight the fact that, in many respects, in Aboriginal Australia the activity of dreaming—that is, dreams as human action in the world, and as social process—is more valued than the actual dream content, or dreams simply as objects. Dreams and dreaming are valued then not only for their contribution to the interpretation of past, current, or future events, but also, due to their mediating and connecting role between human, non-human, and ancestral components of the world, they contribute to the unfolding of reality.

In Aboriginal knowledge, it is clear that dreams and the Dreaming, the Ancestral Law, are closely related to one another. Dreams and dreaming are vital components and expressions of The Dreaming, and, in many ways, all share the same aesthetic. Nevertheless, they represent two structurally distinct levels of reality, and two distinct modes of experience and realms of action that are not to be confused in Aboriginal practice and thought. As we will see, while they are not interchangeable, they certainly stand with each other in a relational complicity.

I shall discuss now some of my understandings of the cultural systems of dreams in the Wirrimanu area, located on the northern fringe of the Gibson Desert, in Western Australia.[7] The Aboriginal community of Wirrimanu (formally the Balgo Hills Catholic Mission, established in the 1940s), and neighboring communities of Yagga Yagga and Mulan, are mostly inhabited by Kukatja and Walmatjari people, but there are also a number of Wangkatjunga, Ngarti, Pintupi, and Warlpiri, whose ancestral lands lie to the south of Wirrimanu.[8] In Kukatja, as in most Western Desert languages, *Tjukurrpa* is the word most commonly used for The Dreaming; that is, the ancestral order. But in contrast with their neighbors, the Warlpiri, who also use the word *tjukurrpa* for dreams, the Kukatja have a distinct word, *kapukurri*, to refer to dream experiences.

Local Dream Theories:
Dreaming as Cognitive, Emotive, and Communicative Experience

For the Kukatja and neighboring groups, a dream occurs when, while a person is asleep, his or her *kurunnpa* (what we would usually translate as one's spirit), which is related to the abdominal (or umbilical) area (*tjurni*), leaves the body to pursue various experiences and encounters and is thus liable to acquire knowledge. The *kurunnpa* (spirit) relates to cognition, volition, and to the expression of emotions (Peile 1997:94). It should be pointed out that the abdominal area, the *tjurni*, is the seat of emotion and *maparn* (medicine-man) power. Thus, for the Kukatja, there is a close relationship between dream experiences, knowledge and understanding, emotion, well-being, and strength (or power). Furthermore, this relation between cognition, emotion and dreams is consistent with the fact that dreams are valued as much for their content as for the impression they leave on the waking dreamer.

In the present context, knowledge is used in a very broad sense: that is, knowledge about the land in terms of hunting-and-gathering resources; knowledge about named sites on the countryside to which the dreamer is related; knowledge about the well-being of relatives living in other communities, or of dead relatives, or; ancestral knowledge, relating then to corpuses of myths and rituals.

"Openness" is a fundamental dimension or skill in this instance and can readily be read as a metaphor for one's receptive, sensitive and communicative qualities. A good dreamer is usually a person who knows how to "open" his or her *tjurni*. Talking one day about her son, Nungurrayi told me, "He is good dreamer, he is open" (showing her abdominal area). For the Kukatja, there are two interrelated means of acquiring knowledge and understanding. First, through the ears, which are seen as the organ of thought (*kulila*), that is, the mind, which stands in relation to whatever is acquired through listening to other people or stories; and second, through the *tjurni,* the seat of emotion, from which the *kurunnpa* departs for dream experiences. In brief, someone who can open his or her ears or abdominal area will no doubt become a knowledgeable person, a Law man or a Law woman. This implies also that one has acquired the strength and the power (*maparn*) to counteract the attacks of malevolent sorcerers (or spirits). Law men and women—that is, those who have mastered the narratives of the *Tjukurrpa* (the Dreaming), those who are well versed in ritual matters—are usually but not necessarily presented as good dreamers.

The relationship that is drawn between dream, knowledge, and (spiritual) power explains also the attitude of younger people whenever I asked them about dream experiences or stories. Here are some of the answers I received then: "You should ask the old people; they know"; or, "The old people, they know how to dream, they know about dreams." In the dream sphere, as in the ritual sphere, the right to speech and the right to knowledge are acquired and recognized gradually, through one's own engagement and participation as hunter, forager, dancer, singer, painter, or dreamer. The fact that the dream realm, as we will see, is closely related to the ancestral realm explains also this attitude on the part of the younger people.

To aid me in understanding dream experiences as a "voyage," a "journey" of one's *kurunnpa* (spirit) out of the body, Nungurrayi, an elderly woman, offered me two analogies, drawing on elements from my own culture. She said that in dreams her spirit travels everywhere, "just like the Holy Spirit."[9] In another example, she said, "When we are dreaming, we are thinking, we are feeling with our *tjurni,* we look at our spirit going away, like in a picture [movie]"[10]; or again, "it is the spirit that goes on walkabout." In Aboriginal Australia, as anywhere else, some individuals are better dreamers than others. There are also a few people who make it a point to store dream narratives, theirs and other's—that is, dreams that they have had or have heard during their lifetime. Such stories can always be useful, individually or collectively, simply as stories (see below) but also as a means for providing information on contextual or unusual events, for guidance or for other purposes. In the Wirrimanu area, individual attitudes toward dreams vary considerably. Some people welcome dream experiences, which they consider "as sweet as tea," as one man put it, while others prefer dreamless nights, thereby avoiding the risks of receiving bad news or unwanted encounters with malevolent spirits or powerful sorcerers. In all cases, though, everybody recognizes the mediating and communicative value and potential of dreaming.

Elizabeth Povinelli (1993:152–160; 1995) has aptly demonstrated how for the Belyuen Aborigines (Northern Territory) the land, elements of the landscape, and named places, as embodiments of ancestral essence and presence, are sensitive and responsive to the immediate products of human hunting activity, like sweat and speech. The same observation also applies in the case of dreams, as a human activity. Thus, when people dream of their country or specific sites, or when, before going to sleep, they express their intention to travel to their country while dreaming (either simply to visit a specific area or to meet dead relatives), they not only show that they are caring for their country but they are also contributing to the well-being of that country and thus to the reproduction of local resources (in their intrinsically linked cosmological and physical dimensions). A good illustration of this notion is contained in the words of Napangarti, a middle-aged woman, who, while talking of plant resources at Munggayi, her country, said to me, "This is good country, we are good dreamers." Obviously, Napangarti is not implying that dreaming itself allows for the production and the reproduction of local resources. But rather that dreaming is a way of thinking, caring, feeling, and relating to the country that, in turn, is sensitive to such human's attention and might respond positively. Dreaming, as a mode of experience and a daily activity, is a part of local theories of human action. It is a form of engagement (though by far, not the only one) and thus one aspect and expression of Ingold's "poetics of dwelling" within the world. This example also shows the permeability and consubstantiality between the bodily self (i.e., the person), and the landscape as a sentient entity that is permeated with ancestral agencies and essences (Poirier, in press).

These considerations now lead me to the communicative potential of dreams that also highlights this aspect of permeability and thus receptivity between the person and his or her surroundings. In Aboriginal Australia, as in many other societies around the world, dreams are the privileged space-time of communication between humans and ancestral beings, or between humans and the spirits of the dead (see below). But the point I wish to stress here is how dreams can be a shared experience. In the Wirrimanu area, it was not uncommon for two individuals to say that they had shared the same dream. Both dreamers usually have shared the same camp overnight and found themselves in the same dream setting and action.[11] There were also instances when, as other dreamers dreamed, they decided to enter yet another person's dream or were attracted to the action occurring in a dream setting. For example, an elderly woman once told me that she feared that some male relatives of hers who were sleeping nearby might, during their dreams, have heard her singing sacred-secret songs in her own dream (in this case, men's songs usually forbidden to women); she took great care then in singing very softly. Love magic songs are another example of how dreams are perceived as a space-time of higher receptivity. The beloved will hear a suitor's love song in his or her dreams and thus be attracted to the singer. For the Mardu, a Western Desert group living at Jigalong, Robert Tonkinson (1970, this volume, Chapter 5) has given good examples of how the medicine-man can reconnoiter with less experienced people in their dream travels to their country and thereby protect them against malevolent spirits.

These various examples and considerations have demonstrated how, for the Kukatja and neighboring groups, dreams and dreaming enter the field of human action. This is, I might say, part of local knowledge and cultural objectivity. All that has been said about dreams and dreaming is also consistent with the local notion of the person as separable (as when one's spirit leaves the body during dreaming), as permeable to and consubstantial with nonhuman agents and essences, and composed of multiple relationships (that some might call "identities"). It must also be said that these relationships, that is, one's ancestral, social, ritual, and territorial networks of affiliations and responsibilities are intrinsic to the bodily self rather than extrinsic (Poirier 1996). In other words, they are constitutive of one's personhood. It is in that sense that we can say that the local notion of the person is also "dividual" (Strathern 1988, Bird-David 1999). Furthermore, such relationships are emergent; that is "they are not totally given but must be worked out in a variety of social processes" (Myers 1986:159), and dreaming is one such processes. As events and as human actions within the world, dreams and dreaming are one expression of sharing relationships between people and the land (and named sites), as exemplified once again in Napangarti's comment, "This is good country, we are good dreamers."

Dream Sharing and Dream Stories

Surprisingly enough, and even though dreams and dreaming might be highly valued in local discourses and practices, Aboriginal people do not systematically share their dreams—quite the contrary. For the sake of respect for one's autonomy, or so I guess, very seldom would people ask others what they had dreamed the night before. Only in cases of illness or crisis would the elders or the medicine-man ask explicitly the people concerned to share their dreams. Otherwise, it is up to individuals to decide whether or not they wish to share their dreams, depending first on the dream content, but also on their mood, the context, the emotional impression left by the dream, or the dream's narrative value. In spite of this, it was quite frequent for people to share, at will, their dreams, mostly around the campfire where friends and relatives had gathered for morning tea.

Dream narratives usually begin by specifying temporal and spatial references—that is, when and where the dream actually occurred. Such references can, at times, be precise to the point of including the time of day or night when the dream occurred (during an afternoon nap, at midnight, in the middle of the night or at dawn); in which camp it occurred and who was sleeping near by; and even, occasionally, the position of the sleeper/dreamer in terms of the four cardinal points. Such temporal and spatial specifications obviously offer a number of avenues for interpretation. Furthermore, by identifying several of the topographical or physical elements appearing in the dream itself, the dreamer usually knows where his or her spirit actually traveled during the dream. If the dreamer is unable to situate the dream action, those who are listening to the narrative will try to identify the named site or the community visited. Such identification seems to be crucial, and, indeed, some people felt uneasy when they were unable to identify where the dream action actually occurred. Identification of the place of the dream action is a consideration that is consistent with a reality of Aboriginal sociality, whereby named places and one's relationships with these are of paramount importance in all stories, events, or experiences. However, dream experiences obviously do not always imply that the spirit travels to faraway places. The dream action can also occur in or around the community setting. Moreover, the dreamer can be visited at his or her camp by a dead relative, a foreign sorcerer, or an ancestral being.

For the Kukatja, dream sharing is also the occasion to partake of a "good story." In this society of oral tradition, it must be said that any discourse, like the narratives of events and personal experiences, or the transmission of any type of knowledge (from a simple enumeration, for example, of edible plants, to the telling of the most sacred myth), all are received as "story" (*wankka;* and *turlku,* for sacred songs).[12] In fact, it took me a while to understand why dreams, from the moment one had chosen to share them, were generally qualified either as "good dreams" (*palya kapukurri*) or as "good stories" (*palya wankka*). Even after listening to the most frightening nightmare (the Kukatja have no word or category for nightmares) someone in the audience would often say, "good story this one." This can be explained, I think, by the fact that, in these societies of oral tradition, any story (and dream stories are no exception) has, no doubt, an entertainment value. But there is more to it. A story carries its share of cognitive value, informative potential, and aesthetic flavor, and thus of truth value (*mularrpa*). In fact, dreams are "good" to the extent that they are capable of informing about past, current, or future events that may concern either the dreamer, his or her close relatives, the community or named places (to the extent that these are perceived as sentient entities and are intrinsic to one's ancestral connections); they may also inform on the state of the relationships between humans and ancestors. Thus, even a dream that left a very negative or frightening impression on the dreamer might, upon awakening, be viewed positively for its informative, curative, or aesthetic potential or value.

Here again, individual attitudes vary considerably. For example, younger people are much more vulnerable to traumatic dreams than are adults and elders. One young woman in her early twenties awoke one morning in a state of fright: in her dream, two unknown sorcerers had pointed the bone at her, a clear act of sorcery. Usually, people will try to soothe the fear or the bad impression left by the dream. In this instance, the elder to whom she had narrated her dream (her own father was away from the community at that time) decided that the young woman had to narrate her dream all around. That way, sorcerers who appeared in any subsequent dreams would know that people were aware of their evil intentions, thus causing the sorcerers to back off. It was also a way of allaying the fears of the young woman. As a general rule, learning to deal positively and creatively with one's dream experiences is something that the elders try to foster among the young. The Kukatja world is filled with malevolent spirits, vengeful sorcerers and powerful ancestral beings who can also all be encountered in dreams. Learning to be able to meet these beings face-to-face, either in dreams or in waking life, but also learning to deal positively with one's own fears, is surely an important aspect in the process of socialization among the Kukatja (Poirier 1996).

It should be added also that some dreamers are more sensitive than others to the aesthetic potential of dreams, as the following example testifies. An elderly man dreamt that he was following the tracks of a snake. Suddenly, the snake got up; it was very long and nicely colored. The snake started chasing the man who took refuge in a tree. Frightened, the dreamer woke up. When he told his dream the following morning to the few people present, he insisted on the strong impression of discomfort, but nevertheless concluded his narrative by saying that the colors of the snake seen in his dream will be a good inspiration for his next acrylic painting. He also explained his dream by the fact that his wife had left that night her bag containing women's sacred objects in the camp (rather than in the women's house).

Dream Interpretations

When a dream is narrated, for example around the camp in the morning hours, people will listen to the story but will not necessarily attempt to decipher it or confirm its import via some pre-established or fixed meaning. The dreamer, or somebody else, might make a few comments, or someone might carry on with another story (either a dream, an anecdote, a mythical sequence or a past event), often suggested by the first one. Most of the time, people are satisfied with simply having heard a "good story." However, this does not exclude the possibility that the dream narrative will be shared later on by the dreamer or someone who had heard the story, in another context and with other people, either for its informative potential, or for its narrative or aesthetic value. As with any other story, the dream narrative, and the narrative event taken as a whole, is liable to expand the knowledge of anyone who is prepared to listen. With its potential for meaning, the dream story, like any story, "might generate sense for circumstances beyond the story itself" (Biesele 1986:161). It must be stressed also that the dream does not belong to the dreamer to the extent that it is seldom seen has being addressed solely to the dreamer who considers him- or herself rather as a messenger or a witness of something that, as it is being shared, is liable to become meaningful and relevant to others.

In the local mode of dream interpretation, the intratextual, contextual, and intertextual levels all have parts to play. Unless a dream has left a vivid or unpleasant impression, very rarely do people seek to interpret their dreams upon awakening. As a rule, Kukatja dream interpretation is flexible and open to multiple readings, depending on the context and current events, and on the impression made on the dreamer by the dream. I have not found any dream sign that has a fixed meaning; depending on context, any sign can be read as a good or a bad omen. Dream narratives are essentially open, and there is much room for individual and contextual interpretations. Whenever an interpretation is suggested, it is seldom assumed to be immediately true; only future events might eventually confirm its accuracy. Very seldom do dream narratives and interpretations carry a sense of fate or determinism.

What might seem at first to be a lack of interest in dream interpretation reveals, on closer examination, another local reality, one that became quite evident during my research; the primacy of the activity of dreaming over the dream content. Whenever an unusual, happy, or unhappy event occurred, there would often be someone to say that he or she had dreamt it, either a few days, a few weeks, or a few months before; yet the dream had remained unexplained (maybe even unshared) until the event occurred. Let me give an example here. As a group of people were getting ready to depart for a neighboring settlement in order to participate to initiation ceremonies, their vehicle broke down. For two days, the men tried to repair it, but in vain. On the third day, they finally succeeded in fixing it. As the engine started running again, a young woman pointed at her toddler and said, "Might be that boy had a dream about that car and saw it working properly." As none of the adults present had come forward to recall a dream in relation to the event, she concluded that the child must have dreamed it. The purpose was not to bring attention to the child, but rather to bring the activity of dreaming into relation with the flow of events; the dream itself being one of the events, a prelude to a happy ending, even though no one seemed to recall such dream. In no way am I saying here that dreams are predictive of the future; if that was so the Kukatja would put far more attention into trying to interpret their dreams. It is rather a question of bringing the dream realm into relation with the flow of events.

It appears then, that in the Western Desert, the activity of dreaming (or the dream realm) is party to the unfolding of reality. Dreams are seen indeed as a prelude to significant or peculiar events (births, deaths, accidents, etc.), even though they might only be recalled and interpreted afterwards; that is, after the event actually occurred, someone will often venture to say, "I knew it, I dreamt it." In other words, the Kukatja are confident that regardless of whether or not dreams are remembered, narrated, or interpreted, the dream realm has a part to play in the unfolding of an emergent reality. In my analysis, this is where the juncture, or the relational complicity, between the human, the dream and the Ancestral realms begins to emerge.

By way of illustration of the types of dreams that are seen as preludes to significant events, I will take up two further examples concerning conception and death. Those familiar with the Aboriginal Australian theory of conception will recall that according to the discourse the newborn is "found" or "dreamt" by the mother, the father, or a close male or female relative. In local knowledge, a dream is necessary to validate or confirm the passage of the spirit-child (*kurruwari*) from the ancestral realm to the human realm. It is in dreams that the spirit-children announce their intentions to take on a human form. In other words, the dream allows the process of metamorphosis to take place, even though such dream might go unnoticed or unrecalled by the parents and close relatives. But outside the dream event and prior to or during pregnancy, the spirit-child will also adopt different forms (an animal, a plant, or a natural element) and is often presented as a trickster who enjoys teasing his or her future relatives. It is in such a form—as a game killed by the father, or a plant collected by the mother—that the spirit-child comes into contact with the mother. This aspect of metamorphosis accounts for the permeability and the fluidity of forms, either human, non-human, or ancestral. Though I could certainly go further in the analysis of conception theories and narratives, the intention here is mainly to stress the role of dream as mediator in the process of human conception by validating the passage from the ancestral realm to the human one.

Now it is worth noting that the same holds in the case of death. That is, whenever a death occurred in Wirrimanu or in neighboring communities, often someone would say that he or she had dreamt it. I will give one example. After hearing the news of the death of one of her male relatives from another community, a woman recalled a dream she had had a few weeks before. In her dream, she had seen a spinning stick, and though she felt that such a vivid image was certainly the sign of something, she remained unaware of its meaning, until she heard of the death. From then on, she knew that the dream had come as a prelude to (or a message regarding) the event. It is often said also that such dreams are sent by already deceased relatives who come to announce an impending death. While a close relative is more liable to act as the receptor of such a dream, to some extent it can be anybody who was acquainted with the deceased. Once again, the dream is said to play an active part in the flow of events. The high frequency of references to a dream in the case of a death suggests that, more than simply announcing the event, dreams allow, as the inverse of the process of conception, the passage from the human realm back to the ancestral realm. This is in accordance with the knowledge that, at death, one's spirit (*kurunnpa*) returns to one's country, joining (or merging with) the ancestral essences of the area.

Dreams and the Ancestral Order

In anthropological research and literature (and in our mode of representing Aboriginal Australians), the concept of The Dreaming, that is, the ancestral order, has assumed such a dominant position that it is surprising that anthropologists have not felt the need to inquire further into its relationship with dreams and the activity of dreaming. Even the Aboriginal people I worked with were at first puzzled when I questioned them about their dream experiences. Aware that the whites use the same word "dreaming" to name at once the dream experience and the Ancestral realm (*Tjukurrpa*), and used to seeing them more interested in the latter, some thought I had mistaken these two orders of reality. This became clear to me one day that Napanangka went through the trouble of explaining to me the difference between *Tjukurrpa* and *kapukurri* (dreams). Still wanting however to satisfy my request of dream stories, she choose to tell me a *Tjukurrpa* story in which the heroes have a dream that warn them of a coming danger.

At this point, I would like to look more closely into the relationship between the dream realm and the ancestral realm, or at least those dreams that are said to "come from *Tjukurrpa*." In this context, as in the theories of conception, dreams stand out more as mediating elements between the ancestral and the human orders than as a founding expression (as it is implied with "The Dreaming" or "Dreamtime" translation, terms that, incidentally, are restrictive to the point of being misnomers, but that is another issue). Dreams are conceived of as constituting an intermediate order, a space-time of higher receptivity between humans (as we have seen already) and then again between humans, the land (as an expression and embodiment of ancestral actions and presence), and the ancestral order. Dreams are indeed a favored space-time of communication and exchange between humans and the ancestral beings, or between humans and dead relatives. It is worth mentioning that encountering long-dead relatives in dreams is usually perceived as being a pleasant experience, in which the dreamer may talk, hunt, or sing with a long-dead relative. I have never heard anyone describe such experience as being unpleasant or frightening. And, when dead relatives came to announce a death or an accident in a dream, it was the news of the event that was received as unpleasant, not the encounter itself.

While the presence of ancestral beings can be experienced while awake, and all the more so in ritual contexts where people might feel or hear them, they can usually be seen only in dreams. Dream encounters with ancestral beings obviously have a very special value. It is also in dreams that the ancestral beings or dead relatives reveal new mythical or ritual elements to the living (however, not all dream encounters with ancestral beings have a revelatory dimension to them). In fact, in local discourse it is said that all ritual and mythical knowledge was revealed by the ancestors to humans through dreams. This capacity of dreams for revelation and innovation, whereby pre-existing corpuses of myths and rituals are transformed, also features a definite political dimension to the extent that, more often than not, such dreams serve to validate one's group affiliation to a country (as a series of named sites identified with one or more ancestral beings) and responsibility for it and its associated rituals. The aesthetic and creative dimension of such innovation should not be overlooked, either. Considering the cognitive and communicative value attributed to dreams in Aboriginal Australia, and the role of the dream realm in the unfolding of reality, such dream revelations from the Ancestors represent a hierarchically superior type of dreams. As in the cases of death and conception, revelatory dreams play a mediating role between humans and ancestors. While the elders, men and women, are more inclined to experience such dreams, owing to their complicity and intimacy with the ancestral realm, to their knowledge of ritual matters, and also to their higher understanding of the current socio-political dynamics at stake, the ancestors can also choose to make such revelations to younger people. Obviously, these dreamers will gain in recognition, not so much because of their own creative potential, which is indeed rarely overtly recognized (this volume, Keen Chapter 7), but because the ancestors have selected them as messengers through whom revelations are to be transmitted.

I have discussed at greater length elsewhere (Poirier 1992, 1996) the whole process of revelation and creative innovation, that is, revelatory dreams, in terms of new mythical or ritual elements (in the forms of songs, dances, designs, or story lines), their process of collective recognition and validation, and their eventual insertion into existing ritual and mythical forms, contributing then to their transformations.[13] With these revelatory dreams, considered here as events and as "texts," we can see how Kukatja politics and aesthetics are closely intertwined, and how both are in turn closely intertwined with the acquisition of sacred knowledge "from the *Tjukurrpa*." Dreams and dreaming play thus a prominent role by allowing communication between humans and ancestral beings (and deceased relatives).

A Few Tracks for Further Reflection

Drawing from my data and experiences in the Western Desert, I have written this chapter for the purpose of filling a number of gaps in current understanding of the cultural systems of dreams in Aboriginal Australia. I have striven to bring out, though briefly, considering the scope of the chapter, a number of interrelated points. Among these, there are: (1) the notion of the person as dividual, permeable and composite, which makes for higher receptivity and communication in dreams, among other things; (2) the activity of dreaming, that is, how dreaming, like other human (and non-human) actions within the world (walking, talking, hunting, or singing) is an element in the dynamic production and reproduction of networks of "sharing relationships," or connections, at once social, territorial, and ancestral; (3) the role of "openness" in defining a good dreamer—that is, someone who can "open" his or her abdominal area and thereby gain knowledge about his or her physical, social, and cosmological environment, as a form of "dwelling" or engagement within the world; (4) the dream narrative (and experience) as one that is "open" to contextual and multivocal interpretation and as a barometer providing indications about the state of the world and the state of relationships between the human and the ancestral realms; (5) when people are listening to a dream narrative, they are seldom expecting to learn something about the dreamer, but they do, however, anticipate learning something, whatever it might be, with the knowledge that dreams may indeed contain relevant signs or messages; and (6) the multiplicity of dreams and dreaming, that is as events, as actions, as experiences and as narratives ("good stories"), but also as a mode of knowing and relating.

We are dealing here with worlds where everything is meaningful, where anything may constitute a sign, or is liable to say something, on the state of the relationships between humans, and again between them and surrounding "others" within a sentient landscape. The form of a cloud, the song of a bird, the direction of the wind, the lines on a stone, a tickling sensation on one's body, or a dream are capable of saying something to whoever is willing to decipher it within a framework of cultural idioms, with a touch of improvisation and in consideration of a whole series of contextual and personal variables, including the anthropologist's presence. This kind of hermeneutic of everyday life, which is at times most serious and sacred, at other times quite playful, is open, multivocal, and negotiable. It is a way of being-in-the-world that is primarily dialogic, and a mode of dwelling within the world and of engagement with a sentient landscape. To conclude, I will draw from Bird-David's concept of "relational epistemology," which she contrasts with a modernist epistemology in which knowledge "is having, acquiring, applying and improving representations of things in-the-world." In a relational epistemology, knowledge "is developing the skills of being-in-the-world with other things, making one's awareness of one's environment and one's self finer, broader, deeper, richer, etc." She adds a contrast. "Against 'I think, therefore I am' stand 'I relate, therefore I am' and 'I know as I relate'" (1999:S77–78). I hope to have clearly demonstrated how in Kukatja ontology and epistemology, dreaming is one way to relate, one way to gain knowledge (or to steal sacred knowledge), one of the means by which humans engage and dwell within the world, a world that is not given once and for all, but that is emergent.

Acknowledgments

I wish to express my deepest thanks and gratitude to all those people in the Wirrimanu area who have taught me about dreams and dreaming; I want them to know that I am still learning from their teachings. My thanks go also to the Social Sciences and Humanities Research Council of Canada and to the Australian Institute of Aboriginal and Torres Strait Islander Studies for their financial support. This chapter has also greatly benefited from exchanges with and comments by Roger Lohmann and the other contributors to this volume. I thank them very much. This article is a much revised version of one that appeared in French (Poirier 1994).

Notes

1. I do not mean to say that references to dreams are absent in the anthropological literature: quite the contrary. On the other hand, there have not been explicit and continuous efforts to investigate and conceptualize dreams and dreaming within Australian Aboriginal sociality and cultural construction of experience.
2. "une société aux rêves bloqués, une société désorientée dans le domaine onirique."
3. See, for example, O'Flaherty (1984) and Ewing (1994).
4. Some South Asian and Melanesianist ethnographic writings are quite explicit on the concept of the "dividual" person. See, among others, Marriott (1976) and M. Strathern (1988).
5. On that specific aspect, see Keesing (1982), Brown (1987), and Herdt (1987).
6. In such an ontology of dwelling, "apprehending the world is not a matter of construction but of engagement, not of building but of dwelling, not of making a view *of* the world but of taking up a view *in* it" (Ingold 1996:121, original emphasis).
7. Fieldwork in the Wirrimanu area was first conducted from August 1980 to January 1982, then for one year in 1987–1988, and during two stays of a couple of months each in 1994 and 1998.
8. These different names refer to more or less bounded linguistic and territorial entities. In spite of a few decades of settlement life, these people have

maintained strong ties with and a deep sense of responsibility toward their ancestral lands that are best expressed in the vitality of their ritual life.
9. This comment is most interesting. The majority of the people living in Wirrimanu have, in many ways, always resisted the Christian discourses and practices, and this in spite of decades of the missionaries' presence and sustained efforts. In some respects, their resistance is exemplified in Nungurrayi's comment. That is to say, as opposed for example to Christianized Melanesians who received visits from the Holy Spirit in dreams (see this volume, Lohmann Chapter 10, Robbins Chapter 2), she compares rather her own abilities (as a wandering spirit) to those of the Holy Spirit.
10. In other instances she compared dreams to "telegrams" or to "X-rays" (when a sick person can, while dreaming, observe the inside of his or her body). These different analogies are revealing of the manifold qualities granted to dream experiences.
11. For similar examples, see also Munn (1986:37–38).
12. In societies of oral tradition, "many sorts of knowledge are acquired through hearing the dramatized story of a day's event [including dreams] rather than in a directly didactic learning context" (Biesele 1986:163).
13. On the role of dreams in ritual innovation and transformation, see also, among others, Berndt (1951), Dussart (2000), Glowczewski (1991), and Munn (1986).

References Cited

Bauman, Richard
1986   Story, Performance, and Event. Cambridge: Cambridge University Press.
Berndt, Ronald M.
1951   Kunapipi. Melbourne: F. W. Cheshire.
Biesele, Megan
1986   How Hunter-Gatherers' Stories Make Sense: Semantics and Adaptation. Cultural Anthropology 1:157–70.
Bird-David, Nurit
1999   Animism Revisited. Current Anthropology 40:S67-S91.
Brown, Michael F.
1987   Ropes of Sand: Order and Imagery in Aguaruna Dreams. *In* Dreaming: Anthropological and Psychological Interpretations, B. Tedlock, ed. Pp. 154–170. Cambridge: Cambridge University Press.
Dussart, Françoise
2000   The Politics of Ritual in an Aboriginal Settlement. Washington: Smithsonian Institution Press.
Ewing, Katherine
1994   Dreams from a Saint: Anthropological Atheism and the Temptation to Believe. American Anthropologist 96(3):571–584.
Fabre, Daniel
1996   Rêver: Le mot, la chose, l'histoire. Terrain 26:69–83.

Glowczewski, Barbara
1991 Du rêve à la loi chez les Aborigènes: Mythes, rites et organisation sociale en Australie. Paris: Presses Universitaires de France.

Graham Laura R.
1995 Performing Dreams: Discourses of Immortality among the Xavante of Central Brazil. Austin: University of Texas Press.

Herdt, Gilbert
1987 Selfhood and Discourse in Sambia Dream Sharing. *In* Dreaming: Anthropological and Psychological Interpretations, B. Tedlock, ed. Pp. 55–85. Cambridge: Cambridge University Press.

Hunt, Harry T.
1989 The Multiplicity of Dreams. New Haven: Yale University Press.

Ingold, Tim
1996 Hunting and Gathering as Ways of Perceiving the Environment. *In* Redefining Nature. R. Ellen and K. Fukui, eds. Pp. 117–157. Oxford: Berg.

Keesing, Roger
1982 Kwaio Religion: The Living and the Dead in a Solomon Island Society. New York: Columbia University Press.

Le Goff, Jacques
1985 L'imaginaire médiéval. Paris: Gallimard.

Marriott, Mckim
1976 Hindu Transactions: Diversity without Dualism. *In* Transaction and Meaning. B. Kapferer, ed. Pp. 109–143. Philadelphia: ISHI Publications.

Munn, Nancy D.
1986 [1973] Walbiri Iconography. Chicago: Chicago University Press.

Myers, Fred R.
1986 Pintupi Country, Pintupi Self: Sentiment, Place and Politics among Western Desert Aborigines. Washington: Smithsonian Institution Press.

O'Flahery, Wendy
1984 Dreams, Illusions and Other Realities. Chicago: University of Chicago Press.

Peile, Anthony R.
1997 Body and Soul: An Aboriginal View. Carlisle: Hesperian Press.

Poirier, Sylvie
in press Ontology, Ancestral Order and Agencies among the Kukatja (Australian Western Desert). *In* Figured Worlds. Ontological Obstacles in Intercultural Relations. J. Clammer, S. Poirier, and E. Schwimmer, eds. Toronto: University of Toronto Press.
1996 Les jardins du nomade: Cosmologie, territoire et personne dans le désert occidental australien. Münster: Lit.
1994 La mise en œuvre sociale du rêve: Un exemple australien. Anthropologie et sociétés 18(2):105–119.
1992 Nomadic Rituals: Networks of Ritual Exchange among Women of the Australian Desert. Man 27(4):757–776.

Povinelli, Elizabeth A.
1993 Labor's Lot: The Power, History, and Culture of Aboriginal Action. Chicago: University of Chicago Press.

1995 Do Rocks Listen?: The Cultural Politics of Apprehending Australian Aboriginal Labor. American Anthropologist 97(3):506–518.
Strathern, Marilyn
1988 The Gender of the Gift. Berkeley: University of California Press.
Tedlock, Barbara, ed.
1987 Dreaming: Anthropological and Psychological Interpretations. Cambridge: Cambridge University Press.
Tonkinson, Robert
1970 Aboriginal Dream-Spirit Beliefs in a Contact Situation: Jigalong, Western Australia. *In* Australian Aboriginal Anthropology. R. M. Berndt, ed. Pp. 277–291. Nedlands: University of Western Australia Press.
1978 The Mardudjara Aborigines: Living the Dream in Australia's Western Desert. New York: Holt, Rinehart & Winston.
Tylor, Edward B.
1871 Primitive Culture: Researches into the Development of Mythology, Philosophy, Religion, Language, Art, and Custom. 2 vols. New York: Henry Holt.

7 Dancing "Morning Star," at Milingimbi, 1975. Photo: Ian Keen.

Chapter 7

Dreams, Agency, and Traditional Authority in Northeast Arnhem Land

Ian Keen

In this chapter I attempt to relate Yolngu doctrines of dreaming as revelatory to three rather distinct domains.[1] The first has to do with agency: by contrast with the emphasis on individual authorship in "the West," Yolngu downplay the creative role of the individual. While in Yolngu doctrine an individual is given some credit for realizing a group's ancestral traditions in his or her own way, the main source of religious traditions were the remote *wangarr* ancestors in whose "thought" religious symbols arose. The second domain is Yolngu concepts of mind: it is possible that the downplaying of the creative role of the individual is reflected in Yolngu concepts of the person and mind as discussed by Michael Christie (1983). In Yolngu thinking, there is a greater emphasis on things happening to a person than the person as the initiator of events. Third is the structure of the Yolngu polity in which the control of religious knowledge is a central feature (Morphy 1991; Keen 1994). In this context the chapter examines discussions of authority and "traditional authority" by Nancy Munn, Max Weber, and Maurice Bloch. The structure of Yolngu governance and religious "law," I will suggest, is the central node of this nexus. I put this forward as a rather speculative, exploratory essay—it requires further development, especially concerning the construction of person, agency, and responsibility.

128   Ian Keen

The people referred to as Yolngu in this chapter are the indigenous inhabitants of northeast Arnhem Land, which lies on the coast of the Northern Territory in Australia. Yolngu now combine a cash economy with fishing, hunting, and gathering. Most Yolngu live in three relatively large coastal and island settlements (Milingimbi, Galiwin'ku, and Yirrkala), and three smaller inland settlements, originally established as mission outposts (Ramingining, Nangalala, and Lake Evella), as well as numerous small "outstation" communities or "homeland centres" on traditional lands.[2] The Yolngu are distinguished from their neighbors culturally and linguistically: their languages are of the Pama-Nyungan family of suffixing languages, whereas their neighbours to the south and west speak non - Pama-Nyungan prefixing languages (Yallop 1982).

Before proceeding we need to be clear about the distinction between, on the one hand, dreaming as a process, and on the other "The Dreaming" or "Dream Time" as a creative period in Australian Aboriginal cosmologies and cosmogonies.

Dreaming as Communication with Ancestors

Everyone has heard of "The Dreaming"—it is *the* stereotype of what "traditional" Aborigines are all about. The expression came from the anthropology of Spencer and Gillen (1927). *Alcheringa* means literally "belonging to dream"; but Spencer and Gillen translated the word as "Dream Times" in order to differentiate the creative ancestral period from everyday dreams (Morphy 1997:176). In the cosmology of Aboriginal peoples of the arid zone of Australia, however, the process of dreaming *links* people to the ancestors, as a number of anthropologists have pointed out (see e.g., in this volume, Goodale Chapter 8, Poirier Chapter 6, and Tonkinson Chapter 5).

Warlpiri people studied by Nancy Munn in the 1950s employed a similarly multivalent concept of *djukurrpa* (*djugurba*) which means dream, ancestral times, and ancestral traces and designs. Munn writes:

> The intrinsic ties between a design and an ancestor are based in Walbiri thought upon the origin of designs in ancestral dreams or, for certain kinds of designs, in the dreams of contemporary Walbiri in which ancestors give them designs. The label *djugurba* (dream, ancestral times) expresses this connection between ancestors and dreams. The dream origin of designs is also the ultimate grounds for their efficacy since the ancestors are the original sources of potency in the Walbiri world. (1973:33)

Munn makes it clear that not all personal dreams were thought to be ancestral revelations. One Warlpiri view was that the matrilineal spirit (*pirlirrpa*) could leave the body and travel around, while in sexual dreams the person visited his or her partner's camp, not as a spirit but bodily (1973:33n1).

In the early 1970s, Pintupi people made a stronger distinction between "dreams" and "The Dreaming" as an ancestral domain, although the word *tjukurrpa* signified both of these. The act of dreaming contrasted with experience of the visible, but "The Dreaming" remained a distinct order of reality. The common Pintupi view was that one's spirit traveled apart from the body and observed things not ordinarily within the field of the senses; however, "[s]ometimes individuals are believed to come into contact with the ancestral figures of The Dreaming, who may give them special knowledge, usually of songs and ceremonies" (Myers 1986:51). The significance of dreams was a matter of negotiation—even if a person believed that he or she had come into contact with ancestral beings, others had to be persuaded to accept the claim.

Poirier confirms this separation but connection in the Western Desert:

> These translations (of *Tjukurrpa* as Dreaming or Dreamtime), and their French equivalents, "*Temps du rêve*," "*Temps rêvé*," or "*Rêve*," are essentially analogical and are therefore not completely inadequate. Indeed, the officially adopted Dreaming and Dreamtime facilitate communication between Aborigines and non-Aborigines. But they also imply a simplistic view of a world of representations whose source is to be found not solely in the realm of dreams. The unfortunate consequence of such translations is that they much reduce the local cosmology. However, it is well understood that, drawn as they are from Aboriginal reality, these translations attest to an intimate relationship between the mythical and the dream realm. Even more so when such groups as the Aranda or the Warlpiri . . . use the same term to designate both the ancestral order and the dream experience. These are nevertheless two structurally distinct levels of reality that are not confused in Aboriginal practice and thought, except in their shared epistemology. The majority of Western Desert groups, such as the Kukatja, the Walmatjari or the Pintupi, have a specific word to name the dream experience: *kapukurri*. (Poirier 1996:49, translation by Poirier; see also this volume, Poirier Chapter 6)

Among Yolngu of northeast Arnhem Land the word for dream (*mabuga*) does not refer to the period of creation by *wangarr* ancestors either.[3] Nevertheless, the individual has contact with the dead and remote ancestors through dream or reverie, which is also a process through which new religious forms, such as songs, as well as the meaning of religious symbolism, are revealed (see also this volume, Lohmann Chapter 10 and Robbins Chapter 2).

Dreams that connect people to the ancestors are the concern of this chapter, so it will be helpful first to sketch the character of Yolngu religion.

Yolngu Religion

Yolngu religion and religious change have been quite fully described in the anthropological literature (e.g., Berndt 1952, 1962; Bos 1988; Keen 1978, 1994; Morphy 1984, 1991; Peterson 1972; Slotte 1997; Tamisari 1998; Warner 1937). Yolngu myths encode beliefs about *wangarr* ancestors and other beings who lived long, long ago. Some are believed to have created human groups, implanted the powers that ensure continued reproduction through spirit conception, created social institutions, and established the norms that govern them. The Yolngu believe that many *wangarr* transformed themselves into elements of the land or sea-bed, such as bodies of rock or ochre; left marks of their activities, such as gullies or creeks; transformed their appurtenances, for example turning a digging stick into a tall tree; or live on in the deep waters, perhaps moving with the tide.

Religious practices both describe and "follow" the activities of the *wangarr*, and the objects and places associated with or created by them. The ancestors, the countries in which they left their traces, the groups that they founded, and the ceremonies which follow their activities are strictly divided between the two patri-moieties, Dhuwa and Yirritja. Exogamous patrigroups own the country and the religious forms that are associated with their ancestors. They range in size of up to two hundred members or more, each holding several distinct areas of land (and in many cases coastal waters) as well as the ceremonies, songs, sacred objects, and designs which relate to their land and its *wangarr* ancestors. Members of each group are dispersed among several communities.

A strong characteristic of Yolngu religion is that it is and has been highly eclectic. Indigenous songs and ceremonies have a number of sources: the ceremony called Gunapipi is in a desert style, Ngulmarrk has links with the Ubarr of western Arnhem Land, while Mandayala ceremony is linked to the Mandiwala of the Gulf of Carpentaria. Yolngu have been similarly incorporative in their approach to Christianity, especially since indigenous control of local churches followed the withdrawal of the Uniting Church from an administrative role in the region. To varying degrees, Yolngu have integrated their interpretations of Christian doctrine with ancestral beliefs, and incorporated Christian elements into indigenous ritual forms (see Bos 1988; Slotte 1997; cf. in this volume chapters on religious change in Papua New Guinea, Kempf and Hermann Chapter 4, and Lohmann Chapter 10). Yolngu dreams and visions as revelatory, religious experience concern both *wangarr* ancestors and God.

Yolngu Dreams and Visions

Except for the intrusion of figures from Christianity, accounts from the 1920s to the 1990s of the significance that Yolngu give to dreams (*mabuga*) are remarkably similar. Writing about the late 1920s, W. L. Warner reports that Yolngu attribute illness to bad dreams about someone who has died, or about a grave; singing *garma* (public) songs offers protection (Warner 1937:209, 421). Similarly Yolngu at Ramingining informed Ingrid Slotte in the early 1990s that a ghost of the recently dead may visit in a dream and give the person food or a spear, making them sick, or may repeatedly visit the person trying to strangle them. The *wan'tjirr* purification ceremony helps prevent such visitations (Slotte 1997:218). In some dreams the death of a person is revealed through a visit by that person's *mokuy* (ghost), or by a dream of the dead person's totem (*madayin*) (Slotte 1997:216).

Wangarr ancestors as well as minor totemic beings also visit in dreams. W. S. Chaseling (1957:89) reports the Yolngu belief that ancestors assure sick people in dreams that they will get well. Similarly, people told Slotte how totemic animals visit in dreams to cure illnesses (1997:218–9). People encounter God or Jesus in a dream, often leading to the healing of an illness. One woman recounted to Slotte a dream experienced by her daughter who was sick with dysentery. In the dream two angels sat by her, sounding trumpets, singing and praising. The dreams were supposedly induced by the prayers of her parents, and resulted in the girl returning to good health (1997:217). People dream or have visions of *wangarr* ancestors in the major revelatory ceremony called Nga:rra (Berndt 1952:21–22; Cawte 1993:21).

Somewhat distinct from dreams are what people refers to as "visions," in which they "find" or "encounter" (*malng'marangal*) God, angels, or other beings (Slotte 1997), or in which they see strange events.[4] In his account of the Christian "revival" at Galinwin'ku in Arnhem Land, Robert Bos reports a number of visions:

> A man called Wirriyi (Liyagawumirr [patri-group]) had a vision whilst he was sitting down resting in the evening. He was suddenly gripped by a feeling of panic and saw a great fire start at the point (the old hospital site) and sweep right through the town. The whole landscape was scorched black. But then immediately green grass was growing everywhere. Then he saw Christ holding Galiwin'ku and all its people in his hand. (1988:107)

In a second example:

> Rurrambu tells how in the days before Djiniyini's return on 14 March 1979 [Djiniyini is a Christian leader from Galinwin'ku], a group was gathering at

Bunbatju's house. Suddenly all the leaves on a nearby tree trembled unaccountably. This event added to the sense of awe felt by people at the commencement of the Movement. (107)

Messages given or insights revealed by ancestors or by God may relate to significant things found on the land or in the waters. The following narrative is doubly interpreted; a man's account of events has been retold by an anonymous author cited in Bos (1988:108):

> When things first started to happen [i.e., when the Christian "Revival" commenced], Buthimang, an elder of the Galinwin'ku church, was worried. He prayed earnestly, asking God what it all meant because it was so new. He said the Lord reminded him that Australia was to be set free as a country.
>
> The Yolngu (Aborigines) were experiencing different kinds of freedom—in worship and [in] their relationship with God. God wanted this freedom that the Yolngu had begun to experience to permeate all of Australia so that the whole country would be really free.
>
> Buthimang felt strongly [that] he wanted a map of Australia so that when he prayed about that vision he could give substance to that prayer. Where on earth could he find a map of Australia? He thought of his friend, Djaymila, the spear fisherman and diver. He went to him and said, "You are to find me a map of Australia."
>
> "Where will I find such a map?" said Djaymila. "I don't know," replied Buthimang. "Maybe in the bush. Maybe somewhere."
>
> A couple of days later Djaymila was skin-diving off the air-strip beach. A shaft of sunlight flashed on a beautiful rock deep under the water. He felt drawn to dive and bring it up and on doing so was amazed at the shape of the rock. He took it to Buthimang and said, "Here is your map of Australia."
>
> Buthimang rejoiced at this and shared that he had had a picture of this rock, Australia, covered with water. "The earth shall be filled with the glory of God as the waters cover the sea."

Slotte recounts the following examples of visions. The mother of a sick child prayed to God, then heard God's voice and saw an angel; after that her son recovered. A Yolngu man recalled that he was traveling on a bus in Darwin when he was ill. He saw Jesus in a cloud, after which he went to hospital and got well. Other visions have to do with foreseeing the future, or reveal the presence of the Holy Spirit (1997:221–222).

Young men have explained to me that they gained knowledge of religious things (*madayin*) in dreams or reveries when the spirits of deceased ancestors revealed the meaning of sacred objects and designs (cf. Cawte 1984:237). Galiwirri, a man of about twenty-five, visited me at my house to talk about the Madayin ceremony to be held the following year at which he would refurbish the sacred object. He said that he had been sitting in camp last year with his hand to his forehead and eyes, and had experienced something like a dream, although he was not asleep. He told his father about it who said, "That is sacred [*dhuyu*], your *maḏayin* [sacra, things connected with the ancestors]." It was his *ma:ri'mu* [father's father or father's father's brother] . . . who told him all about it in the dream.

Discussing the possibility of filming the ceremony, he said that he wanted to tell the stories to me and to the people of Canberra. He was knowledgeable of everything but needed to get permission to tell others about the *maḏayin*. Then he qualified that to say that he did not know everything: there were some words that his father had yet to tell him (Keen 1978: 340). Galiwirri did not claim to have "worked out" the significance of the *maḏayin;* rather his insights resulted from revelation.

To sum up, people believe that they encounter *wangarr* ancestors, the Christian deity, angels, and other beings in dreams (*mabuga*), and they undergo experiences with supernatural import in what they call "visions" (using the English word) and; religious truths are revealed in waking dreams or reverie. Truths about the ancestors are "discovered," or are imparted by a deceased predecessor, or by an elder with the requisite rights and authority.

The centrality of dreams and visions in the revelation of religious knowledge is linked to the downplaying of individual creativity.

The Denial of Creativity

Describing people of the Western Desert of the 1960s, Robert Tonkinson writes:

> Local innovation refers to the composing of new rituals through dream-spirit journeys. These rituals, revealed to humans by spirit-being intermediaries of the spiritual powers, invigorate the life of the band because of the great enjoyment derived from them by its members of all ages.

Important for my theme, Tonkinson adds, "Although individuals are denied an innovatory function in ritual creativity, they nevertheless have the vital task of translating piecemeal information into highly structured and integrated ritual wholes" (Tonkinson 1978:113; cf. Myers 1986:52).

Like Western Desert people, and by comparison with Anglo-Celtic Australians, Americans, and the British, Yolngu downplay individual creative powers, at least in the domain of religion, displacing agency onto creative ancestors (*wangarr*). In this regard they contrast strongly with the Tiwi of Bathurst and Melville Islands (this volume, Goodale Chapter 8) with their emphasis on individual creativity.

The late Ba:riya, who lived at Milingimbi and nearby islands, was the male leader of the Liyagawumirr patri-group in the mid- to late 1970s. The following is his commentary (given to me in 1976) on his group's song about *ga:murung,* the larvae of Longicorn beetles. It is one of a long series performed by them for mortuary and purification ceremonies, as well as for initiation and revelatory ceremonies. He refers to the two Djang'kawu sisters, *wangarr* ancestors who created the Liyagawumirr and other patri-groups, their countries, and their ceremonies on their long journey from east to west along the coast:

> Larvae lie in the mud inside the rush-corms, which they eat. The two [ancestral] women got them out with the digging-sticks and put them in the sacred Dilly-bag. The Larvae lay in the *nganmarra* mat as well.[5] The Larvae grew wings [*wana*] and feet, and flew. The Dhuwa [moiety] groups all the way from the east up to here have the same song. Larvae are *gutharra* [grandchildren: wife's daughter's children or sister's daughter's children] . . . and are people—thus said the Djang'kawu [sisters]. We follow the old men and the forerunners: son follows father, father and older brother die, and we copy them. But everything is the thought of the Djang'kawu; the Djang'kawu gave the meaning to Larvae. (Keen 1994:213–214)

Here Ba:riya insists that the ancestors were the source of symbolism.

Dja:wa, a man in his seventies, was the leader of the Daygurrgurr Gupapuyngu patri-group, and also a religious and secular leader in the Milingimbi community as a whole in the 1970s. Of particular significance, I think, was his rejection of a bit of symbolic speculation on my part.

The story of the Marsupial Mouse, *marrawata,* tells how the mouse gossiped first to one group and then another, spreading malicious rumors. This led to an all-out-fight (*ganygarr*) at Ganygarrngura on Howard Island. The warriors entered the mangrove swamps to cut wood for spears, but the leeches in the water attached themselves to the warriors' shins, which bled into the water.

Discussing this story with Dja:wa, I speculated that the warriors' legs were like the mangroves which, when they are cut, "bleed" into the water with their red sap. Dja:wa said that was false (*nya:l*), and reiterated the events of the story. I think the point was that it was not my prerogative, as both junior and an outsider, to speculate on the meaning of the story.

People testify to the truth of narratives about *wangarr* ancestors with reference to an authoritative figure of the senior generation who has or had rights in that subject; the story is true because one's father or mother's brother told one it was true. By the same token men, at least, attributed the absence of knowledge and skill in religious matters to the failure, for whatever reason, of fathers to teach their sons (Keen 1994:249).

Ceremonies that reenact the ancestral events related in myth are "copied" from ancestral times and "follow" ancestral events. (In a discussion with a young man I likened a ritual to theatre; he corrected me by saying that Yolngu did not make them up, rather they are "from the beginning.") When performing ancestral dances, a person becomes identified with the *wangarr* ancestor (see also this volume, Tonkinson Chapter 5, on the Mardu).

While Yolngu take the inner significance of religious forms to be an ancestral given, nevertheless they recognize innovation in outer forms (see Warner 1937; Berndt 1962; MacKnight 1972). Howard Morphy, for example, discusses innovation in painted designs that come to be included within a patri-group's corpus (1991:207).[6] Steven Knopoff (1992) and Peter Toner (2001, chapter 12) have described versions of *manikay* songs called "new" (*yuṯa*), some of which are "found" in dreams. These are performed in a song series, following the established versions. "New" songs have several characteristic features, including references to contemporary events as well as ancestral events. However, the basic content and musical style is similar to the established songs:

> A singer generally invents a *yuṯa* after some emotional or otherwise exceptional event which can be metaphorically related to a particular song subject. The singer uses the song text of that song subject as the basis for his *yuṯa* version, adding additional text in the form of two identical unison chorus sections. The texts of the choruses refer to the contemporary inspiring event, often in some oblique way such as the use of the kinship terms of the people involved. The end result is the drawing of some comparison between the original song subject and the contemporary event. (Toner 2001:12)

However, *yuṯa* songs are regarded as having been "found." In another work Toner quotes Bangana Wunungmurra who said of *yuṯa manikay*, "that doesn't mean that it's new . . . I mean, the song's been there . . . it's been there for a long time. . . . [*yuṯa manikay* don't] change the whole picture . . . whatever you make up, it still talks about that . . . song, that has been there for a long time, and the words are still there" (Toner 2000:20).

As a link between people and ancestors, dreams and visions are an important medium for the revelation of religious knowledge, and the creation of legitimate new forms. The next section examines the relationship between this revelatory process and aspects of Yolngu concepts of mind.

Creativity and Concepts of Mind

The denial of creativity in a religious context appears to be reflected in features of Yolngu dialects. According to Michael Christie (1983), these features imply the mind is seen as a passive arena in which things happen, as much as the locus of actions on the part of the person (cf. this volume, Lohmann Chapter 10, on concepts of the self). Christie sees this passivity as characteristic of demeanor in a ritual context as well.

Christie (1983) has written about Yolngu ways of expressing intention, personal control, and responsibility. For native speakers of English, knowing, cogitating, understanding, condemning, and forgiving are all deliberate actions, whereas remembering, recognizing, forgetting, and disliking are things that happen to a person rather than intentional actions. Yolngu dialects do not make the strong contrast between the person as an agent and as someone to whom things happen. Where speakers have a choice between what Christie calls a "highly intentional" verb and its "less intentional" counterpart, they tend to prefer the less intentional verb. Yolngu dialects have pairs of verbs equivalent to the English pairs talk/ask, see/look, and hear/listen. In each pair, the second verb represents a "more purposeful" version of the first. In this respect English and Yolngu languages are alike. However, "whereas an English speaker would say 'He was asking for tobacco,' the Yolngu speaker would more often say 'Ngayi ga wanga ngaraliw'—He was talking for tobacco. Similarly, they would say 'I am seeing for matches,' rather than 'I am looking for matches'" (1983:268). Christie sums up that:

> the strict differentiation in English of words denoting highly goal directed action (look, listen, ask) from those denoting less intentional action (see, hear, talk) is not found to the same extent in Yolngu matha [language]. The attribution of intentionality is blurred, and in practice, where there is no ambiguity, the form connoting less intentionality is preferred. (1987:268)

In Yolngu verbs denoting cognitive activities, Christie suggests, "the conscious self-regulated intentional aspects of cognition are deemphasised." There is no way in Yolngu dialects to refer specifically to purposeful as opposed to unintentional cognitive activity. "All references to cognitive activity are ambiguous as to the purposefulness of the thinker" (1987:269). The word *marnggi,* "to know" or "to be knowledgeable," meant to have experienced something, even by accident, as well as to understand or know by personal cognitive effort.[7] He adds other examples:

guyanga	to cogitate purposefully; or to worry, remember (involuntarily)
dharangan	to understand (by virtue of making an effort); or to realize, recognize
moma	to fail to understand (in spite of efforts to work something out); or to forget, fail to recognize

Christie suggests that the same ambiguity obtains in the retrospective attribution of purposefulness. In each of the following cases, Christie thinks, the word can be used without any ascription of culpability:

gulinybuma	condemn (for wrongdoing); or dislike
gora	ashamed (feeling personally responsible for wrongdoing; or shy, bashful
bay-lakarama	forgive (for wrongdoing); or forget, ignore

Christie hypothesizes that this ambiguity allows for a high level of indirectness in everyday speech, which facilitates harmonious relationships (see also Eades 1982; Liberman 1985; Myers 1986). Moreover, Yolngu dialects inhibit the speaker's ability to perceive and therefore to exercise personal control or take personal responsibility over his or her behavior.

Christie's analytical contrasts between, on the one hand, highly intentional, purposeful, and goal directed, and on the other, less intentional, unintentional, accidental and involuntary, are most convincing in the following: know/have experienced (*marnggi*), cogitate/remember (*guyanga*), understand/recognize (*dharangan*), fail to understand/forget (*moma*), forgive/forget (*bay-lakarama*). The contrast in all these cases lies between the person as active as against the person as someone to whom something happened.

Other cases are less convincing. Consider say/ask (*wanga*): the contrast here is between a non-specific speech act (say, talk) and a more specific speech act (ask). In the case of condemn/dislike (*gulinybuma*), the contrast is between an action (condemn) and an attitude (dislike). In the case of ashamed/shy (*gora*) the contrast has to do with etiology. A person feels that way because of what the person did and other's reactions to it, as against a person feeling that way because he or she is that kind of person.[8]

Christie's analysis presupposes that there are universal senses, which are expressed in English yet are suppressed or ambiguated in Yolngu dialects. It may be the case, however, that the contrasts drawn in English rely on culturally specific concepts of the person and of mind in which thought *can* be conceived of as an action. In spite of these reservations about Christie's analysis, aspects of Yolngu languages do appear to embed a picture of the person as an arena in which things happen rather than as the locus of the origin of actions.

Christie relates these features to Yolngu norms of participation in rituals—and school—in which the individual reproduces forms rather than engaging in purposeful, goal-oriented behavior. Education research in Arnhem Land by Christie (1983) and Stephen Harris (1984) suggests that the Yolngu approach to learning is non-didactic. In some contexts it is passive: an initiand in a ritual ought to be quiet, not ask questions, look and listen when told. Certainly people learn by long exposure to practices such as songs and dances, although learning is active in the sense that a person learns by doing and copying how others do things. Yolngu children tend to think of school as similar to ritual—if one has been through the experience then one comes out schooled at the end.

Two rather different (though related) explanations have been proposed, then, for these features of Yolngu language and thought. The first has to do with indirectness and the maintenance of harmonious relations; the second is about demeanor in rituals and schools. Both have implications for agency—the person as actor or as acted upon. Language is structured and used in a way that minimizes the perception of persons as imposing on or controlling others; rituals and schooling are thought of as domains in which those who learn are somewhat passive receivers of experience.

I propose that the concepts of mind and person that these features of Yolngu dialects imply are *also* consistent with the idea that creativity in ritual is the result of dreaming and reverie happening to a person, and that legitimate religious knowledge has been handed down from generation to generation, ostensibly unchanged in essence. This brings us to the structure of the Yolngu polity, and "traditional authority."

Dreams and Traditional Authority

In one way, the revelatory aspect of religious experience needs little explanation; a person is hardly going to claim to be the innovative creator of religious truths. But it is less obvious why the creative and interpretive role of the individual is so strongly denied.

One relevant fact is that sacra are collectively owned as the property of patri-groups (*ba:purru* or *mala*) (Keen 1989, 1994). When new paintings and sand-sculpture designs are accepted, they become part of a patri-group's corpus (Clunies Ross and Hiatt 1977; Morphy 1991). While the individual's particular style is recognized, the forms of what they produce must conform to convention and their production (of paintings, songs, and dances) is normally subject to surveillance by others (Morphy 1991). People of a sub-group may make and perform a limited selection from the total complement of a group's sacra, and within that, individuals are responsible for particular versions of designs and have particular sacred objects in their keeping.

A person does not have the right to reproduce the religious forms belonging to another group. Even the strong rights of a person in the sacra of his or her mother's and mother's mother's groups are constrained. Within the patri-group, rights to perform (and so to make knowledge manifest) are subject to age and seniority. The most knowledgeable are said to be among the older men and women, to whom the young defer.

The point I wish to stress here is that if an individual coins a "new" item within genres of expressions to do with the *wangarr* ancestors and related beings, it necessarily becomes part of the collective property and responsibility of the patri-group.

Law, Ritual, and Traditional Authority

Maurice Bloch (1974) links what he sees as the absence of individual creativity in ritual to the structure of traditional authority. This expression comes from the work of Max Weber, whose ideal type of "traditional authority" does not entirely fit the pre-colonial Yolngu polity, but some features are germane:

> A system of imperative co-ordination will be called "traditional" if legitimacy is claimed for it and believed in on the basis of the sanctity of the order and the attendant powers of control as they have been handed down from the past, "have always existed." The person or persons exercising authority are designated according to traditionally transmitted rules. The object of obedience is the personal authority of the individual that he enjoys by virtue of his traditional status. (1947:341)

Weber goes on to outline the authority of the chief and personal retainers. The chief's commands are legitimized partly in terms of traditions and partly by his own decisions, such as to confer "grace." Importantly, Weber remarks that:

> It is impossible in the pure type of traditional authority for law or administrative rules to be deliberately created by legislation. What is actually new is thus claimed to have always been in force but only recently to have become known through the wisdom of the promulgator. The only documents which can play a part in the orientation of legal administration are the documents of tradition; namely, precedents. (1947:342)

(In Chapter 2 of this volume, Joel Robbins discusses a contrasting Weberian concept, that of charisma, in relation to Melanesian big men).

While they have never had "chiefs" with the power to command, Yolngu regard "law" (*rom*) not as a human creation but as emanating from the *wangarr* ancestors. Law is objectified and distantiated. The ancestors were the source of law, of which not only the rules governing social conduct, but also the performance of ceremonies and the making of sacred objects, are instantiations. *Rom* is "the right way" or "proper practice" rather than simply a body of rules and, in one sense of the word, it is grounded in religion.[9] Religious forms are law, and, like law in general, are not made by persons but reiterate what was "in the beginning." Yolngu themselves contrast the law of *balanda* (white people), which is made up and constantly changed, and *yolngu rom*, which does not change.

Munn (1970) discusses the character of ancestral objectification in a discussion of Warlpiri and Pitjantjatjara religious practice. She argues that it is the transformation of ancestors as persons ("subjects") into "objects" in the form of features of the landscape, sacred objects, and designs inscribed on the body that underpins the structure of authority.

The linkage of religious law to traditional authority has an obvious connection with Bloch's (1974) argument about the relation of ritual to traditional authority. Bloch sought a corrective to the Saussurian analysis of religious symbols by relating ritual enactments of intoning, song, and dance to political language. Briefly, he argued that formalized language is impoverished, for many of the options of form, style, vocabulary, and syntax are diminished by contrast with "everyday" language. Formalized communication is the sign and tool of traditional authority because in a political situation, where formalized speech is the norm, the inferior must accept what is said if he or she is to remain within the rules of appropriate behavior. In this form of communication the propositional content is reduced so that only the illocutionary force remains. The effect of this is to make what is said beyond argument. The political leader is also restricted by this effect, so that formalized language must be complemented by everyday speech.

Bloch points out that this formalization is pushed even further in religious rituals:

> The almost total lack of individual creativity which is involved in singing a song means that the fixity of the feature of articulation that we had noted for political oratory is present to a much greater extent. . . . [T]he fact remains that the propositional force of all song is less than that of spoken words in an ordinary context. The songs sung by groups of people in unison which characterize so much of ritual are particularly extreme examples of lack of individual creativity. (1974:70)

As the formalization of communication in the Merina (indigenous Malagasy) circumcision ceremony increases, the elders become depersonalized and "transformed into representatives of the dead," and each gradually loses the identity of particular elder to become the "eternal elder" (1974:78). Bloch sees this depersonalization as the automatic result of formalization, with its increase of repetition and ambiguity. Formalization removes what is being said from a particular time and place, and from the actual speaker, creating a supernatural being which the elder gradually becomes or speaks, for the elder "is transformed into an ancestor speaking eternal truth" (78). Traditional authority works by making a power situation appear as a fact of nature, indeed, Bloch ends by speculating that the origin of religion lay in this special strategy of leadership.

Much of what Bloch writes is applicable to Yolngu rituals, in which participants (but not only elders) identify with *wangarr* ancestors, ghosts, and other beings. Singers and dancers act *as* the ancestors in ceremonies that reenact ancestral events. Bloch remarks that not all song completely rules out creativity, and, indeed, Yolngu religious songs of the *manikay* genre do allow a considerable degree of freedom to the singer. They are notable for the amount that participants are able to communicate through the choices they make within the constraints of song, dance, and design—about the significance of the occasion, the identity and affiliations of the dead or an initiand, about political alliances, and so forth (Morphy 1984; Keen 1994). Moreover, song and dance are vehicles for the expression of deep emotion relating to particular personal experience (Tamisari 1998). Nevertheless, the elements and their significance are taken to be ancestral givens, as aspects of *rom*, "law."

Bloch links religious language to agency and the structure of governance. I think that it is possible to trace quite specific links between dreaming, ritual, and the structure of the Yolngu polity. The Africanists of the 1940s (Fortes and Evans-Pritchard 1940) referred to polities akin to that of the Yolngu as "acephalous," and described what they "lacked"—notably specialized institutions of government. In northeast Arnhem Land, people of a wide region more or less agree to a shared body of law (*rom*) governing social relations—land holding, relations of production, the control of technology, marriage, exchange, dispute settlement, and so on. Within constraints now imposed by the Australian state, it is up to individuals and their close kin to take redressive action for what they see as breaches of law which are against their interests, so that those who are able to recruit the strongest support are more able to press their interest (Keen 1994).

It is in this context of a regional order of law grounded in the ancestors that individual agency is downplayed. The genius of the social order is that people of a wide region can more or less agree to a body of legitimate law without legislators and in spite of the autonomy of kin groups. The assertion of individual powers radically to reinterpret its foundations would threaten that order.

Conclusions

In this chapter I have suggested that by comparison with "the West," Yolngu downplay individual creative powers in the domain of religion: religious forms and their significance originate with the *wangarr* ancestors and other beings, rather than the intellectual effort of individuals. A legitimate and central means for innovation is revelation through dream or reverie in which the individual has contact with the dead, and in which new religious forms such as songs, as well as the meaning of religious symbolism, are revealed. Yolngu claim to encounter God, angels, and other beings in "visions" that are also sources of religious revelation.

The downplaying of creativity is reflected in features of Yolngu dialects as discussed by Michael Christie, which embody a picture of the person as an arena in which things happen, rather than as the originator of actions. These kinds of features have been linked to indirectness in interpersonal interaction, and to approaches to ritual and schooling. I suggested that this picture is consistent with the idea that religious creativity is the result of things happening to a person, such as the experience of dreams and reverie linking the person to the ancestors.

The revelatory process and the downplaying of agency are linked to the structure of the Yolngu polity, I have argued. Sacra are collectively owned as the property of patri-groups, so that new designs and songs, if accepted, become part of a group's corpus. In this way individual production is subsumed under collective ownership and ancestral authorship. Weber's ideal type of "traditional authority," in which it is impossible for law to come about deliberately through legislation, and in which what is new is claimed always to have been in force, captures something of the character of the Yolngu polity. Regional cooperation in rituals reproduces a domain of legitimate ancestral law that is indeed not legislated, and that is objectified (and distantiated) in the form of ancestral traces in the landscape, songs and dances, sacred objects, and designs. No group has or had the power to establish enduring dominance and to become lawmakers, and there is no over-arching governmental body. It is up to individuals and their kin to enforce their interpretation of law in their own interests; nevertheless, anarchy does not prevail, for there is a shared, legitimate order. It is in the context of a regional order of law grounded in the ancestors that individual agency is downplayed, I have suggested, for the assertion of individual power to radically reinterpret the foundations of law would threaten that order.

Jane Goodale's case study in this volume provides indirect support for the links that I am drawing here, for the Tiwi acknowledge and encourage individual creativity. Furthermore, Goodale in Chapter 8 writes that they "do not consider knowledge to be sacredly derived or secret in essence or symbol, nor do they believe that certain knowledge only rightfully belongs to certain groups" (163). Tiwi draw a more indirect relationship between the creative ancestors and current religious practices than do the Yolngu.

In Yolngu thought, *wangarr* ancestors (including Christian figures) are the ultimate source of religious forms and structures. Symbols are not the ideas of living persons, but the "thought" of the ancestors. As Nancy Munn writes of Warlpiri cosmology, "The designs are forms external to individual subjectivity that are thought of as having originally been part of subjective experience, that is, of the interior vision (dream) of ancestors" (1973:33; cf. this volume, Lohmann Chapter 10).

But if *wangarr* ancestors are modeled after persons in the Yolngu imaginary, then perhaps Yolngu doctrines imply that the "ideas" embodied in symbolic equivalences came to the ancestors rather than being actively "thought" by them. Certainly, things *happened* to *wangarr*—they did not create the world out of nothing in six days; the world pre-existed them. Events that befell them gave the world its present shape. I say "befell" because the signs and substance of ancestors now in the land and waters are often the result of things that happened to them, of accidents, or the unintended consequences of their actions, rather than deliberate creative acts. The downplaying of agency (like those turtles) goes all the way down.

Notes

1. I am grateful to Roger Lohmann, the organizer of the conference sessions, and to Sylvie Poirier, for their detailed comments on the original paper, and to other participants in a lively conference session in Hawaii.
2. Yolngu means "person" or more specifically "man" in the Yolngu languages. It denotes an Aboriginal person by contrast with a European (*balanda*), Japanese (*djapani*), etc. The word also signifies more generally any person with a black skin. "Yolngu" is now generally accepted by researchers to refer to the people and culture of northeast Arnhem Land, and so has replaced "Murngin," "Wulamba," and "Miwuyt," all of which have more specific referents.
3. I have carried out fieldwork in northeast Arnhem Land between 1974 and 1976, and for shorter periods between 1980 and 1987 (see Keen 1994).
4. Yolngu use the English word "vision" for experiences with a specifically Christian content, although they can also be referred to as *mabuga*, "dream."

5. A dilly-bag is a general-purpose ovoid basket made by women of twined strips of pandanus leaf, with a string handle. A large version decorated with lorikeet feathers, carried in ceremonies, is held by the Liyagawumirr group as a sacred object. A *nganmarra* is a conical mat, about 1500 cm in diameter, formerly used by women as an apron, crib, mosquito net, sunshade and work-surface. Louise Hamby is currently carrying out research on the manufacture and significance of baskets and other fiber objects in Arnhem Land.
6. Among the neighboring Gidjingarli people, who share similar religious forms with the Yolngu and participate with them in performances of rituals, a man in a mother's mother's brother relation (*anmari*) to members of a patri-group has a key role in mediating the acceptance of new sand-sculpture designs into that group's sacra (Hiatt and Clunies Ross 1977:133).
7. In Yolngu doctrine being knowledgeable (*marnggi*) comes from experience; after a person has been present at a ritual, for example, one can say that the person "knows" the ritual. However, knowledge is also linked to performance. A person is judged to be "extremely knowledgeable" (*mirrithirri marnggi*) of some domain, according to their capacity to perform in that domain-paint the designs, perform the dances, sing the songs, remember and call out the names in the appropriate order, and so on (Keen 1994:253). Furthermore the concept of *marnggi* implies social competence and rights rather than simply the content of the mind (Harris 1984:44ff). People say that a person "knows" a ceremony even after experiencing it only once. However, a claim to be knowledgeable and to be able to impart that knowledge depends on such factors as group membership, gender, and age. A person might deny being knowledgeable, or affirm being only a little knowledgeable about something belonging to another group, where an older person of their group has the prerogative of being knowledgeable.
8. The example of *gora* brings out translation problems in Michael Christie's analysis. Two adults in certain relationships, especially mother-in-law and son-in-law, and brother and sister, are obliged to be *gora*—to avoid social intercourse. It is not so much a matter of the kind of person one is (a shy person) as obligations between two people. (Indeed all Christie's contrasts rely on the adequacy of his translations).
9. *Rom* has a number of related meanings including the usual way of doing things, habitual dispositions, and customs, as well as practice grounded in the *wangarr* ancestors.

References Cited

Berndt, R. M.
1952   Djanggawul. London: Routledge and Kegan Paul.
1962   An Adjustment Movement in Arnhem Land. Paris: Mouton & Company.

Bloch, Maurice
1974   Symbols, Song, Dance and Features of Articulation: Is Religion an Extreme form of Traditional Authority? European Journal of Sociology 15:55–81.

Bos, Robert
1988   Jesus and the Dreaming: Religion and Social Change in Arnhem Land. Ph.D. thesis, University of Queensland.

Cawte, John
1984   The "Ordinary" Dreams of the Yolngu in Arnhem Land. Australian and New Zealand Journal of Psychiatry 18:236–43.
1993   The Universe of the Warramirri: Art, Medicine and Religion in Arnhem Land. Kensington: New South Wales University Press.

Chaseling, W. S.
1957   Yulengor: Nomads of Arnhem Land. London: Epworth Press.

Christie, Michael
1983   The Classroom World of the Aboriginal Child. Ph.D thesis, University of Queensland.

Clunies Ross, Margaret and L. R. Hiatt
1977   Sand Sculptures from Arnhem Land. In Form in Indigenous Art: Schematisation in the Art of Aboriginal Australia and Prehistoric Europe. Peter Ucko, ed. Pp. 131–146. Canberra: Australian Institute of Aboriginal Studies.

Eades, Diana
1982   "You gotta know how to talk...": Information Seeking in South-east Queensland Aboriginal Society. Australian Journal of Linguistics 2(1):61–82.

Fortes, Meyer and E. E. Evans-Pritchard, eds.
1940   African Political Systems. Oxford: Oxford University Press.

Harris, Stephen
1984   Culture and Learning: Tradition and Education in North-east Arnhem Land. Canberra: Australian Institute of Aboriginal Studies.

Keen, Ian
1978   One Ceremony, One Song: An Economy of Religious Knowledge Among the Yolngu of Northeast Arnhem Land. Ph.D. thesis, Australian National University.
1989   Yolngu Religious Property. In Property, Power and Ideology in Hunting and Gathering Societies. T. Ingold, D. Riches, and J. Woodburn, eds. Pp. 272–291. London: Berg.
1994   Knowledge and Secrecy in an Aboriginal Religion: Yolngu of Northeast Arnhem Land. Oxford: Clarendon Press.

Knopoff, Steven
1992   *Yuta manikay:* Juxtaposition of Ancestral and Contemporary Elements in the Performance of Yolngu Clan Songs. Yearbook for Traditional Music 24:138–153.

Liberman, Kenneth
1985 Understanding Interaction in Central Australia: an Ethnomethodological Study of Australian Aboriginal People. Boston: Routledge & Kegan Paul.

MacKnight, C. C.
1972 Macassans and Aborigines. Oceania 42(4):283–321.

Morphy, Howard
1984 Journey to the Crocodile's Nest. Canberra: Australian Institute of Aboriginal Studies.
1991 Ancestral Connections: Art and an Aboriginal System of Knowledge. Chicago: Chicago University Press.
1997 Empiricism to Metaphysics: in Defense of the Concept of the Dreamtime. *In* Prehistory to Politics: John Mulvaney, the Humanities and the Public Intellectual. T. Bonyhady and T. Griffiths, eds. Pp.163–189. Melbourne: Melbourne University Press.

Munn, Nancy
1970 The Transformation of Subjects into Objects in Walbiri and Pitjantjatjara Myth. *In* Australian Aboriginal Anthropology. R. M. Berndt, ed. Pp. 141–163. Nedlands: University of Western Australia Press.
1973 Walbiri Iconography: Graphic Representation and Cultural Symbolism in a Central Australian Society. Ithaca: Cornell University Press.

Myers, F. R.
1986 Pintupi Country, Pintupi Self: Sentiment, Place and Politics among Western Desert Aborigines. Washington: Smithsonian Institution Press.

Peterson, N.
1972 Totemism Yesterday: Sentiment and Local Organisation among the Australian Aborigines. Man (NS) 7(1):12–32.

Poirier, Sylvie
1996 Les jardins du nomade: Cosmologie, territoire et personne dans le désert occidantal australien. Münster: Lit.

Slotte, Ingrid
1997 We Are Family, We Are One: An Aboriginal Christian Movement in Arnhem Land, Australia. Ph.D. thesis, Australian National University.

Spencer, B. and F. J. Gillen
1966 [1927] The Arunta: A Study of a Stone Age People. (2 vols.) Oosterhout Anthropological 28.

Tamisari, Franca
1998 Body, Vision and Movement: In the Footprints of the Ancestors. Oceania. 68(4):249–270.

Toner, Peter
2000 Ideology, Influence and Innovation: The Impact of Indonesian Contact on Australian Aboriginal Music. Perfect Beat: The Pacific Journal of Research into Contemporary Music and Popular Culture. 5(1):22–41.
2001 When the Echoes Have Gone: A Yolngu Musical Anthropology. Ph.D. thesis, Australian National University.

Tonkinson, Robert
1978   The Mardudjara Aborigines: Living the Dream in Australia's Desert. New York: Holt, Rinehart and Winston.

Warner, W. L.
1937   A Black Civilization: A Social Study of an Australian Tribe. New York: Harper and Brothers.

Weber, Max
1947   The Theory of Social and Economic Organization. T. Parsons, ed. New York: The Free Press.

Yallop, C.
1982   Australian Aboriginal Languages. London: André Deutsch.

8 Rachel Puruntatamer, chief mourner at grave/memorial ritual, painted to disguise herself from the ghost of the deceased. Photo: Jane Goodale.

Chapter 8

Tiwi Island Dreams

Jane C. Goodale

Introduction

The Tiwi (numbering approximately 2,000) live on two Islands, Melville (5,700 sq. km) and Bathurst (2,070 sq. km) separated by a narrow strait from mainland Australia and skirted by the strong currents of the Arafura Sea. They have no near linguistic relationship to mainland language groups. Under the Lands Rights Act (NT) of 1976 they regained legal possession of all their traditional lands. They govern these islands through the Tiwi Land Council. They have always resisted visitors to their island, in the past often killing them outright (Hart, Pilling, and Goodale 1988). With only bark canoes they rarely ventured across Clarence Strait to visit the mainland people whose hunting smoke they could barely see on exceptionally clear days. Before the 1788 invasion of the mainland by the British, and until the twentieth century, the Tiwi world consisted only of Tiwi people of the same language and all of known relationship to others.[1]

It is because of this isolation from others that the Tiwi appear to contrast with other mainland Australian cultures and societies. For example, they lacked the characteristic Australian hunting toolkit (e.g., the spear thrower, boomerang, small hafted stone or glass spear points, stone knives, and scrapers). They hunted with fire-hardened and -shaped spears crafted using crudely chipped stone ax heads and finished off with clam (cockle) shell scrapers. In the organization of society, the Tiwi recognized named groupings of matrilineally related persons (clans/sibs) grouped through fission and fusion into exogamous phratries. Matrilineal moieties as are found on the mainland are thought by some writers to be a recognized feature of traditional Tiwi society; however, they are not recognized by most of the Tiwi at Milikapiti. They may for some Tiwi today represent a diffusion of ideas imported from recent mainland contact. The matrilineal clans/sibs are chartered in The Dreamtime, but the higher matrilineal orders are not. Similarly, the patrilineal land-owning groups have no Dreamtime existence. They do, however, have significance today.

The English words "dreaming" and "Dreamtime" have been used by Australian Aboriginal and non-Aboriginal people to refer to a complex aggregation of concepts and behaviors. These characteristic belief systems concern the origin of the world, of all the relationships between humans and other animate and inanimate inhabitants of that universe, and of all natural laws governing the universe. The role of ancestors (interchangeable in human and non-human forms) who inhabited the world in the distant past is remembered in myths and rituals. In some parts of Australia, the travels of specific ancestors along tracks are encoded in geographic features of the landscape, representing particular actions and/or physical characteristics of those ancestors. In historical and contemporary art and in ritual dances and actions, ancestors are often represented in highly symbolic and/or more realistic form. Several authors in this volume, including Poirier (Chapter 6), Tonkinson (Chapter 5), and Keen (Chapter 7) discuss the more commonly known manifestation of the concept among the mainland cultures (see also Lee and Daly 1999). The Tiwi concept differs in significant ways.

The ancestress of all animate life and features of the islands landscape, who circumnavigated the islands, separating them from the mainland, is unconnected to any mainland ancestral being. She is now the sun (*Pukwi*) rather than the snake of the mainland (this volume, Keen Chapter 7). Her descendants are severally responsible for the major rituals, *Kulama* and *Pukamani*, which are focused on the passage of individuals (male and female) throughout birth, life, and death. In these rituals, the ancestor-creators are not the major focus and are given little attention. Rather, the less remote ancestral beings, the spirits of those who have recently died, are the co-performers at these rituals. In the art and dances that I witnessed in 1954, I saw no representation of the creative ancestors; however, today in the contemporary art being produced on commission and for gallery exhibition, the major creative ancestors are a major source of inspiration.

I found the Melville and Bathurst Islanders (the Tiwi) had little concern with dreams per se. With the exception of men, who responded to a direct question concerning their hunting for yet to be born children in dreams (see below), my data comes principally from being in the right place when a particular dream had significance to the dreamer and was discussed by others also involved. Such dreams were rare and memorable. In these dreams, the dreamer's contact was most likely to be the spirit of deceased relative, not the remote ancestors.

History of Contact

The British attempted settlement in 1826 on Melville Island near Pirlangimpi, but it was unsuccessful and abandoned in five years, leaving behind a legacy of water buffalo and horses. The first permanent foreign settlement (1911) was the Sacred Heart Mission at Nguiu, Bathurst Island. This was followed by a church-sponsored permanent settlement, established at Pirlingimpi (Melville Island) in the late 1930s. In 1945 the last permanent community, Milikapiti, was established as the Government Native Settlement of Snake Bay, on north Melville Island. During World War II, Snake Bay was a navy and air force base.

Owing to differences between mission and government goals in their administrations during the twentieth century, the three communities vary in their interpretation of the world, including their understanding of past traditions. I believe that before the outside world had a major impact on their culture, there were also significant differences between local groups geographically distant from one another. I believe that the gross differences seen today between Nguiu (on Bathurst) and Milikapiti (on Melville) may reflect both these older differences and the more recent differences in development policies in the two communities. At Nguiu the church had an early and strong impact on the beliefs and rituals of nearby local groups whose members were attracted to the mission, particularly by the opportunity it offered for educating the children in English and white culture. Here the mission personnel were dedicated to a slow but steady development and change in the hands of personnel who were there to stay. A half-century later, in 1945, Milikapiti (on Melville) drew most of its residents from the local groups most geographically removed from the mission, where even today Christian influence is minimal. Development since the early 1940s has been in the hands of a succession of offices and agencies under the Commonwealth and Northern Territorial governments, characterized by an ever-changing personnel and national policy. Because of the variation between communities in the past and the present, I restrict my remarks here to those I collected among the Milikapiti residents and draw on the work of others.

Palingari—The Dreamtime

The Tiwi have had many anthropologists residing among them beginning with Sir Baldwin Spencer in 1911 and, to mention only a few of those who followed, Hart (1928–29) and Pilling (1953–1954), all of whom worked at Nguiu (Bathurst Island); Mountford (1954), Robinson (1986–1987) and myself (1954, 1962, 1980–1981, 1986–1987, 1995, 1996–1997, 1999) at Milikapiti (Melville Island); Grau (1980, 1998), and Venbrux (1986) at Pirlingimpi. In spite of differences between the communities, it is interesting that when it concerns The Dreaming (*palingari*), and the importance of one's dreaming (*yirruma*) (discussed below) there is little variation among the communities or disagreement among their anthropologists.

The creation myth is known to Tiwi of all ages. The following is a composite obtained in 1954.

> In the beginning of the Dreamtime a woman, *Pukwi* [the sun] came out of the sky, walked about the land, and made all the animals, birds, insects, trees, and other plants. Behind her as she walked fresh water bubbled up eventually surrounding Bathurst and Melville (separating them from the mainland). Then she separated the Islands from each other walking down Apsley Strait. At the end of this journey the ancestral Jabiru speared her and her urine made the water salty. Later one of her children called a big meeting of all animate beings and told them to where to "sit down."

Typically these sit-down places are in shallow water and can only be seen during neap tides. They are the Tiwi equivalent to mainland "sacred sites" and are matrilineally distinctive sources for groups of unborn Tiwi (*pitapitui*) who may be born into the living world. The sites are also sources of related non - human life.

The Tiwi use the word *pukwi* (sun) to refer to their matrilineal affiliation, referred to in English as "skin group."[2] Most but not all of these skin groups are identified with ancestral figures of The Dreamtime, for example, jabiru, crocodile, march fly, and bloodwood tree; while others refer to inanimate features, for example, fire, stones, mud, and rain. With the exception of *Pukwi,* the mother of all things, who circumnavigated the islands, none of the other ancestral figures are noted for traveling; rather they are associated with the spirit-children at sacred sites. They are responsible for their animate and human existence in the real world, and some are noted for having initiated certain customs of life, ceremony, and death.

Purukupali is the most important of these creative ancestors, for he instituted everlasting death for all and forever. As any child or adult Tiwi can tell you:

After his son Djijini died having been neglected by his mother, Bima, and her lover Tjapara, Purukupali refused Tjapara's [the moon's] offer to take the child and bring him back to life in three days choosing to fight him from one end of the island to the other where he killed the moon. Thereafter, Purukupali took his dead son in his arms and walking backward into the sea declared that as his son had died and would never return, so would all Tiwi. Tjapara of course came back as the moon and Bima became the curlew. (cf. Goodale 1994 [1971]: 236–237)

Purukupali has significance for men for he symbolizes a primordial relationship between fathers and sons in an otherwise matrilineal world.[3] The film "Mourning for Mungatopi" begins with a Tiwi woman telling of her father's death shortly upon returning from directing his favorite son's funeral rituals. She relates how her father told her that in dying he was "following" his youngest son (as had Purukupali). Many years later (in 1995) I was shocked to hear from another daughter of this man how her brother, upon hearing that his own son had drowned, lay down and announced he too would die "to follow my son as my father did." He died within 24 hours.

Bima, the errant wife of Purukupali, is "followed" by women as they balance motherhood and sexuality with marriage to much older men. In the past when this pattern of marriage was still extant women would commonly find lovers among the young men. They told me they would say to their husband, "I am a bad woman," using the words spoken by Bima to her husband. Bima turned into the curlew, whose song is her lament.

Purukupali and Bima are the most common ancestral figures depicted in contemporary, not traditional, carvings, prints, and paintings (see below). Purukupali is also credited with telling people at his own funeral ceremony to sing and dance and paint all things they see around them, thus endowing all Tiwi with a creative spirit and challenge. Unlike many mainland Aboriginal groups, the Tiwi do not attribute the designs they create to Purukupali or other ancestral figures. However, while the events and figures in the Palingari may inspire the artist, the designs, songs, and dances are attributed to the creative individual artist or performer (see below).[4]

Dreams *(Piyapiya, Majirripi)*

Dreams (commonly called *piyapiya*) were rarely discussed. I was told that the ancestral figure Malijanini walked about the earth and taught people to sleep. When they sleep their *imanka* (spirit, shadow, reflection, photograph, film) may walk about and visit with other spirit beings. By far the most frequent encounter is with ghosts or spirits of "recently" deceased Tiwi (*mabidituwi*), who may also be seen during wakefulness.

Mobidituwi are described as having wings like flying foxes and long, claw-like nails. At night they will clutch at the throat and the person will become a little bit sick—it will feel like a sore throat. In the morning the person feels completely well. *Mobidituwi* sit near their graves on stones. They are white by day and black at night (invisible). They are cheeky fellows. They are there after death and during all subsequent death rituals, performing dances in parallel to those of the living. *Mobudituwi* may also be seen in their "living" form by close relatives. The very young and very old are considered particularly vulnerable to being kidnapped by spirits of the deceased (Goodale 1954 fieldnotes). At the grave site, following a burial, these vulnerable young and elderly relatives are introduced to the ghost as they jump over the grave or, with assistance, step over the mound. As they do so, they ask the ghost to leave them alone.

The ghost remains close to the grave area until the final (*iloti*) rituals are performed many months later when carved and painted poles are set up to mark the grave. Until this is done the grave area is surrounded by fire to keep the ghost from leaving, and the area is tabooed for hunting in order to reserve it as a hunting ground for the ghost. The ghost, however, is lonely and seeks out the weak whom he will try to make ill and die. He typically makes them "deaf" (unresponsive, unconscious) and, if not found by others, they will die. When found, hot leaves are pressed on their ears, then they can hear and respond to their saviors.

In 1962, a middle-aged man related his encounter to me:

> A *mobuditi* [male] stole me when I was thirteen years old. At eight o'clock my [dead] brother came. I saw my father, all grandmothers, and all mothers who were dead. There were four women and me in one camp. Women go to get water. Try to give me some water. I say, "No, I go myself." Went a mile or so to the swamp. Walked down and went for a swim. Came up from swim and someone [his dead brother] grabbed me, kill [hit] me, take me to where big mob *mobuditi*—all young women go hunting—sit down, head in hands and put me in the middle. PB's dead father came after—light fire in grass and make camp and fire go right around. A *mobuditi* (my step-brother) came and he, my brother, call out, "I got him, my brother here." All listen and carry me and stand me up. All wives of my step-brother are very happy, "We got brother's wife." All dead men. I camp there overnight. Mother finds me and gives me sugarbag (honey) and possum. All men go hunting geese and call out, "Come up brother, he still here." Women take care of me and cook a new goose. Two brothers and wives sleep in a circle around me. In the morning men get more geese. Call out again, "Cook goose, possom [sic] and sugarbag for him." All tired now, lay down. Old woman sleepy. I told them I go

get water for the old woman. I jump over all sleeping people, get two *tulini* [water containers] and two geese. I go swim and climb out and meet my mother who takes me to the camp. The *mobuditi* all run away. CC's father came up and chucked a spear at the *mobuditi* and they all ran away. (Goodale 1962 fieldnotes)

When a mature woman or man dreams of deceased spouse(s) or lover(s) the dreams are usually sexual. This is considered a very bad omen and one should, upon waking, immediately spit on the fire and also tell someone about the dream in order that the dream not become reality. In the following case a deceased spirit was seen by several individuals, some while asleep, others while awake.

In 1980, R. dreamed she copulated with her dead husband, M. and, when she woke, she didn't tell anyone, as she should have, nor did she spit on the fire. Later that same day another woman while awake saw the deceased M., riding in a Toyota. The ghost M. got out of the truck and said to her, "If I see any children on the road I will run over them." Her husband called out, "Who are you talking to?" She told him she was talking to M. and sat looking at the door. "It's not a dream," she told her husband. She told all children to stay out of the road and she also went to R. and told her to look after her children. R. replied, "He [my dead husband] is around here." The next day her six year old son was stung by a sea wasp while playing in the shallows with his friends. He died instantly. In this case, it is interesting that a woman told me that she saw the ghost of M. while she was fishing at Tjiberapu six months before the boy was stung. He (the ghost) came and called for R and her son. (Goodale 1980 fieldnotes)

Spirits of the deceased become less cheeky as time goes on. A woman told me that her dead son came to her in a dream. She asked him why he came and he replied, "I just came to see you. *Nimbangi* [goodbye]" (Goodale 1981 fieldnotes).

Finally, ghosts may indeed be helpful to living descendants. When one approaches an older grave site one should "call out" to the local *mobudituwi* (who are always so located) saying, "We are your children and grandchildren, we come here and we are hungry." The *mobudituwi* should then bring food close so people can find it easily. They may or may not give a sign or be seen. In 1962, I interrupted two men in deep conversation. When I asked what they were talking about one said, "We are planning that when one of us dies we are going to help (not hurt) the other. For example, if he dies first he will warn me if there is an alligator [crocodile] close by, and he will hit a tree to show me where the possum sleeps in it's hole" (Goodale 1962, 1980 fieldnotes).

In 1981, we were hunting in an area where there is a large multiple grave site.[5] That day everyone found some kind of food: my sister as she sat down found a nest of turtle eggs just under her right elbow; accompanying men speared six stingray; a couple hunting together in the mangroves found a number of large crabs and other mob arrived with fish. As we were eating this banquet, a young boy of twelve remarked, "My grandfather must really have heard me." One of the adults immediately said that it was a good thing that he had "sung out" because they, the parents, had forgotten to announce their presence. A man then remarked that he had seen a crocodile swimming away which then changed direction and returned and now he reckoned that was the sign made by the ghost, although at the time he didn't know what to make of it.

Dreaming, Land and Country, and Spirit Children

The act of dreaming has its closest relationship between what a Tiwi calls "my *yirruma*" (my Dreaming) and the dreaming action by their fathers in seeking or hunting for them while they were living as *pitipitui* (spirit-children) in the sacred places identified with his country.

I was told that a father could only hunt for and dream an unborn child when he was in his own territorial country (*tungarima*) defined as where his own deceased father was buried. If he had trouble in finding his children, the *mobuditi* (ghost) of his own dead father would help him. A man told me in 1954:

> My father been die when I little boy. By and by I get wife. Father see I no got pikanini. He get *pitapitui* (dream-child) from Karslake Island in my country and bring them to me. We are crossing a mangrove swamp and the water was deep. Pablo go ahead. I couldn't cross so I go sleep in the mangrove. Five girls come up. "Papa," they say, (I had five girls. Four been die. R. was behind.) I say, "Come along. I go back to Darwin. One night I be asleep. A spear hit me on the head. I wake up. I think wife hit me on head. I slap her. "You been kill me," I say. "No," she say, "I been asleep." I point to my head and say, "Look here, I got hurt." She say, "No, no. I no hit you." I think then maybe pikanini. (Goodale 1994 [1971]:141)

As the fathers became more mobile in recent times, so did their unborn children. Another father told me:

> I had a dream in which I saw my unborn son in a canoe, killing a turtle. I then went to Darwin and my wife stayed behind and my dream son followed me and said, "You are my father, but who is my mother?" [When a man has a

number of wives of different matrilineal skin groups, this is an important question.] I told him that his mother was P. Later P. told me that she was pregnant. (Goodale 1994 [1971]:141)

In 1954, I asked a mother of four whether a man ever dreamed his child before his wife told him she was pregnant. In answer I was told the following story:

A man [she gave his name] dreamed of his unborn child who was crippled. The *pitapitui* told his father that although he was firstborn, he had been crippled during an aerial attack during World War II and had to go first to America to be treated for his leg. "But," he told his father, "when I am healed I will come back to be born. Meanwhile I'll send my younger siblings first." When he was eventually born his father recognized him because of his crooked leg. (Goodale 1954 fieldnotes)

Venbrux (personal communication) obtained a version of this story in 1986 from a Pirlingimpi resident.

I found it significant that, when I asked what the *pitapitui* looked like, men said "like children playing in the shallows," but women were singularly unresponsive and I do not believe they ever see *pitapitui* in their dreams (Goodale 1954 fieldnotes).

Some older men told me, in the late 1990s, that they dream of their unborn children particularly while asleep in, or dreaming of, their country. But whenever I asked young fathers about this experience they only referred me to their own fathers. While it is possible that grandfathers are dreaming their grandchildren to send to their sons today, I never specifically checked this out (Goodale 1999 fieldnotes).[6]

The Tiwi, however, still conceptualize themselves as living in three parallel worlds or as having three kinds of existence: Before birth, they are *pitapitui* living and playing in and about the shallow watery sacred sites created in The *Palingari* (Dreamtime). After their fathers have found (dreamed) them and they are born to their mothers, they exist in the living world associated with the surface of the land and sea until death. After death they become *mobudituwi* (ghosts) and join other deceased living, invisibly for the most part, in the air, atmosphere, or sky. All Tiwi come from the world of the unborn, pass into the world of the living, and eventually pass into the world of the deceased—and never, since Purukupali, go through this sequence twice.[7] Fathers and one's patrilineal kin are principally responsible for the two transitional actions—into and out of the living world.

Dreaming as Father's Skin-Group and Country

Before and after birth a Tiwi is a member of her or his mother's matrilineal skin group (*imunga*). But once born, the child is also said to have "come out of" the father's matrilineal skin-group which the child refers to as his or her dreaming (*yirruma*). The matrilineal skin group is exogamous and preferred marriage for both men and women is to a spouse in their dreaming (*yirruma*) or their father's matrilineal skin group. It was, and to a large extent still is, appropriate to marry someone also affiliated with one's own territorial country (*tungarima*). In reference to the discussion above, concerning the role of grandfathers in helping their sons find children, it should be noted that, if tradition is upheld, a proper marriage is between individuals who are in each other's dreaming (father's skin group) and also belong to the same country. This will result in grandfathers and their grandchildren being in the same skin group and country. The ideal of endogamous country marriage was of course not the reality over time, or for all individuals, but the marriage exchange and personal attachment to one's dreaming (*yirruma*) to land and country was still very strong in the 1990s.

Before modern township settlement, one's country was where one's father's grave was located and marked with distinctive carved and painted grave poles. With township living (and dying), country affiliation has shifted to being the same as one's father's. The townships, however, still reflect in their population people's desire to live as close to their country as possible and geographical affiliation remains politically and socially important. The Tiwi use the word *timani* as a gloss for "dreaming," "land," and "country."[8]

Yirruma (Dreaming)

What is important is that the phrase "my dreaming" (*yirruma*) refers not only to one's father's matrilineal affiliation, but to additional and important features of one's own and one's father's country. These may be animal, vegetable, mineral, or aspects of weather, for example, jungle fowl, black cockatoo, blanket lizard, *ningawi* (mangrove spirits), whirlwind, king brown snake, thunder, horse, sailing ship, lightning, rain, possum, dingo, crow, geese, buffalo, cycad. Obviously not all of these are ancestral beings who populated the landscape during the Dreamtime (*palingari*). Some have been incorporated from the more recent past (ship, buffalo, airplane, e.g.).

An individual may have up to half-a-dozen dreamings passed on to him or her by paternal kin and through affiliation with a country, but usually two or three of them are emphasized by the individual, and he or she may be said to have a special relationship with the selected or emphasized dreaming. My Aboriginal sister wept when one of the buffalo herd, which was her dreaming, was shot, and she refused to eat its meat (Goodale 1980 fieldnotes). A man of the mangrove spirit (*ningawi*) dreaming can go into the mangroves without fear of these spirits (Goodale 1954 fieldnotes). When one of these dreamings is seen during the day or in dreams at night, it may foretell of coming events. A jungle fowl seen sitting on a tree one day was said to be the ghost of a man of jungle fowl dreaming who was recently deceased, and children were cautioned from throwing stones at it lest they come to grief (Goodale 1997 fieldnotes).

> One day a very heavy cloudburst was seen advancing across the bay and threatened a group of us playing cards in front of the house of a woman who had rain as one of her dreamings. She immediately got us inside her house and armed us with sticks, pots and pans to bang on the iron sides of the house. Her son and I were cautioned not to watch the black line of rain approach for if we did our (then) living parent(s) would die. The line of rain approached within 20 yards, stopped and slowly receded. Gary Robinson, another anthropologist working in a different part of the community where there was no one with rain dreaming, told me that night that everyone he was with was drenched! This convinced me of a special kind of relationship between the living and their individual dreamings. (Goodale 1980 fieldnotes)

Dreaming in *Yoi* Song and Dance

Tiwi may honor their dreamings (*yirruma*) by not eating them, or by feeling sorry for them when they are injured or killed. Tiwi may also "mark" their dreaming(s) (*yirruma*) by expressing them in song, dance, or visual art production. In dance one's dreaming is marked by members of a patrilineal dance group (also called *yirruma*). These dances, initially created by a patrilineal ancestor, are the most frequent performed at a mortuary ritual (*pukamani*). The *yirruma* dance will feature the special features (the walk, physical appearance, activities, etc.) of the dreaming of its originator.

One's dreaming is marked[9] in performance by a male member of a dance group who sings a composition about his dreaming. When other men take up the phrase, the leader is joined in dance by other men and women of the same *yirruma*. Songs marking dreamings were a major part of the rituals in 1954; for example the following was sung by a man of *Ningawi* (mangrove spirit) dreaming at his father's funeral.

> Coming strongly, pushing outwards, I am *Ningawi* boss.
> Newborn *Ningawi* lies on the ground. The Cockatoo calls "Someone is coming."

> I push aside the branches of the mangroves with my hands.
> Flies are looking at me, says the newborn's mother.
> Flies are climbing on my shoulders.
> *Mudati* [sea eagle] says, "Visitors are coming."
> We throw spears to see who throws furthest.
> One leg is up as he prepares to fly. (Goodale 1954 fieldnotes:224)

Whereas the song was a composition by the singer expressly for the occasion he punctuated each line of the song with a performance of the *Ningawi* dance. It was his father who invented the distinctive dance steps marking *Ningawi*, and both his sons and daughter have the right to dance *Ningawi*. The singer's sisters and brothers helped him in the dance, while a man and/or woman of the Cockatoo and then of the Sea Eagle dreamings/*yoi* danced their *yoi* to the appropriate lines of the song's composition.

In another 1954 performance a man of flying-fox dreaming sang:

> A big mob of flying foxes.
> You look, a big mob of flying foxes.
> The flying foxes are out in the late afternoon eating the blooms of the stringy-bark and woolly-bark trees.
> Cook the flying foxes and dry them in the sun.
> Hit them where they are thickest and break many wings at once.
> We can't cross the river because the crocodiles are in it.
> Look out! The sea eagle [*mudati*] dives upon the flying foxes.
> She catches them in her claws and eats them. The rest fly away.
> No leaves in the trees. The foxes have flown away. (Goodale 1994 [1971]:295)

After each line the *yirruma* group danced flying fox, joined where appropriate by members of other dance groups to depict the dreamings involved.

Some songs recorded in 1954 made reference to remote *Palingari* ancestors, but these were not common. Below is one sung by a man at his daughter's *pukamani*:

> Pukwi sits down along the middle water at Aringgo.
> Pukwi pretends to make the cheeky, bitter yam.
> Muriupianga and Uriupunala are sisters.
> An old woman digs the cheeky (*kulama*) yams and makes a fire and cooks them.
> Two sisters dig the cheeky yams.
> Muriupianga said to Uriupunala, you carry the cooked yams. (Goodale 1994 [1971]:293)

Singing (not dancing) is the major performance of the annual *Kulama*, an initiation ceremony focussed about the cheeky *kulama* yam which symbolizes pre-initiates (adult children) and is participated in by fully initiated men and, in the past, women. To become a fully initiated Tiwi and able to participate in adult ritual life one must learn to compose many new and original songs to be sung, without any faltering or mistakes in the poetic form of the language, throughout the three day *Kulama*.[10] During the first night of the ritual the men make songs about close kin who have recently died, while the last day's songs are about *pitapitui* (spirit children).[11] Recent ghosts (I am not sure about dream-children) are always present in the atmosphere surrounding ritual, and they join in the ritual with the living, unseen but always present.

In the late 1990s there still were a few old people (males and females) with the linguistic fluency in Old Tiwi language to compose songs and new dances for the *Kulama* and to sing at the truncated funeral rituals. Today, most of the songs and dances performed during the burial and memorial rituals mark the dancers relevant category of relatedness to the deceased person (fathers, mothers, sibling, and spouses) rather than their or the deceased's dreaming (*yirruma*). The kinship marking dances may possibly be more basic, perhaps older and more "traditional." But dances marking dreamings are still being passed on to younger participants who perform them energetically when the occasion calls for it. They are frequently performed in non-ritual ceremonial occasions, such as a visit from the chief minister, a dedication or opening of a new township building, and for parties on the occasion of birthdays, marriages, or departures. The latter are usually held in the township social club. Today as in the past these dances have kept pace with the changes occurring in their world. There are now not only buffalo, horse, and sailing-ship dreamings and dances (introduced in the nineteenth century), but also airplane, cyclone, prisoner, and thumb-print (to mark a worker getting paid) dances. Creativity and skill in song and dance is still remarked upon by all Tiwi present.

Painting and Carving

In the past, painting was done on the body, on bark baskets, and on funeral poles. Red and yellow ochres, white clay, and black charcoal were the only pigments used. The occasions for body painting were to mark transitions of a girl's puberty or of young adults through stages of initiation rituals and, for the fully initiated, to mark the stages of the *Kulama* yam ritual. Painting on the body was also done to disguise close kin from the spirits of a recently deceased relative and to mark off those under behavioral restraints due to being *Pukamani* (tabooed individuals). In 1954, I also saw young women decorate their bodies to "make them look good" for their lovers. The designs marking a young girl during her first menstrual period, and those marking the annual progression of initiates in the various levels of the yam (*Kulama*) ritual, were the same for all, set in the *palingari* by Purukupali.

However, body designs in connection with *Pukumani* rituals are highly original, being the creation of the individual being painted or who is doing the painting. Some people select designs marking their dreaming (*yirruma*), others purely abstract designs, but all agree the idea is to effect a disguise so that the *mobuditi* of the deceased will not recognize them. Some people experimented with new designs for each funeral ritual; others repeated designs. These body works took a full day to paint in 1954, but today only one or two individuals paint themselves so elaborately. Body designs live on, however, in the male and female figures carved, painted, and decorated with beards and armbands representing appropriate funeral attire and on portraits of Purukupali and Bima; sometimes Tjapara painted on bark or paper, or made as prints for exhibit and sale by the artists of the art centers.[12]

The artists of Milikapiti who produce works at Jilamara, the art center, are the only Tiwi producers still using only traditional ochres. Their work may be seen in museums in major cities in Australia, most European countries, and America. There has been considerable debate among the art center managers, galleries, and other outsiders about whether Tiwi art designs have a basis in the Dreamtime, as they do in Yolngu and Kukatja (see this volume, Keen Chapter 7, and Poirier Chapter 6) and other major art centers on the mainland. Tiwi artists (and their anthropologists) both in 1954 and consistently as late as 1999 emphatically say "no!" A Tiwi design is abstract and comes from the mind of the artist. Because artists work in groups they are influenced by others in the group and over time styles may be come regionalized as well as the work of artists who are considered "outstanding" by their fellow artists (see Goodale and Koss 1967). Jilamara welcomes anyone who wishes to submit art, but their works are judged by the all-Tiwi executive board who decide when a piece is "finished." If it is not finished it goes back to the artist for more work before being offered for sale. Purukupali's charge to paint things around them also gives them leeway today to paint realistic forms attractive to buyers, such as their dreamings and figures depicting ancestral beings, which I never saw painted in the 1950s.

Conclusion

The Tiwi see their world as having three dimensions of being. There is the dimension of those who live now (Tiwi), the dimension of the yet-to-live (spirit children), and the dimension of those who have once lived (ancestors and ghosts). Individuals in all three dimensions exist in the present and, according to people I have talked with, spend their days hunting, collecting, eating, and having sex. We the outsiders can only accept as being equally real and valid experiences which our Tiwi friends recount telling of their interactions, while awake or in dreams while asleep, with beings on the same or in another dimension. Sometimes these interactions involve all three dimensions—when, for example, a deceased father's father helps his living son find a yet-to-be-born child. During these interactions there is always some danger, just as there is in everyday encounters with others.

Tiwi value individual achievement and originality. All Tiwi are given the opportunity to express originality in song, dance, painting, and carving. Inspirations are personal experiences with the world they see around them and include things that have their origin in the *Palingari* and also in the historic times and today. Representations of one's father's matrilineal group and country encoded in one's "dreaming" are symbols to be used in traditional dance by the *yirruma,* and some are restricted to holders of the same dreaming for representation in modern paintings and carvings. All other images are available for representation by anyone. This is quite distinct from rights to representation of symbols of the individual creative ancestors held by their descendants, as is common on the mainland.

Another distinction between Tiwi and mainland groups is their concept of knowledge. The Tiwi do not consider knowledge to be sacredly derived or secret in essence or symbol, nor do they believe that certain knowledge only rightfully belongs to certain groups. Rather knowledge exists, I believe, primarily in the living and dreaming world and is there to be found by those who hunt for it. This was the stated reason that, in 1954, all parents welcomed the establishment of a government school at Milikapiti with open arms. Adults told me, and expressed in a number of songs, their expectation that, once their children acquired white knowledge, they would be equals with the whites.

Knowledge of the living world is one mark of a male or female person's prestige and is the basis for respect of elders as well as the basis of their power. But it is not knowledge that they pass on to their children, for each generation must find it on their own and achieve their own level of prestige and power. Like that of the big men in Melanesia (see this volume, Robbins Chapter 2 and Tonkinson Chapter 5), Tiwi prestige is individual. Their knowledge is rarely used to benefit anyone else even within the same household. In the Tiwi Islands there is no one who claims or is claimed by others to possess specialized knowledge of sorcery or healing. They are in fact quite apprehensive when on the mainland of sorcerers and their skills. Tiwi men in the past were mainly after the prestige that came through skillful negotiation with others for valuables (in their case wives and or mothers-in-law (Goodale 1994 [1971]). However, negotiation skills were not characteristic of the *palingari* ancestors. Rather, ancestors both remote and historic frequently fought with each other (cf. Purukupali and Tjapara), and it is by taking direct action against another that Tiwi today follow *palingari* ancestors of yesterday (see Venbrux 1995).

Having worked both among the Tiwi and among the New Britain (Papua New Guinea) Kaulong (Goodale 1995), I have spent many hours trying to make the Tiwi fit into both Australia and Papua New Guinea. Like some Melanesians they ritualize the yam, but conceptualize it very distinctly from rituals of these northern neighbors. It is more likely that the yam was significant at some time to some Arnhemlanders, for it is found among the cave art of Kakadu. Like many Melanesians, the Tiwi value individual achievement politically and socially over the status of any group other than the extended family. Tiwi consider that their origin was in what they call The Dreamtime (*Palingari*). This is in some respects similar to mainland Aboriginal groups, but Tiwi differ significantly in how they view the behavior of and their relationship with these ancestral beings.

I have speculated, mainly to myself, that the Tiwi represent a very early manifestation of Aboriginal culture isolated from many events and developments on the mainland in prehistory and more recently. They have the world's crudest tool kit (Oswald 1976), the simplest social organization (with no sections, subsections or moieties), a Dreamtime which is neither secret or sacred, an initiation ritual emphasizing linguistic skill and lacking circumcision and subincision, and an independence from necessary cooperation of any kind with other non-Tiwi speaking groups. How much of this represents an islander's, rather than a continental's, view of the world is debatable.

Notes

1. I have carried out fieldwork among the Tiwi since 1954, making six trips in all: in 1954, 1962, 1980–1981, 1986–1987, 1995, 1997, and 1999.
2. The number of skin groups has varied from as few as eleven to as many as twenty-two over the 100+ years recorded in the literature. The fluctuation is due both to fission and fusion (Goodale 1994 [1971]; Pilling 1957) as Tiwi marriage politics of exchange of women as mothers-in-law or wives dictated.
3. I asked an artist, who in 1980 was uniquely experimenting with a naturalistic style, to draw pictures for me of people engaged in various common ac-

tivities (hunting, fighting, woman and child, etc.). Alone in the set, the artist's depiction of man and child was immediately identified by all as Purukupali and his dead son, the artist showing Djijini lying still as a board in the arms of his father. I had hoped to use these pictures to elicit stories but, with this one exception, found the experiment a failure.
4. There are other beings of the *Palingari* who now appear in animal form: for example, *Tokombini* (Yellow Honey Eater), *Kuperani* (Frilled Lizard), and *Purukagini* (Owl). The origin of *Maratji* (Rainbow) and two other beings, the dangerous Ningawi who lives in the mangrove and the trickster Paramanua, who lives in holes in the ground are all dangerous. The first, Rainbow, is dangerous to young babies and women, and Ningawi and Paramanua will steal living individuals and try to incorporate the living in their worlds by giving wives to stolen men. This is also characteristic of the *mobuditiwi* ghosts.
5. These graves are featured in the films made in the 1970s on request from the Tiwi titled "Goodbye Old Man" (70 minutes), directed by David MacDougal, and "Mourning for Mungatopi" (53 minutes), directed by Curtis Levy. Both are available from the Australian Institute of Aboriginal and Torres Strait Islander Studies (AIATSIS), P. O. Box 553, Acton, Canberra ACT 2001, Australia.
6. Proper marriage is still considered to be between two exogamous matrilineal skin groups (marrying into the father's skin group) with the same country affiliation. Thus, ideally grandfathers and their grandchildren would be in the same country and skin group.
7. Newborns who die are thought to try again another time and return.
8. My country is also referred to as my *mirrakupupuni*.
9. In an unpublished analysis, I found that the deceased's dreaming (not his matrilineal skin-group) was danced the majority of times by patrilineal and matrilineal kin (Lecture given to Philadelphia Anthropological Society, 1960).
10. In the 1954 ceremony, and traditionally, only men dug the yam out of the ground and did all the necessary soaking, slicing, cooking, and so on required to make it edible. However, in 1986, the women (wives of the performing men) dug the yams. They said it was because only they knew where the yams were and the men would botch the job.
11. The *Kulama* yam is an androgynous symbol and throughout the ritual changes from male to female. I have presented my published symbolic analysis of this ritual to Tiwi who agree with me that it represents life as they know it—it is who they are (Goodale 1982).
12. In the past, the funerals were a major art gallery that formed a setting for songs and dances: the carved and painted poles were largely original and abstract (see Goodale and Koss 1967). Today the carved funeral poles have become more elaborate with acquisition of steel axes, chain saws, and multi-sized chisels. These carvings are now commissioned for local graves, and sold through the art centers on the open market. Because "meaning"

sells, for the outside buyer the carver frequently carves one of his own dreamings or a pole depicting Purukupali, the ancestral figure who created the first funeral for his son. A number of poles in Australian museums depict Purukupali with and without his dead son or wife. The dreamings of Jabiru, the stork, or Irikupe, the crocodile, are commonly carved. My young Tiwi "brother," a talented carver, gave me a life-sized, 20-pound owl carved out of ironwood (the hardest wood on the island) and delicately painted in original ochres. "This is to remind you that Owl is our (inclusive) dreaming, our land, and our country." He also carves less-than-life-sized human figures painted and decorated for a funeral ritual marking Owl's features.

References Cited

Berndt, Ronald M. and Catherine H.
1964 The World of the First Australians. Chicago: University of Chicago Press.
Goodale, Jane C.
1959 Tiwi Women. Ph.D. thesis, University of Pennsylvania.
1994 [1971] Tiwi Wives: A Study of the Women of Melville Island, North Australia. Prospect Heights: Waveland Press.
1995 To Sing with Pigs is Human: The Concept of Person in Papua New Guinea. Seattle: University of Washington Press.
1999 Tiwi. *In* The Cambridge Encyclopedia of Hunters and Gatherers. Lee, R. B., and R. Daly, eds. Pp. 353–357. Cambridge: Cambridge University Press.
Goodale Jane C. and Joan Koss.
1967 The Cultural Context of Creativity among Tiwi. *In* J. Helm, ed., Essays on the Verbal and Visual Arts: Proceedings of the 1966 Annual Spring Meeting of the American Ethnological Society. Seattle: University of Washington Press.
Grau, Andree
1983 Dreaming, Dancing, Kinship: The Study of Yoi, the Dance of Tiwi of Melville and Bathurst Islands. Ph.D. thesis. The Queen's University of Belfast.
Hart, C. W. M., Arnold Pilling, and Jane Goodale.
1988 The Tiwi of North Australia, 3rd Edition. New York: Holt, Rinehart, and Winston.
Lee, Richard B. and Richard Daly, eds.
1999 The Cambridge Encyclopedia of Hunters and Gatherers. Cambridge: Cambridge University Press.
Mountford, Charles P.
1958 The Tiwi: Their Art, Myth and Ceremony. London: Phoenix House in association with Georgian House.

Oswald, Wendell H.
1976   An Anthropological Analysis of Food-Getting Technology. New York: John Wiley & Sons.
Venbrux, Eric
1995   A Death in the Tiwi Islands: Conflict, Ritual and Social Life in an Australian Aboriginal Community. Cambridge: Cambridge University Press.

9 The construction of an effigy of the dead called a *tau tau*, associated with *nene'* spirits, who often visit people in their dreams. Photo: Douglas Hollan.

Chapter 9

The Cultural and Intersubjective Context of Dream Remembrance and Reporting

Dreams, Aging, and the Anthropological Encounter in Toraja, Indonesia

Douglas Hollan

Dreams are personal symbols in Obeyesekere's (1981) use of that term, in that they carry meaning at the cultural and psychological levels simultaneously. Dreams cannot be understood without knowing a great deal about the cultural frames, meanings, attitudes, and beliefs within which they are constructed and interpreted. And conversely, dream thoughts and imagery may illustrate or reveal a number of important cultural themes or processes. But it is equally true that dreams are not rigidly determined by cultural processes. People do not merely register or reproduce cultural meanings and beliefs in their dreams; they use, manipulate, and transform those cultural resources in personally creative and expressive ways. And so dreams also reveal or illustrate, through culturally influenced symbols and imagery, the wishes, desires, preoccupations, concerns, and life circumstances of individual dreamers (for surveys of other contemporary views of dreams in cultural context, see Kennedy and Langness 1981 and Tedlock 1987, 1994).

My earlier work on Toraja (South Sulawesi, Indonesia) dreams is based on these assumptions. I have examined Toraja beliefs about dreams and I have discussed how Toraja use dreams to express and make sense of their life experience (see especially Hollan 1989, 1995 and Hollan and Wellenkamp 1994, 1996). For the most part, I have used reports of past and present dreams from a number of different people to illustrate shared aspects of social experience, and to suggest interpersonal concerns and anxieties that are common to many or most Toraja throughout their lives.

In the present chapter, however, I focus more narrowly on individuals' reports of dreams from their near or distant past—reports that are very common in a place like Toraja, Indonesia, where many people believe that dreams may be predictive of future events.[1] Such reports are complex communications that may express, in a condensed and intermingled way, concerns and preoccupations from both past and present. To the extent that a dream report actually is constrained and shaped by the images, thoughts, and feelings of the original dream experience, it tells us something about the dreamer's life and preoccupations at that time. Such preoccupations may or may not be characteristic of later stages of life.

But the remembrance and report of a past dream experience must be prompted by some stimulus in the present. Thus, it is also an expression, directly or indirectly, of current interests and preoccupations. These include, I argue, those that may be peculiar to the dream reporter's current stage of life or which may be related to the circumstances in which the remembrance and reporting occurs. The experiencing and reporting of a dream in a psychotherapeutic setting often communicates, overtly or covertly, information about the dreamer's relationship to the therapist, as well as to other people in the dreamer's current life. In just the same way, the reporting of particular dreams (and not others) in an anthropological setting may reveal how the respondent experiences the anthropologist as well as illuminate other aspects of the dream reporter's current life.

I illustrate these points by examining a series of nine dreams reported to me by Nene'na ("Grandfather of") Limbong,[2] a wealthy and high-status Toraja elder, during the course of a single, long interview session. This session was the last of a series of six open-ended, freely flowing interviews in which I asked Nene'na Limbong to report and reflect upon his life experiences. I begin by presenting a brief ethnographic description of the Toraja. I then report Nene'na Limbong's dreams (and his interpretations of them), followed by a discussion of how they are to be situated within the wider context of Toraja understandings about dreams. I conclude by relating the dreams to Nene'na Limbong's advanced stage of life and to the intersubjective context in which the dreams were collected.

The Toraja

The Toraja are wet-rice farmers who live in scattered villages and hamlets throughout the central highlands of the province of South Sulawesi in Indonesia.[3] They are famous throughout Indonesia, and now throughout much of the world, for their elaborate and complex funeral ceremonies.

Most Toraja currently consider themselves to be Christians. However, their religious and existential beliefs are still influenced by traditional ideas about the power and significance of ancestral figures, *nene'*, and spiritual beings referred to as *deata* (see Hollan 1996). As we shall see, many Christian Toraja still encounter *nene'* and *deata* in their dreams, and many still believe that such entities intervene directly in human affairs. For most Toraja villagers, the question is not, "Which spiritual beings, including the Christian God, actually exist and which do not?," but rather, "Which of these beings, at any given moment in one's life, has the power to influence the course of one's fate and fortune?"

Toraja society is organized hierarchically, and social position and status are reckoned through both heredity and the competitive slaughter of buffalo, pigs, and chickens at community feasts (Volkman 1985). Many younger Toraja now leave the highlands to find work in the urban areas of Indonesia. But it is not uncommon for them to send much of their cash income back to the highlands, where it is used by their families in the competitive staging of ever larger and more elaborate feasts. These large and spectacular community feasts have, in turn, attracted ever larger numbers of international tourists in recent years, and tourism has now become a major industry in certain parts of the highlands.

The Dreams

As part of an open-ended interview process I conducted with seven Toraja men,[4] I asked respondents to report some of their past or present dreams to me. I discovered that most respondents, including Nene'na Limbong, usually reported dreams from their past that had proven to be prophetic in some way. The idea that a certain kind of dream experience may be predictive of future events is one that is widely held in Toraja (see below). Thus it is not surprising that respondents reported such dreams so frequently, since they are the ones that are thought to be most meaningful and significant from a Toraja point of view.

Below I present nine dreams that Nene'na Limbong reported to me during the last of our six interviews together. Like all but one of the other interviews, this one was conducted in my research house and residency, with only Nene'na Limbong and myself present. The small, barren wood-frame house with split, porous bamboo walls and floors provided an atmosphere of relative privacy and intimacy. We sat close together on a woven reed mat, my tape recorder placed between us. Although Nene'na Limbong was approximately seventy years old at the time I interviewed him, he was lean and agile from working in the steeply terraced rice fields, and he found it easier to sit on the floor for long periods of time than I did. Sometimes he and I ate and drank as we talked. Our conversations were always casual and unhurried, sometimes lasting up to two hours or longer. Some of the interviews occurred in the evening. If so, Nene'na Limbong would spend the night with us rather than attempt to navigate the treacherous, mountainous paths back to his own hamlet.

I present the dreams in the order in which they were reported, along with the questions, if any, I used to elicit them. I present as well Nene'na Limbong's interpretations of the dreams, since eight of the nine were thought by him to be prophetic. My purpose is to give the reader a sense of how and under what conditions the dream material was collected before turning to the discussion outlined above. Nene'na Limbong's dream reports are taken directly from our tape-recorded interviews together, but I have edited several of them heavily for clarity and brevity. I have placed direct questions and probes in italics and explanatory comments in brackets.

I begin the interview by asking Nene'na Limbong if he can remember any dreams from his youth.

Dream 1: When I was still young, before I was married, I dreamed that I climbed Mount Tagari. And in my dream, the top of the mountain was flat. But I knew that I was on Mount Tagari. I opened my arms and one arm reached as far as Makale in the south and the other as far as Buruppu in the north.

Meaning of Dream 1: It foreshadows that I would become a respected leader who would be asked to help settle disputes all over Tana Toraja.

I ask if he can remember any other dreams from his youth.

Dream 2: When I was still young [around 17 or 18, before he was married], I dreamed that there were many people, like at a feast. I sat on a mat while the people swarmed about me, petitioning me. Then my stomach started coming out of my mouth, pouring onto the mat in front of me. It didn't stop until it was all out on the mat. I awoke, startled and afraid.

Meaning of Dream 2: It meant that when I became an adult, I would become an expert on traditional customs and a divider of meat at feasts. When I divide meat at a feast, words come out of my mouth just like my stomach does in the dream, "Here is the piece for A, here is the piece for B, here is the piece for C."

Any other dreams from your youth?

Dream 3: I dreamed that I was in a crowd of people. A tall pole had been placed in the ground in front of us. An important man came who ordered people to climb the pole. I hid while a few people tried to climb the pole, but failed. Finally the man saw me and ordered me to climb. When I got to the top I said, "All of you people here, whatever I order you to do, you will do." And they answered, "Yes."

Meaning of Dream 3: I had that dream three years before I became head of the village. It meant that I would eventually become head of the village.

I ask if he has had any other frightening dreams, like dream 2. [I am trying to get a sense of what he might be anxious or afraid about.]

Dream 4: Once I dreamed that I was on the edge of the ocean with a group of people. We were ordered to jump into the sea! I saw many people jump and drown. Finally, I was ordered to jump. I threw myself out, but I didn't drown! I found myself sitting on a mat, floating on the ocean.

Meaning of Dream 4: Later I realized that the ocean was the hospital. Over the years, I have seen many people go to the hospital and die. But when I was very sick and stayed in the hospital for forty days, I survived. The dream foreshadowed that I would survive my illness.

All of these dreams are "good" dreams [in the sense that they all portended good fortune]. *Have you ever had a dream that foreshadowed misfortune?* [Note that he responds by reporting another "good" dream.]

Dream 5: I was already an adult and had children when I had this dream. I dreamed that I was in an open field with many other people, and we saw a plane approaching that was carrying bombs. Then the plane dropped its bombs and I was hit and fell to the ground! Many of the people I had been standing with were also hit, but some were not. Those who survived began to say, "Nene'na Limbong is surely dead." But an hour after I had been hit and fallen, I stood up! I stood up and showed myself to the people in the field and I said, "I am not wounded. I am not hurt. You can see for yourselves." And then I was just like normal.

Meaning of Dream 5: It foreshadowed the deaths of my parents and first wife, all three of whom died within a period of seven years. During that time I had to sacrifice many buffalo at their funerals. But I was able to survive financially without having to sell off my land. The dream portended that I would survive that hard time without losing my wealth or position.

I remember you once told me a dream you had that led you to flee to Ujung Pandang.

Dream 6: When guerillas were still active around here [in the aftermath of the Indonesian revolution], I used to sleep away from home in the forest or by the river. Once I dreamed that I had been stabbed and thrown in the river.

Meaning Dream 6: It foreshadowed my death at the hands of the guerillas, so I fled to Ujung Pandang.

I have heard people talk about tauan *[nightmares]. Have you ever had a* tauan?

Dream 7: I went to sleep about 10:00 P.M., but my eyes were still open! But my body was already asleep. But my eyes were still open and I could see. I thought, "Oh, what is this?" Then it came. It came and trampled on my stomach! Then it trampled on my hands and legs. I wanted to say something, but I couldn't speak! I wanted to yell, but nothing would come out. I was frightened! And my heart inside was pounding [he speaks louder to convey his sense of fear and anxiety]. So my heart was pounding, beating hard! People die from experiences like that! *They can die?* Yes, die, because of the restricted breathing. *And the spirit that jumped on you, was he/she a man or a woman?* A woman. *And what did she look like?* Like a human, but her hair wasn't tied up. Her hair was very long. [Women unbind their uncut hair only in very private contexts, such as bathing and lovemaking, and when they are possessed by spirits during the course of special rituals.] I was very frightened to see her. But I saw her with my own eyes! I have seen many people die because of an experience like that, because they can't fight back and they can't survive.

Have you ever had a dream in which one of your ancestors came to you? [I ask because I know that this is supposed to be a common dream experience in Toraja.]

Dream 8: One time I dreamed that my dead father came and tried to take me away with him! He came to me and said that he wanted to take me because my time in the village was up and I had to go. I said, "I don't want to go!" But he grabbed my arms and tried to take me. He said, "I must take you." But I said that I didn't want to go. "It's not time for me to follow you!" But he grabbed my arms and tried to take me. I struggled with him and he tried to grab me. I was sitting at the front of the rice barn, but he dragged me away. But I continued to struggle. As he dragged me by the front of the house [directly opposite from the barn], I wrapped my legs around a stone and held on. Then I was able to pull my arms away and I ran! After that, my father left and I didn't see him again.

Meaning Dream 8: This was a "bad" dream that may have foretold my death. But I went to a dream expert who was able to change the dream so that my father didn't really want to kill me. Instead, it was a reminder from my father that he was hungry and wanted to be fed. So I went out and sacrificed a pig for him.

Have you had any other really "bad" dreams? [I am still trying to ascertain how often he experiences frightening or unpleasant dreams. Note again that he responds not with another "bad" dream, but with one that again could be seen to foreshadow some type of good fortune.]

Dream 9: One time I dreamed that my throat had been cut! There was a man who cut my throat. I fell down dead! And I was very frightened. I woke up frightened thinking, "I'm dead!" A man cut me with a machete and I fell down dead and my eyes went dark. Then my body was cut up and distributed to A and B and C [he whispers in a low, terrified tone of voice]. "Oh, this is my body being cut up!" But I could see it happen! I was cut up and distributed [voice continues low, quiet, horrified]. I was very frightened.

Meaning Dream 9: The dream really meant that I would eventually slaughter many buffalo and become an important man.

Toraja Beliefs about Dreams

Let me begin by placing Nene'na Limbong's dreams and interpretations within the larger framework of cultural attitudes towards and beliefs about dreams. Many of the Toraja I have worked with identify three types of dream experience. The first type are dreams that occur frequently, are recalled only in fragments, and usually have something to do with the previous day's activities. The second type are nightmare-like experiences in which the dreamer sees or experiences something that is terrifying and struggles to cry out or awaken. The third type, referred to as *tindo,* occur relatively infrequently but are unusually vivid and easy to recall.

Most people seem to think of the first type of dream as a form of nighttime thinking in which the mind continues to mull over the events and activities of the previous day. These dreams usually are relatively emotionless, and people do not seem to think or worry about them much. Note that Nene'na Limbong does not include any of these dreams among the nine he reports to me.

Nightmare experiences, called *tauan,* can be divided into two subtypes. In one type, the dreamer relives an unpleasant or disturbing experience from waking life, often an incident from the previous day. What distinguishes this type of dream from the nocturnal thinking mentioned above is the intensity of the negative emotion that permeates the dream. The second type of *tauan* are thought to result from encounters with malicious spirits. Malicious spirits of various kinds usually are invisible to humans, but they may manifest themselves in people's dreams. Such face-to-face encounters are thought to be "real" experiences which in fact validate the existence of spiritual beings in the world. The dreamer who is the victim of a spirit attack nightmare often experiences a sense of motor and verbal paralysis (as the spirit attempts to restrain his or her movement), suffocation, and an overwhelming sense of dread and anxiety. Dream 7 above is an example of a typical spirit attack nightmare in Toraja. It resembles closely the widespread "sleep paralysis" dreams discussed in Simons and Hughes (1985).

Dreams that are unusually vivid and easy to recall, but which may occur infrequently, are called *tindo*. Like nightmares, many of them are thought to be "real" experiences in which the dreamer communicates with the souls of other sleeping humans or with spirits, gods, or deceased ancestral figures.

The dreamer's soul either wanders off to meet with these other entities, or these other entities come to visit the soul of the dreamer. Such dreams are of special interest to the Toraja because many of them are thought to be predictive of future fortune and misfortune. *Tindo* that have an unusually strong emotional tone, either positive or negative, or those that are easily understood using conventional interpretations are more likely to be considered prophetic than those that are not. In practice, of course, it is difficult to show that a *tindo* has not been prophetic in some way, since usually one can find some correspondence between a dream and the unfolding of future events.

Conventional interpretations of *tindo* are based on sets of symbolic meanings and equivalences. For example, it is widely believed that dreamers will eventually receive in waking life whatever an ancestral figure presents to them in a dream, or whatever that gift or object represents symbolically. Conversely it is widely believed that dreamers will eventually suffer the loss of whatever is taken away from them by an ancestral figure in a dream, or whatever the taken away object may represent. Note that interpretations of *tindo* are never clear-cut and unambiguous because it is never completely certain whether the objects and events experienced in a dream should be interpreted literally or metaphorically. It is because of this ambiguity that people may remember and analyze their *tindo* long after they were experienced, waiting for clarification or confirmation of their meaning.

While the idea that a dream can or must be interpreted metaphorically at times would appear to contradict the belief that many dreams are real experiences, none of my respondents made comment on this. This indicates, I believe, that even dreams that cannot be interpreted literally are considered "real" in the sense that they are caused or sent by actual ancestral spirits or correspond closely to objects or future events in the actual world (see also this volume, Lohmann Chapter 10 and Robbins Chapter 2).

When it appears that a *tindo* portends misfortune of some kind, one may enlist the services of a dream expert who can neutralize or reverse the original, ominous foreshadowing. Such people are known for their clever interpretations of dreams, but they do not receive any special training in dream interpretation, nor do they hold a special role or title. For example, the foreshadowing of a dream in which an ancestral figure carries away a chicken, which ordinarily would mean that the dreamer will suffer the loss of a domestic animal or child, can be manipulated so that the dreamer actually will receive a chicken sometime in the future. This can be done by making an offering to the ancestral figure who is associated with the ominous message, thereby insuring his or her favor in the future. This is the process Nene'na Limbong goes through after experiencing dream 8.

We see, then, that eight of the nine dreams that Nene'na Limbong reports are of the *tindo* variety. This is significant because I asked him to tell me about his dreams, not just *tindo*. He believes that all eight have foreshadowed significant events in his life. Dreams 1, 2, and 3 all foreshadowed that he would eventually become a leader of his village. Dreams 4, 5, 6, and 9 all foreshadowed that he would survive a misfortune. Dream 8 actually foreshadowed that he would die prematurely, but he was able to have this negative prophecy changed into a positive one.

Nene'na Limbong readily pronounces a meaning for each of the *tindo* dreams he reports. (Dream 7 is a *tauan* spirit attack nightmare and its meaning is self-evident.) However, I cannot be certain as to how or when he arrived at these interpretations. Some of the meanings he reports correspond closely to what other Toraja would consider to be conventional interpretations, and so he may have apprehended them almost immediately upon awakening. For example, dreams 1 and 3 are exactly the kind of dreams a high-status person is expected to have in order to validate a claim to high office. Most Toraja also would agree that the meaning of dream 6 is obvious, especially given the dangerous and uncertain times in which it was experienced. Nene'na Limbong's interpretation of dream 9 also has a conventional ring to it, given its straightforward reversal of fortune and the commonness of its images of buffalo slaughter.

But the remainder of the dreams do not lend themselves as readily to conventional interpretation, and Nene'na Limbong may have taken days, weeks, or even years to negotiate and eventually to settle upon their meanings. For example, he claims that dream 2 also foreshadowed his rise to positions of esteem, but unlike dreams 1 and 3, it is charged with fear and dread. Further, the connection he draws between the disgorgement of his entrails and his later entry into the meat divider role is less than obvious, even from a Toraja point of view. He almost certainly developed his interpretations of dreams 4 and 5 long after he experienced them. Neither lends itself to conventional interpretation, and conceivably both could have been linked to a vast number of future events. Nene'na Limbong could have settled upon their "exact" meaning only after he had survived a long hospital stay (dream 4) and after his parents and first wife had all died (dream 5).

I am not suggesting by this discussion that the Toraja make a hard and fast distinction between dream interpretations that are "conventional" and those that are not. From a Toraja point of view, all *tindo* experiences require interpretation, and the meaning of any given dream experience is always somewhat ambiguous and open to reinterpretation. I am merely suggesting that most Toraja find some kinds of dream experience much harder to understand than others, and that it is the former that require most interpretive time and effort.

What Are the Dreams About?

Focusing for a moment on the actual imagery and content of all nine dreams taken as a whole, and using Nene'na Limbong's interpretations as commentaries upon, or associations to, these images and content, we see that two primary and sometimes overlapping themes emerge. In dream 2, 4, 5, 6, 7, 8, and 9 Nene'na Limbong is threatened by some bodily assault or disintegration that leads to the experience of fear and that does or could lead to his death. In dreams 1, 2, 3, 5, 6, and 9, there is a representation of, or allusion to, a status concern of some kind. Dreams 1, 2, and 3, according to Nene'na Limbong, all correctly foreshadowed that he eventually would become a high-status and respected leader.[5]

The reference to status concerns in dream 6 is indirect. The dream expresses Nene'na Limbong's fear that he would be attacked and killed by guerillas in the aftermath of the Indonesian revolution. What is unspoken here is that Nene'na Limbong would have felt particularly vulnerable at that time because he would have been seen by the rebels as a wealthy individual who had cooperated with the Dutch. The dream is therefore both a representation of his status (he is worthy of attack) and an expression of his fear that his status could be taken away from him.

The themes of status and death anxiety overlap in dreams 2, 5, and 9 as well. In all of these dreams, Nene'na Limbong suffers some kind of bodily assault in the context of status enactment. In dream 2, he loses his entrails as he attempts to respond to his clients' petitions. In dream 5, expectations that he fulfill his ritual obligations become as destructive and damaging as an aerial bombardment. And in dream 9, his achievement of status through the sacrifice of buffalo is linked to his own bodily disintegration and death.

Elsewhere (Hollan and Wellenkamp 1994, 1996) I have suggested that the Toraja pay a psychological price for their participation in family and social networks that emphasize status competition and the extensive use of reciprocity to maintain relatedness. Nene'na Limbong's dreams offer a window onto some of these widespread social anxieties, anxieties that for the most part are culturally "hypocognized" (see Levy 1973, 1984)[6] and suppressed, if not repressed, in daily life. But the intensity of anxiety that we find in these dreams, and the graphic nature in which it is depicted, is also related more specifically to Nene'na Limbong's social position. Born to an aristocratic family and subject to innumerable social obligations and responsibilities, throughout his life he has struggled even more than most to assert and hold on to his status and sense of self worth, even as the hereditary privileges to which he clings come under increasing attack in the political economy of modern-day Indonesia.

But let us now place the dreams back into the immediate context in which they were elicited. When we do, we see that they are not only expressive of past and lifelong preoccupations and concerns, but also much more contemporary ones as well.

Old Age in Toraja

Nene'na Limbong was approximately seventy years of age when I interviewed him. By Toraja standards, he had already lived a long life, and he had already survived several very serious illnesses. My talks with him came, then, at the latter stages of his life, as he was experiencing old age and as he was adjusting to its possibilities and limitations.

What is old age like in Toraja (cf. Counts and Counts 1985)? In general, as Wellenkamp and I have noted (1996:168–182), life becomes less work-driven for older people, as their children become adults and begin to provide the primary economic support for the family. As physical strength declines, older people may slowly begin to disengage from heavy labor in rice fields or gardens, but they usually continue to help out with other less strenuous household tasks such as drying rice, cooking or washing dishes, and looking after young children. Some, like my respondent Nene'na Tandi, look forward to the day when they imagine they will be fed and cared for the way young children are, and they find relief in not having to be so responsible for the well-being of others.

Old people may also begin to enjoy a behavioral freedom that younger people do not. They may, for example, more openly threaten or strike misbehaving children and in other ways take advantage of younger people's reluctance to criticize their behavior. And they may begin to take on and enact certain political and religious roles that were too time-consuming to perform when they were younger.

But people's reactions toward becoming older and more dependent are ambivalent. Many older people bemoan their declining energy and strength. They recognize a growing gap between what they wish or desire to do and what their bodies are physically capable of accomplishing. And, while their opinions and advice may be valued and sought after even very late in life, they become aware of a growing social isolation—as beloved parents, relatives, and friends die and children move away or grow apart. As in later childhood (see Hollan and Wellenkamp 1996:50–56), life often ends with an awareness that one cannot have all that one would hope or long for.

Toraja culture encourages older people to develop a philosophical attitude toward their own deaths—to accept, for example, that human life must always end at its predestined time and that in any case, the life of the spirit continues in heaven or in Puya, the land of the dead. But such equanimity is not always achieved. Old people may become frightened or unsettled by the prospect of their own bodily decomposition or by the thought of being buried in the same cave or tomb with others. Older Christians sometimes fear the possibility that they may end up going to hell rather than to heaven (Hollan and Wellenkamp 1996:175–182).

Although Nene'na Limbong denied to me that he was fearful of or worried about the nearing of his own death, like other older people I knew, he did seem to be acutely aware that he was getting older and that he no longer had the energy or strength he once had. This weakening of mind and body was particularly upsetting to him because it was interfering with his efforts to complete two important public projects, the building of a new road into the village and the construction of a new grade school. He had often bragged to me about the many public improvements that he would be remembered for after his death, and he was beginning to worry that perhaps he would not be able to bring these last two projects to a close before his health gave out.

Even near the end of his life, then, it was important for Nene'na Limbong to assert his status as a leader in the village, to command the respect and cooperation of others, and to prove to himself and others that he was still a force to be reckoned with. Indeed, I now see more clearly than I have in the past that he was struggling, if not raging, against the dying of the day. Here in his seventieth year, he had become aware that his time was running out and that he was losing his grip on his position in life. This, in turn, was leading to a renewal of efforts to enact status and to fend off social oblivion.

I would now argue that we cannot understand why Nene'na Limbong remembers and reports these particular dreams, and not others, without taking into account his advanced years and the particular problems he faces as a result of those years. When taken as a whole, the dreams express a concern with status enactment and the threat of death or bodily disintegration—the very issues that Nene'na Limbong struggles with here at the end of his life. But the dreams and their interpretations also assert, over and over again, that status challenges can be overcome and that one can persevere and survive even in the face of death and bodily assaults of all kinds. These are important and reassuring lessons for a weakening, older man who has been challenged to review his life course and the direction in which it is heading.

The Intersubjective Context of Dream Reporting

I have argued that we cannot understand this corpus of dream reports without relating them to the challenges and problems that Nene'na Limbong was confronting when I collected them. But let us carry this one step further.

One of the challenges Nene'na Limbong faced at this time in his life was how to relate to a relatively young (at that time), white, male, American anthropologist who was asking him to review and comment upon his life experience. How did the nature of my relationship to Nene'na Limbong effect his reporting of these particular dreams, if at all?

Nene'na Limbong was introduced to me as one of the most important members of the village in which Jane Wellenkamp and I were to conduct an extended field study. He was one of the oldest members of the community, he was its wealthiest citizen, and he was considered by many to be its most knowledgeable scholar of local language, culture, and religion. He was also an important political figure, and was influential in the village's dealings with outside people and governments. I knew very shortly after meeting him that I wanted him to be one of my primary respondents and collaborators.

On the surface, almost all of my interactions with Nene'na Limbong were very polite and cordial, if not formal. I saw him as a high-status elder, deserving of deference and respect on my part. I wanted and needed him to help me with my project, and I was willing to do almost anything to encourage his cooperation. Because he was old enough to be my father or grandfather, I think I also cast him in this role. I was hoping and expecting that if I treated him with kindness, deference, and respect, he would in turn, in a fatherly or grandfatherly way, help me through my anthropological rite of passage.

But how did Nene'na Limbong view me? What kind of stimulus was I for him? At the time I conducted the interviews, my understanding of this was limited. At that time, I imagined that he probably was flattered by my interest in him, and that he viewed me as a much younger, relatively harmless young man who was open to his teachings and influence. Only after thinking about my relationship to Nene'na Limbong for many years now, and after rereading my journal notes and relistening to tapes of my interviews with him, have I come to realize how much more complicated our relationship was.

In addition to tape recording my interviews with Nene'na Limbong, I kept a journal of my interactions with him and of my thoughts about how the interview process was unfolding, including noting such things as Nene'na Limbong's emotional tone and displays, as well as other aspects of his nonverbal behavior. In one of my first notes to myself, I write that he talks a lot about his accomplishments, as if to impress me and as if he is aware that his life is coming to a close.

As I go through all of this material again, I realize how often Nene'na Limbong was directly and indirectly asserting his status with me, or trying to make certain that I really did comprehend what an important and high-status person he was. I realize, too, how worried he was that I might misjudge or misrepresent him in some way. In the first interview or two, he is very cautious about how he presents himself and the material that he discusses, as if worried that I am waiting for him to make a mistake. He also makes several flattering comments about my own status, how he knows that I must be a very important person myself because otherwise I would not have been given the time and money to come to Tana Toraja. In the second interview, he tells me how many people have told him how intelligent he is and how he could have become a professor himself if he had ever been given the chance.

We begin to see here that I am anything but an innocuous, neutral stimulus for him. Despite my youth, he is comparing his status to mine, and he is assessing whether I acknowledge his own relative importance.

In later interviews, this indirect communication over our relative status continues. In one, we are discussing what it would be like for him to come to the United States. He is excited about the idea, and I am encouraging his fantasy by telling him that he would learn a lot and enjoy himself there. As I get carried away in this dialogue, I naively seek to dispel any fears he might have about going to a place like the United States by trying to reassure him that the United States is filled with many different kinds of people from all over the world. He would not have to worry about standing out by looking or acting Indonesian because there would be many others there who would look or act the same.

As I listen again to this interview, I realize that I enflamed Nene'na Limbong's anxiety rather than extinguished it. He fears I am telling him that he would look no different than any other American and begins to worry that people would be indifferent to him, that they would not be able to recognize what an important person he is. He then tries to reassure me that such a mistake could never happen in Tana Toraja. In Toraja, he says, everyone just assumes that foreigners are aristocratic because they have a lot of money and can travel. They could never be mistaken for low-status or unimportant people.

Status issues became involved in our scheduling negotiations as well. Nene'na Limbong would repeatedly cancel our scheduled interviews, or just fail to show up for them, but would then appear at our door unexpectedly or complain to me in a half-joking, half-serious way that I was neglecting him. Although scheduled appointments in Toraja are rare and are always subject to last-minute change or cancellation, there was something more going on here. He was keeping me off balance, and in so doing, he was asserting the prerogative of a high-status person. He was indirectly communicating to me that we met at his pleasure, not mine. It was his way of keeping me in my proper place.

But I would often misread the message back then. I would convince myself that Nene'na Limbong really did not want to help me, in violation of my own, unfair expectations of him, and that I could not continue to waste my time with him. I would start to withdraw from our interactions which, I now think, would lead him to believe that I was trying to assert my own status and dominance over him. He would then drop by my house again unexpectedly or jokingly accuse me of neglecting him, and so pull me back into enacting my mentoree, lower-status role, and so on.

I want to underscore again that my relations with Nene'na Limbong were always cordial and friendly. The status rivalry I describe here was very subtle and mostly out of our conscious awareness. I recognize it now only because I have gone back to the records of our interactions together and have examined them closely. But however subtle and indirect, the tension was there, and helps to explain why the interview process unfolded in the way it did.

The dreams, then, can also be read as indirect communication to me—the young, inexperienced, and sometimes inept anthropologist, who by my very presence challenges Nene'na Limbong to enact his status and sense of himself in a particular way. The dreams can be seen as an indirect association to our problematic and complex relationship (cf. this volume, Kempf and Hermann Chapter 4). They assert not only to Nene'na Limbong himself, but also to me, the wealthy, white foreigner, that Nene'na Limbong is a man of renown and that this renown was fated by the gods and ancestors and was foreshadowed in his early youth. They further assert that although his status and renown have been challenged in many ways at many different times throughout the course of his life, he has always been able to rise above the challenges and persevere. And so they assert that the challenge my presence and questions pose can be overcome as well.

Discussion and Conclusion

The remembrance and reporting of dreams is a complex communicative act that may express concerns and preoccupations from both past and present. For my purposes here, I have focused on what these acts can tell us about a dreamer's present preoccupations and concerns. I have noted that the remembrance and reporting of dreams can be related not only to a dreamer's current stage of life, which is shaped in significant ways by cultural patterns and expectations, but also to the immediate circumstances in which the remembrance and reporting is stimulated.

Dating back at least as far as Devereux (1967), a number of researchers have pondered how the intersubjective nature of fieldwork affects the kind of data anthropologists collect and report, and how this selective collection and presentation of data affects the development of social and cultural theory (see, for example, Briggs 1970, 1981, 1998; Rabinow 1977; Crapanzano 1981; Kracke 1979, 1981, 1987; LeVine 1981, and Ewing 1987, 1997). Waud

Kracke, in particular, has been concerned with such issues. Reflecting on his own fieldwork and that of others, he notes:

> The nature of the crisis or adaptation facing each informant as they came to the interviews must have made some difference as to what aspects of their personality came to the fore, which childhood memories surfaced, or generally what they talked about and how they saw it. Awareness of an informant's personal motives for participating must help anthropologists evaluate information they get from an informant, not only when the information is of such a personal nature as I was looking for, but even when it is more abstract social and cultural data. (Kracke 1981:272)

I have suggested that the major adaptation facing Nene'na Limbong at the time of our interviews was the aging process and his inexorable movement toward physical and social decline. He was a man who was still fighting this decline, and who was not yet ready to relinquish his place in life. I have suggested, as well, that the kind of person I was (white, male, relatively young and wealthy), and the kind of questions I asked, tended to intensify Nene'na Limbong's awareness of this problem in adaptation, not dissipate it.

In Nene'na Limbong's case, the immediate intersubjective context of the challenges of aging and the confrontation with an anthropologist brought to the fore, as reflected in his reported dreams, lifelong interests and concerns about the acquisition and retention of status and authority. After all, he had been born into a wealthy, high-status family, and he had begun dreaming (literally) about becoming an important person even as a relatively young man. Further, as a high-status and wealthy person, he possessed tangible resources and prerogatives that were worth struggling to hold on to.

This was not the case for other old people I knew, however. For example, Nene'na Tandi, another of my primary interview respondents, had never been able to acquire and command the kind of resources that Nene'na Limbong had. He had been born into a relatively poor, commoner family, he had been unable to have children (a major source of wealth and prestige in Toraja), and all of his attempts to acquire wealth through travel and commerce had failed. For someone like Nene'na Tandi, old age tended to diminish concerns about status and prestige, rather than intensify them. Wanting to take advantage of an older person's right to greater economic and social dependency, he once told me that he just wished to be taken care of, the way a prized fighting cock is fed, stroked, and groomed. And none of the dreams he reported to me suggested status or death anxiety.

Nene'na Limbong copes with the demands of the present by drawing upon resources from the past. Although he exercises a certain amount of "choice" in this process—remembering some dreams, forgetting others—this freedom is not unlimited. He cannot just confabulate a past to suit his current needs. The dreams he reports to me are ones that have haunted him for many years. They have been told and retold over the years, their details evolving and changing. And surely the dream as narrated is not the dream as experienced. But just as certainly, in a culture that values dreams and encourages their remembering, the dream narratives are not infinitely malleable either. They are constrained by vivid images, from different stages of Nene'na Limbong's life, that express a powerful and consistent emotional truth—his need for validation of his status, rank, and prestige, and fear of its loss. The circumstances of the present allow Nene'na Limbong to revisit and rework the past, including his past dreams, but they do not allow him to escape it.

When anthropologists collect dreams in other cultures, they must be aware of the stimuli they provide potential dream reporters. How does their appearance, age, nationality, gender, wealth, education, personality, and presentation of self effect what the reporters experience and remember? Conversely, how do the current life circumstances of dream reporters, including their age and stage of life, lead them to experience the anthropologist in the ways they do? Only by paying closer attention to the intersubjective nature of the fieldwork setting can anthropologists fully appreciate the complexity of the dream communication process, with its intricate intermingling of past and present, word and image.

Acknowledgements

I wish to thank all of those who participated in the ASAO dream seminar over the last two years, from whom I learned much. In particular, I wish to thank Sylvie Poirier and Florence Brunois for their thoughtful comments on an earlier draft. I am especially grateful to Roger Lohmann who organized the dream seminar and who provided me with detailed and incisive comments on earlier drafts of this paper.

Notes

1. There are of course many places in the world, including several of the societies discussed in this volume, where people believe that dreams can be prophetic. The Toraja certainly are not unique in this regard.
2. "Nene'na Limbong" is a teknonym meaning "the grandfather of Limbong." Although a bit long and unwieldy, I use this term throughout the chapter because it is the name used by all of Nene'na Limbong's friends and family to refer to him and the term that Nene'na Limbong uses to refer to himself. As well, it alerts readers to the significance of parenting and kinship in the construction of Toraja personal identity. It is, however, a pseudonym.

3. There are only two large market and administrative towns in Toraja, Makale in the south and Rantepao in the north. As I have noted, the vast majority of Toraja still live in relatively isolated villages and hamlets.
4. These interviews were conducted in 1982–83. All of the interviews were conducted in Bahasa Indonesia, without the aid or presence of an interpreter. For further information on the details of the interview process, see Hollan and Wellenkamp 1994, 1996.
5. As I note above, it is expected that individuals of high status would have experienced such dreams during their youth, and it is common for aspiring individuals to cite such dream experiences as part of their claim to, or validation of, high office or status.
6. Levy argues that cultures shape personal experiences not only by starving them of cognitive and linguistic representations, which he refers to as "hypocognition," but also by categorizing and labeling them in great detail, which he refers to as "hypercognition." These processes represent two different ways of shaping and controlling emotion and personal experience. In the latter, awareness of certain types of experience is heightened and focused by drawing close attention to them. In the former, experience is flattened or made difficult to access through lack of representation.

References Cited

Briggs, Jean L.
1970   Never in Anger. Cambridge: Harvard University Press.
1981   In Search of Emotional Meaning. Ethos 15:8–15.
1998   Inuit Morality Play: The Emotional Education of a Three-Year-Old. New Haven: Yale University Press.
Counts, Dorothy Ayers and David R. Counts, eds.
1985   Aging and Its Transformations: Moving Toward Death in Pacific Societies. Lanham: University Press of America.
Crapanzano, Vincent
1981   Tuhami: Portrait of a Moroccan. Chicago: University of Chicago Press.
Devereux, George
1967   From Anxiety to Method in the Behavioral Sciences. The Hague: Mouton.
Ewing, Katherine P.
1987   Clinical Psychoanalysis as an Ethnographic Tool. Ethos 15:16–39.
1997   Arguing Sainthood: Modernity, Psychoanalysis, and Islam. Durham: Duke University Press.
Hollan, Douglas
1989   The Personal Use of Dream Beliefs in the Toraja Highlands. Ethos 17:166–186.
1995   To the Afterworld and Back: Mourning and Dreams of the Dead among the Toraja. Ethos 23:424–436.
1996   Cultural and Experiential Aspects of Spirit Beliefs among the Toraja. *In* Spirits in Culture, History, and Mind. J. M. Mageo and A. Howard, eds. Pp. 213–235. New York: Routledge.

Hollan, Douglas W. and Jane C. Wellenkamp
1994   Contentment and Suffering: Culture and Experience in Toraja. New York: Columbia University Press.
1996   The Thread of Life: Toraja Reflections on the Life Cycle. Honolulu: University of Hawaii Press.
Kennedy, John G. and L. L. Langness, eds.
1981   Issue Devoted to Dreams. Ethos 9:249–390.
Kracke, Waud
1979   Dreaming in Kagwahiv: Dream Beliefs and their Psychic Uses in an Amazonian Indian Culture. Psychoanalytic Study of Society 8:119–171.
1981   Kagwahiv Mourning: Dreams of a Bereaved Father. Ethos 9:258–275.
1987   Myths in Dreams, Thoughts in Images: An Amazonian Contribution to the Psychoanalytic Theory of Primary Process. *In* Dreaming: Anthropological and Psychological Perspectives. B. Tedlock, ed. Pp. 31–54. Cambridge: Cambridge University Press.
LeVine, Sarah
1981   Dreams of the Informant About the Researcher: Some Difficulties Inherent in the Research Relationship. Ethos 9:276–293.
Levy, Robert I.
1973   Tahitians: Mind and Experience in the Society Islands. Chicago: University of Chicago Press.
1984   Emotion, Knowing, and Culture. *In* Culture Theory: Essays on Mind, Self, and Emotion. R. A. Shweder and R. A. LeVine, eds. Pp. 214–237. Cambridge: Cambridge University Press.
Obeyesekere, Gananath
1981   Medusa's Hair: An Essay on Personal Symbols and Religious Experience. Chicago: University of Chicago Press.
Rabinow, Paul
1977   Reflections on Fieldwork in Morocco. Berkeley: University of California Press.
Simons, Ronald C. and Charles C. Hughes, eds.
1985   The Culture-Bound Syndromes: Folk Illnesses of Psychiatric and Anthropological Interest. Boston: D. Reidel Publishing Company.
Tedlock, Barbara, ed.
1987   Dreaming: Anthropological and Psychological Interpretations. New York: Cambridge University Press.
Tedlock, Barbara
1994   The Evidence from Dreams. *In* Psychological Anthropology. Philip K. Bock, ed. Pp. 279–295. Westport: Praeger.
Volkman, Toby
1985   Feasts of Honor: Ritual and Change in the Toraja Highlands. Urbana: University of Illinois Press.

10 Adiabo and Jim Alosi, some of whose supernatural encounters are described here, and Robert, a boy knowledgeable in traditional myths. Photo: Roger Lohmann, 1995.

Chapter 10

Supernatural Encounters of the Asabano in Two Traditions and Three States of Consciousness

Roger Ivar Lohmann

Dreams and the supernatural are perhaps the two cultural realms most infused with imagination. The Asabano of Papua New Guinea's Sandaun Province share with one another numerous accounts of supernatural experiences that occur not only in dreams, but also in trance and alert awareness. I collected many of these during fieldwork among them in 1994–95. Nearly twenty years earlier they had abandoned their traditional religion and adopted Baptist Christianity. Supernatural encounters experienced in pre-conversion times influenced the content of later experiences in Christian times. Both indigenous and exogenous cultural forms are found in each person's experience, and spirits of local and foreign myth borrow characteristics from one another. Likewise, memories of supernatural experiences in one state of consciousness shaped and encouraged such experiences in other states. In a daily cycle, memories of the day's events or "day residues" shape dreams, and memories of dreams or "night residues" shape waking experiences, particularly those that rely heavily on imagining.

The Asabano

The Asabano are an ethnolinguistic group of about 200 who inhabit the forested valleys of the stony Fu and Om Rivers to the south of the Schatteburg Mountains, near the center of New Guinea Island. They are swiddeners and small-scale pig-raisers, who until shortly after the first government contact in 1963 lived a semi-nomadic life, circulating among preferred hamlet sites in their territory. In 1995 they lived in two relatively permanent hamlets near the Duranmin airstrip.

My work with the Asabano focused on asking people what sorts of experiences convinced them to accept religious beliefs (Lohmann 2000a; 2001; 2003c). Frequently my informants told me of direct encounters between themselves and mythological beings that seemed to prove the existence of these spirits.

Asabano traditional religion was based on gender separation and male initiations, marked by a variety of tabooed foods and secret myths and practices. Of special relevance for this discussion are two indigenous assumptions. First, the Asabano say that human beings possess a body, a "big soul" responsible for generous and kind behavior, and a "little soul" responsible for selfish and belligerent behavior. In alert life, "when walking around," the body, the big soul, and the little soul are together and can travel somewhat arduously over the landscape. In "spirit work" trance (*alomowdu namodinedu*), body and souls are stationary while communicating with supernatural beings. In dream sleep (*aluma*) the body and the little soul are immobile and the big soul is able to leave and move about with great ease to visit and observe the activities of humans and spirits. Asabano thus distinguish states of consciousness based on the degree of mobility of the body and its associated little soul, the location of the big soul, and intention regarding contact with supernatural beings. Asabano generally consider perceptions in all of these states to be valid and genuine as sources of information. Dreaming in particular offers Asabano the freedom to travel about safely and to see supernatural beings, who are usually be hidden from plain view (on this and other characteristics of supernatural beings in general, see Lohmann 2003b).

A second significant assumption is that the landscape is populated with a variety of supernatural beings. These include (1) spirits of the dead who can be either positively or negatively disposed toward the living; (2) wild, humanoid, and powerful beings called *wobuno* who are often benevolent; (3) place spirits, or wicked beings associated with trees, stones, and bodies of water; and (4) witches, or shapeshifting cannibals controlled by anthropophagic animal spirits residing in their intestines. Asabano can perceive all of these beings during dream, spirit work, and alert consciousness.

In 1974, a Papua New Guinean missionary from Telefomin named Diyos came to live with the Asabano and founded a Bible college. Converted as a child by the Australian Baptist Missionary Society, he became a pastor. Diyos was driven by religious experiences in which he perceived God to be speaking to him. These encounters occurred in alert consciousness, for example, when he was walking along and heard God call his name, and during late night prayers in what might have been dream or trance states, in which he saw visions and heard God's voice (Wapnok 1990). He settled on his life's work with the Asabano, supported by his wife, Mandi, who is a renowned "Spirit woman"—one who contacts the Holy Spirit during spirit work and dreams. Diyos and Mandi presided over a revival movement that began in 1977 and saw the conversion of the Asabano and neighboring peoples including the Urapmin (this volume, Robbins Chapter 2). The revival featured perceived encounters with the Holy Spirit and other figures of Christian mythology, which motivated the conversion of the community.

Conversion has meant the banishment of the fairy-like *wobuno,* on whom Asabano used to rely for help. Some have lumped the *wobuno* with the malevolent spirits of trees and stones and written them off as "Satan's family." Christians who had earlier formed close relationships with *wobuno,* however, saw them as either capable of conversion or as angels.

The Asabano consider experiences in dream and trance to be real perceptions, not mere imaginings. This is not to say that they believe perceptions in such states are flawless reflections of the world. Rather, these experiences are valid in the same way that perceptions occurring during the waking day are relatively trustworthy. The state of consciousness in which a supernatural experience occurs is relevant because it provides information on the location of the person's big soul at the time.

Supernatural encounters are frequent; nevertheless, they are odd and exciting. They are long remembered, the source many tales around the hearth, and can have long-lasting effects on the attitudes and beliefs of both experiencers and those who hear their narratives.

In the narratives I collected, dreamed supernatural experiences involved encounters with a message-bearing deity, a wild spirit, or a dead person. In spirit work, generally undertaken publicly and accompanied by involuntary shaking, some experienced dreamlike encounters with spirits who displayed visual scenes or auditory messages. Experiencers felt spirits were beside or inside of them, telling them what to say or, in the Christian tradition, producing glossolalia. Alert religious experiences frequently consisted of brushes with witches in animal form, glimpses of ghosts, or hearing strange sounds indicating the presence of supernatural beings. Some individuals recounted extended interactions with supernatural beings when alert.

Asabano share narratives of supernatural encounters in the same contexts as they do other entertaining stories—when walking or resting together. While they appreciate dream narratives as a source of knowledge, one may choose whether or not to share them. In contrast, because information from spirit work experiences is explicitly sought, accounts are expected. Before contact, men took care not to reveal references to secret mythical elements to the uninitiated; however, this did not prevent a general sharing of at least the outlines of the experience. In contrast, in the Christianized community of the 1990s, religious experiences were shared in church services (cf. Curley 1992; this volume, Robbins Chapter 2). In this context, Asabano easily shared narrative accounts of their religious experiences with me.

Supernatural Encounters in Dreams

I have strange dreams. At night I dream women come and take me away; or evil spirits come to kill me and I can fly. I don't turn into a bird; I just fly. I think in dreams the spirit goes and the body stays. So the things we dream really happen. When I'm totally asleep, and I want to go to the bush, and stone and tree spirits want to kill me, I just fly. In dreams it's safe; I move about well.

—Obai, a young man

Sleep, for Asabano, is a time when the bonds between body and big soul are unbuttoned. The gravity that fights against people as they walk trails over mountains can be turned off at will, and one's big soul is free to wander unencumbered to visit friends and relatives far away (cf. Merrill 1987:202). Simolibo, a pragmatic man in his thirties, told me he believed that dreaming literally frees the soul, citing one of his dreams in which he walked on water with a bow and arrows and then flew up to a tree branch and looked around. A dream provides ease of contact with spirits because Asabano conceive of them as being separated from people by geography. So to gain freedom to move about grants access not only to other living people, but also to the dead, to spirits, and, since the 1970s, to the Christian god. These beings, in Asabano cosmology, inhabit the same dimension as people, but like wild animals are capable of hiding themselves.

Since dreams often involve sightings or encounters with supernatural beings, they provide information about the spiritual causes of current problems and previews of the future. People recognize that dream images are not necessarily literal sensory perceptions but can be symbolic. Asabano understand dream symbols to be cryptic messages, displayed by spirits in response to prayers. In this sense, dream symbols are analogous to linguistic messages: a form of communication used by the spirits.

Indigenous Supernatural Encounters in Dreams

Before conversion, Asabano religious dreams included encounters with *wobuno;* tree, stone, and water spirits; the dead; and witches. These contacts included meeting spirits, witnessing their actions, and being shown events distant in time or space. Most of the dream narratives I was able to collect refer to post-contact (1963) dreams; however, many were based on the indigenous religious idiom.

Many of these dreams took the form of responses to prayers and offerings. For example, an older man named Omahu told me that he used to make offerings to *wobuno,* and later in dreams they would display images predicting his hunting success.

> When I wanted to hunt, or if I was eating something good I had to give them something too. Now too, I see them in dreams and then I kill animals. If I dream that I kill a man, I will go and kill a pig. If I cut a banana, I'll kill an animal. The *wobuno* show me these things in dreams. When I have dreams like this I don't have to go far. When I went to the forest, I gave the *wobuno* something and I would see a dream, then I'd kill animals. If people went to the forest and I said they would come with animals, they would. If not, they wouldn't. The *wobuno* gave me these thoughts and I would talk.

Dream messages provided information on where to hunt, and what causes, in the form of intentional actions of supernatural beings, were responsible for misfortunes. "Before the revival, when a man was sick, people would dream that a tree spirit or other thing had hurt him," a community leader named Yalowad told me.

> When we had these dreams we would know the cause. I too had dreams about the tree spirits. When I dreamed of the *wobuno* they would give me pigs. They could talk to me. The tree spirits would also give us animals. I myself have dreamed when someone was sick that the tree spirits made him or her sick. I would dream that someone just like a man talked to me and told me, "Tomorrow you will kill animals." When this happened, I would kill something soon afterwards.

As they were seen as real experiences rather than fantasy, even the supernatural dreams of children were taken seriously by all (cf. Reynolds 1992:27–28). In the process of coming to terms with the world in which they find themselves, Asabano children are often frightened by their parents' stories of malevolent beings lurking in natural objects. It is often in their dreams that they initially encounter these ogres. Such images remain with them throughout life when they go on to perceive these beings in other dreams, during spirit work, or in waking life. Lonika, a 12-year-old girl, told me of a nightmare she had involving one of these malevolent spirits. "Once I dreamed my mother was washing clothes, and a stone spirit grabbed me strongly by the neck and pulled me under the water. I got a stone and hit him, and he yelled. He let me go and went into the water. He was like a baby. I was afraid" (cf. Lohmann 2000b:96).

Such terrifying experiences are all the more harrowing when elders tell children that dreams can predict the future. Mamsbo, a young woman, said her grandmother Blogoi told her, "If you see dead people in dreams, you will die soon." In practice, few awaken after seeing a deceased acquaintance with a clutching certainty that they will soon perish. However, several people told me that after they had seen dead people in their dreams they became sick, but with proper care and offerings to spirits of trees or stones (or since conversion, prayer to God) they recovered. A dream of dancing ancestors indicates a coming death, for the dead must be celebrating that one of the living will join them. When the dead are seen to put on their finery, play drums, sing, and dance dreamers perceive this not as cryptic symbolism, but as a case of eavesdropping upon their doings (cf. this volume, Stewart and Strathern Chapter 3).

Seeing the dead was often, at the very least, a tense and uncomfortable experience. Martin, a student at Telefomin High School, told me of a dream in which he saw his deceased uncle. "Once when I was at Telefomin I dreamt after Agadai had died. I told him, 'This arrow that belonged to you is mine now.' He answered, 'No, it's mine.' I answered, 'You're dead already, why do you want to get your arrow back?' He was mad and pushed me. I thought it was real and then woke up. I think he truly came and talked to me."

Martin acknowledged that though he thought at the time that he was in an alert state and that the experience was "real," he discovered himself to be mistaken when he really achieved alertness. Still, he reaffirmed the reality of the dream experience by stating that the encounter had in fact occurred.

The dead were not always greeted with dread in dreams, for they could provide for their families. An old man named Baraiab told me about a dream he had long ago. "I was asleep, and I saw my [deceased] father Omai coming. He gave me a taro and told me, 'You eat this taro and then go watch at a bird house.' Upon waking, Bledalo [an elder] did this, and then he saw a pig come and he shot him, and that pig had lots of fat." Wild pigs are generally lean, so in this case a fat pig indicates that the dead had cared for it.

Dream encounters with witches were always frightening. Asabano feared perhaps nothing more than these utterly evil and unpredictable monsters, existing as dual entities in a macabre symbiosis of human and animal spirit. Witches are all the more horrible because they kill and devour their own family members. A young woman named Maria told me that while dream traveling she witnessed witches attack an elderly man as he worked in his garden (see Lohmann 2000b:88).

Interestingly, no one described successful witch attacks upon themselves in a dream; the few dream attacks described were upon others. In fact, the girl's dream of a stone spirit's grabbing and attempting to drown her is a rare example of being directly attacked by any type of supernatural being in a dream. By contrast, among some peoples spirit attack dreams are a familiar genre (this volume, Hollan Chapter 9, see also Tonkinson Chapter 5, on spiritual danger in dreaming). No adults expressed the possibility of dying in a dream, though they often learned about dangers and opportunities existing in waking life. The relative safety of dreams contrasts strongly with the dangers faced in alert life. Dream life provided an ability to move about freely, witness important events, and even speak to supernatural beings. The safety Asabano feel in dreams is a consequence of their ability to move quickly and hide, their increased agility made possible by leaving the body behind.

Christian Supernatural Encounters in Dreams

Indigenous supernatural beings continued to appear in dreams following conversion to Christianity, but played a different role. *Wobuno* were derided by young people as demons, but defended by a few older men as angels, or at least as sharing human capabilities of joining with God's side against Satan. They apparently feature less frequently in dreams since conversion, since the Holy Spirit has taken over their function as hunting aids.

Christian Asabano continued to hold place-spirits responsible for a great deal of sickness and death, and dreams remained a valuable source of information on their activities. The dead, though still sometimes producing fear in dreams, often reassured loved ones that they are well, and urged them to keep the Christian faith that they might be reunited in heaven. "They come and tell us how they are in dreams," said Sumole, a middle-aged man who told me of a recurrent dream he has of his wife Nene, who died after giving birth to their son Isaac. "She comes telling me, 'Don't worry about me: just believe and pray. If you worry about me you will go to hell. Take care of the children.' I see her face, and it's different—she has the same features, but white skin and straight hair. When I see these dreams I'm not afraid, I just think a lot and worry."

Sumole's reference to the change in his wife's complexion and hair type reflects a common idea in Melanesia that the dead become Europeans (cf. Lepowsky 1989). This belief arose in response to contact with people of European descent who exhibited the traits expected of the dead such as fantastic powers and generosity. Pictures depicting Jesus and angels as white have furthered this idea, and dreams of white spirits provide, in Asabano sensibilities, solid evidence of its truth.

Wosono, one of the few older women living, described a dream in which her dead friend appeared to her with a figuratively expressed message. This friend was Sumole's wife Nene, a deeply Christian woman who had engaged in spirit work. "Nene had died and I went to Tabubil and I was worried about her—my friend—and had a dream. She came to me with a machete, and said, 'Don't worry about me. You must hold this knife in your right hand firmly and walk.' It wasn't a real machete, but it was the word of God. It is able to cut all the evil spirits."

The murderous deeds of witches continue to be witnessed in dreams, but often dreamers construe these dream images as being shown to them by the Holy Spirit. Thus, characters from Christian mythology have joined the Asabano dreamscape and taken over the role traditionally played by *wobuno*. They show current events in other places and indicate what actions in waking life will result in a payoff. For example, they can show or tell dreamers where to go hunting. "The Holy Spirit will tell me in a dream in the night that I'll kill an animal," said Muluasi. "So I believe it, and say 'Thank you.' I don't see the Spirit's body; I just hear the talk. He shows me these dreams. He will tell me, 'You will kill a cassowary.' So I know the Spirit is with us. We don't give him offerings [as were given to *wobuno*], we just ask."

The Holy Spirit can also show which malevolent beings are responsible for particular misfortunes, as Bledalo, an elderly man, explained:

> If you see a dream when a person is sick in which the Spirit tells you your soul is at a certain stone or tree, you must plant a cross there and pray and the person will get better. The Spirit of the Lord said, "When you get sick you must plant a cross like this." In the Bible it also says to do this. When the revival came down the Spirit showed us here, before we didn't have this.

More rarely, Jesus appears to remind dreamers of the importance of following Christian principles, and to demonstrate the truth of Christianity. These dreams were very significant in the initial conversion of the Asabano because they provided experiential evidence of God's existence. At the time of my fieldwork, such dreams served to strengthen faith in Christianity's supernatural beings, removing the temptation to rely on traditional spirits. More rarely, indigenous mythological beings appeared in dreams that affirmed dreamers' Christian identity. Perhaps these are guilty reminders with which people present themselves when they fear they are backsliding. For example, Jim Alosi, a student at Telefomin Vocational School, dreamed that he encountered the Old Woman or *Semodu*, known regionally as Afek (Craig and Hyndman 1990), who in myth changed the land and founded human groups in the region.

I was at Telefomin, and in the dream I was holding a magic piece of ginger to attract girls—you put it in your pocket. I was standing with a man in the Telefomin hospital. Then I saw a fairly old light skinned [a reference to her being deceased] woman come in. She came to fight with us two men. She asked us, "Do you belong to me or to Jesus?" We answered that we belonged to Jesus, and she was mad and took a swipe at me. I avoided her blow. We kept fighting, and eventually I told her, "I don't belong to you, I belong to Jesus" repeatedly. I was holding up my thumb [a symbol of defiance]. Then I woke up. I went to the school manager, a Christian man, and he asked me lots of questions about how I felt. I said I had this magic ginger in my house. He told me God was showing me this, "So you have to throw it away." I went and got it, and we prayed, and I put the ginger into hot water and threw it outside to get rid of the power inside.

Several people described dreams in which they spoke with angels, Jesus, or God and were shown around heaven. Such dreams usually depicted Christian beings as whites offering the dreamer room and board in flower-bedecked, European-style houses on condition of strong faith.

In dreams of both indigenous and introduced supernatural beings, religious discourse of waking life is translated into nocturnal imagery of encounters with spirits that seem to independently corroborate the truth of that discourse while elaborating on it in novel ways. Remembered indigenous religious dreams and dream narratives shape Christian ones, and vice versa. Christian and indigenous mythical beings come to life in Asabano dreams, revealing their changing relationships to one another. Thus, the Holy Spirit behaves like the *wobuno,* and the Old Woman responds to Christianity's challenge.

Spirit Work

They would smoke and shake: this was the wobuno *showing them where a pig was. They went and shot the wild pig, made a house, and ate the pork with sago.*
—Usakaliamo, an older man

We Spirit women, the Holy Spirit tells us what is making a person sick and we can fix it. So this makes me think the word of God is true. God himself showed me spirit work. God makes my skin shake and makes me hot and all sorts of good thoughts come up in me. Before they would smoke and the wobuno *would sit on their backs: this is just like that. This happens in church or at home, only occasionally, when we are in a group it happens or if I am upset and give a strong prayer to God this happens. My mother Alinbodo could be possessed by* wobuno, *but not I. Before there were a lot of men doing this and only a few women. The spirit work just came from*

> nowhere to all of us at the revival time. We Spirit women don't go to school, we just pray and God gives us the true answer.
> —Wosono, an older woman

While not all dreams are religious, the spirit work trance is exclusively a venue for spiritual encounter in which people hear voices and see visions. Spirit work has qualities of both trance and possession trance. It is like trance in that the spirits encountered are not necessarily perceived to enter the body of the spirit worker. Those who experience it do not report amnesia, which is usually associated with possession trance (Bourguignon 1973:15; Winkelman 1997:412–413). However, spirit work is like possession trance in that it is associated with involuntary shaking or collapse. It is also generally a public spectacle, sometimes purposely induced, and the supernatural beings contacted are sometimes perceived to mount or enter the body. While many Asabano have religious dreams, only a minority have had spirit work experiences.

Indigenous Spirit Work

Traditional spirit work involved intentionally inducing an encounter with *wobuno* by smoking tobacco in order to heal a sick person or get information. While *wobuno* have physical form, their souls, like those of human beings, can move about and come close to people. A middle-aged man named Kanau explained how *wobuno* spirit work, a form of shamanism, was done:

> Before, when someone was sick they thought a stone or arrowhead shot by a witch was inside the sick person. The sick person would point to where it hurt. A man or woman would smoke, begin to shake just like when the Spirit of God possesses a person, and then he or she would be able to remove the object. The *wobudu* [singular of *wobuno*] comes and talks with the man or woman, who sees the *wobudu* and the *wobudu* can tell him or her what's wrong, and then he or she translates. This kind of person was called *dobsosaiyadu sonowa naleadu:* a person who smokes and can see. A man or woman would stand next to a *wobudu*, speak, remove the object, show it to the sick person, and throw it away. He or she was a friend of the *wobudu*.

While only shamans were able to heal people with the help of the *wobuno*, many more people smoked and shook to get information. Baraiab told me that one of his nicknames was Fugod, the name of a *wobudu* who spoke through him.

> They gave me this name when I smoked with men. *Wobuno* used to give movement to men, like [Christian] spirit work, when they smoked. They

would sit on our backs and put wind into us and tell us things, like where to hunt. One of these *wobuno* gave me this name. He possessed me—I spoke the name. We would rest, and then we would wake up and smoke and they would come. This was only occasionally done, but was done in public [in front of the women]. I haven't seen *wobuno,* but when we smoked our bones shook. At that time they gave me thoughts and told me what to say.

Smoking to invoke a euphoric quivering feeling, which was interpreted as the presence of *wobuno,* was the only recognized form of trance or possession encounters with supernatural beings. While tobacco is not native to New Guinea, it reached the Asabano through trade probably centuries before contact.

Christian Spirit Work

The role of spirit work dramatically expanded during the period of religious excitement surrounding the community's conversion of Christianity. Especially during the peak of the revival, men and women broke into unintended trance without any chemical impetus. Instead of tobacco, the catalyst appears to have been heightened excitement, for these bursts of Christian spirit work occurred in response to impassioned prayer and preaching at church services.

Bledalo, like many others, had a spirit work experience in church at the climax of his conversion, but no further experiences.

> When I fell down at the revival and closed my eyes, the Spirit said to me, "You must leave old customs and plant crosses when people are sick." Since then I haven't seen anything. In my vision I saw a picture of Jesus, like in a book, and he told me and others this. Jesus's hair was like yours [brown and at the time, long and straight]. This man Jesus was standing with his hands at his sides in a beautiful place, and was watching over the bodies of the people who had fallen down. *I saw my own and others' bodies on the floor below.* Jesus said, "Look at your bodies down below." Then he said, "It's been a long time already, you people go back," and I got up. [emphasis added]

Unlike traditional spirit work, Bledalo's vision included a dreamlike out-of-body experience. Moreover, while traditional *wobuno* spirit work produced primarily auditory messages, Christian spirit work, especially at the height of the revival, included dreamlike visual imagery. Kanau, a former Bible college student, described his initial Christian spirit work experience at the revival's beginning in 1977.

> When the revival came down I changed. I saw the Spirit of God kick all the men, making them fall down. I myself got a hot face, felt weak, and fell down.

My eyes were open, and I saw Jesus standing with a book; the Spirit was there and God was there, and I thought, "It's true, the Child of God is there." This was the first time of the revival when Diyos was speaking at the Bible college. I saw the Spirit. My eyes were staring blankly; then *I saw something like a dream.* Jesus was standing by a cross and holding a Bible and the Spirit said, "You people believed in false gods before; it's not true, Jesus is number one, you must believe in him and the Spirit must be in your belly." Yadu [the Old Man of traditional mythology] is not true. I was down for three or four minutes. Some got up after a minute or two, *as they didn't understand spirit work.* [emphasis added]

Note here that dreamlike Christian spirit work had to be learned. Dreams aided the socialization process. Sesi, a young mother, seemed scarcely to make a distinction between dreaming and Christian spirit work.

When I did spirit work or dreamed, the Lord would tell me, "If you go to this place you will get something." I would go and find edible insects or snakes, fish, little birds, or bandicoots. These presents the Lord would give me. Some people sang and were happy. In the beginning I would just pray, but then once I felt really hot in the belly, and my arms and legs moved. The others held me. He [the Lord] didn't show me anything at first. Later he showed me light and flowers moving and babies holding flowers and singing "you come." I also saw a room in a house with lots of white cloth. I was happy and wanted to fly. But then it would move back out of reach.

First I saw other women like Mandi and some Oksapmins doing spirit work. I thought they must be pretending, but then it happened to me. I didn't see the Man [God], but I just heard his words.

In 1995, men rarely claimed to have ongoing spirit work experiences. Traditional shamans were typically male, although women also engaged in *wobuno* spirit work. "When the revival broke," both men and women continued to have spirit work experiences. Since the revival, however, the vast majority of people engaging in spirit work have been women, to such an extent that people who "work spirit" are known by the generic Tok Pisin term *Spirit meri.*

Worldwide, women are more often involved with spirit possession than men. Susan Sered (1994:186–190) and others have suggested that some common aspects of girls' socialization, such as greater emphasis on being open to deep relationships and the experience of penetration during sex and pregnancy help account for this propensity to allow the perceived entrance of another will into one's body. However, beliefs in multiple, mobile souls and spirits that can enter and leave one's body would lead men as well as women to expect and thus experience shifting control of their bodies by various supernatural beings (see Lohmann, 2003c). Nevertheless, I suspect that Asabano women have been dominant in Christian spirit work mainly because they are better able to achieve this kind of openness to the idea of being entered by a spirit than are men. So why were men more able to do spirit work in the past? A major change is the abandonment of a chemical aid to trance. Tobacco is not used to induce Christian trance, having been replaced with enthusiastic prayer with closed eyes. While many men were able to do Christian spirit work in the height of revival excitement, the enflamed religious enthusiasm and expectation of Holy Spirit manifestations aided spirit work induction even in the absence of tobacco. With the routinization of the church, however, women are left with a greater general ability to achieve possession states unaided, and thus have become the central participants in spirit work. Indeed, Asabano themselves say that women do spirit work because they are more frequently given this "gift of the Holy Spirit," while men usually are not.

By the mid-1990s, spontaneous spirit work in church had all but disappeared, replaced by more purposeful invocations of the Holy Spirit through collective prayer by a small number of Spirit women. Spirit women intentionally induce trance through these fervent prayers in order to obtain help from the Holy Spirit in diagnosing the spiritual cause of illnesses. Spirit women continue to cite traditionally believed causes of illness such as soul capture by malevolent spirits and witchcraft, and add to this cause the burden of individual sin, which is understood to spontaneously cause a health-damaging malaise. The focus of spirit work appears to have moved from hunting to healing, perhaps reflecting its shift from male to female participants, as women do not hunt large animals. However, Magao, an elderly woman who felt she was a nascent Spirit worker, said the Holy Spirit tells her where her husband should hunt, though usually in dreams after saying a prayer.

While *wobuno* shamanism was a form of classic spirit-guided removal of disease-causing objects from the body, Christian spirit work healing, like dreams, only provides information as to the cause of an illness (see Lohmann 2003a). Instead of directing people to make offerings to the offending spirits, Spirit women prescribe prayer and ritual cross planting if an external spirit is indicated, and confession of sins if internal sin is the pathogen.

Christian spirit work perceptions tend to mimic dreamed experiences in that there is out-of-body travel and visions as well as the audible messages that traditional *wobuno* spirit workers experienced. Pictures and descriptions of Jesus in the Bible and pastors' descriptions of paradise as a place with good houses and food inspired visual dreams in which these wonderful places were actually seen. Asabano drew on their dream experiences as a model of Christian spirit work. Thus, there is a causal chain, from hearing a sermon, to dreaming the sermon into imagery, to experiencing spirit work (cf. Tuzin 1997: 151).

Supernatural Encounters in Alert Consciousness

I saw a witch in the forest when I was watching in a bird blind. There was a bandicoot walking after me and I was frightened and ran away. I know it was a witch because bandicoots never walk in the daytime.
—Lemek, a boy of about 14

Asabano also encounter spirits when they are awake and alert. They recognize supernatural beings in scenes that reveal volition out of place (Lohmann 2003b), such as animals behaving in humanlike fashion. Such knowledge comes from previous enculturation, past experiences in dream wanderings, messages from supernatural beings in past spirit work, or past spirit encounters in alert life. Asabano also recognize the presence of supernatural beings by their own emotional reaction of a shiver or fear, awe, or joy—emotional salience that is also a characteristic of dreaming.

Indigenous Supernatural Encounters when Alert

As was so for dreams, waking life was sometimes punctuated by brief, unsought encounters with *wobuno,* place-spirits, witches, and the dead. Some individuals also recounted extended interactions with supernatural beings who appeared to them while in an alert state. Walen, a former traditional shaman, described many encounters with *wobuno* to me. In fact, he said that he is himself a *wobudu,* having been exchanged for a human baby at birth. Because of this, his "eyes are open," and he was able to see those who usually hide, as indigenous supernatural beings are supposed to do under normal circumstances. He regularly met with members of his *wobuno* family in the bush, and visited their village, which he described as a modern wonderland of cars, roads, and European-style houses (cf. this volume, Kempf and Hermann Chapter 4).

Walen said he can no longer visit the *wobuno* around his home at Duranmin since he reluctantly abandoned them for the revival movement. However, when visiting the nearby town of Tabubil he has seen some individuals whom he recognized as *wobuno* working as mechanics. They gave him money, which further indicated that they were not really strangers. "They are in Tabubil; they work over there. They mix with us and work over there. They fix cars, they come and go."

Few Asabano had such direct meetings. Those who did described the *wobuno* as essentially human, but more powerful, and interested in hiding from people. Because of their secretive power and cloaking abilities, most people who do believe they have caught glimpses of *wobuno* base their conclusions on fleeting impressions. Daniel, a bright boy of about twelve, said his grandfather taught him to recognize *wobuno*:

> He told me that anywhere in the bush, trees, or mountains there are *wobuno*. The *wobuno* women are the prettiest. That's all he said, but I believed him. I believed it because if you go up to the lake in the mountain you will see something in the water, and you will see something in the trees. I haven't seen any. I just see what they're doing—thick smoke coming out from the mountain, but then when I checked it there was nothing there, so I think they exist.

In contrast to *wobuno,* place spirits are wicked and not to be trusted—they are easily offended, and injure or kill people by grabbing their souls or shooting them with sharp bones as they walk by. The sick think back to where they were when they first felt a shiver or fear or an uncomfortable feeling, interpreting this as a clue to discerning the spirit responsible for their misfortune in order to bargain with it.

Walen is one of the few who told me he had seen place spirits while awake.

> Tree spirits, stone spirits, yes, before when I was young I could see them. They have sharp claws and big eyes. Their eyes are like glass, gaping and huge. They have ugly glasses too. Yours are good, but theirs are no good. No good. They are black and utterly repulsive. They have long, long fingers.

Feeling spooked upon hearing a strange sound or witnessing an oddly behaving animal was generally interpreted as proof that a witch was on the prowl in animal form. It seems that everybody has a story about their narrow escape from a witch, and the accounts I heard always began with a description of an animal's odd actions. Simply feeling afraid for no clear reason was also cited as indicative of witch activity.

How does one know one has encountered a supernatural? Bercovitch (1989) describes a witch sighting among the neighboring Nalumin. A strange noise in the night caused terrible certainty that it was lurking nearby. I was present when Jim Alosi encountered a witch—he was clearly quite alert and attentive to the sights and sounds in the environment. We were camping for the night in a bush shelter when he heard a bird call and immediately became gravely concerned that a witch was just outside. I asked him how he knew that this bird indicated a witch, and he replied that this bird species never sings at night. I responded, with a bit of good-natured sarcasm, that obviously this bird *does* sometimes sing at night, since he had just heard it, and therefore I doubted that it was in fact a witch in avian form. Jim found my attitude amusing but dangerously naive.

The effect of witnessing witches in waking life is not limited to uncomfortable feelings. Adiabo, a man in his 30s, told of a more involved event.

> I was walking alone. Then a bird sat near on a tree and sang. I was very scared. I quietly moved and hid behind a tree. I saw one of our mothers, Alu, hiding there behind a tree. She wanted to kill me. I wanted to shoot her, but she ran away and I went home. Then one day Pita's mother Sialo died, and we buried her. That night, everybody was sleeping except me. I shone a light on the grave, and saw Alu looking there. I wanted to get the gun, but it was far away. Alu was sitting on the grave. If a person becomes a witch it is hard for them to stop. We kill animals too; we are used to it and it's hard for us to stop.

Witches are notorious for eating the corpses of the dead—the people they have killed—as hunters eat the animals they kill.

The little souls of the dead also can be encountered at their own graves. On the day of a funeral, I joined the men who went to the cemetery to dig the grave. We were talking in an ordinary manner, when Sokiale, a normally cheery man, said we should be quiet lest the dead be annoyed and decide to take more people.

The big souls of the dead can also be encountered, particularly in areas surrounding their ghostly villages. A teenage boy named Ansep said, "They talk loudly, you can hear them. Cars too, and roosters crowing. I've heard it when I went to cut sago there."

Indigenous forms of alert supernatural encounter centered most commonly on fearful apprehensions, indicating a justified sense that the bush is a dangerous place to be. Walking about, one might encounter enemies with their bows and arrows or traps set by witches or place spirits.

Christian Supernatural Encounters when Alert

Christian Asabano continued to encounter indigenous supernatural beings. Since most young people rely on the Holy Spirit rather than the *wobuno* for aid, they no longer figure prominently. However, a few people like Walen who had a greater investment in traditional religion continue to encounter them and consider them positively oriented toward people. The belief in place spirits and their generally negative attitude toward people continues. People no longer make offerings to influence them, but rather rely on the intervention of God for protection. I heard reports that Spirit women saw them in trance, but not when alert. The ever-present witches were perceived frequently at the time of my fieldwork. While many older people told me that the dead can only be seen in dreams, one day during my stay several schoolchildren saw Tlisela, a young woman who had recently died, standing beside the path on their way home from school. She was standing behind a tree, they said, but quickly disappeared.

With the arrival of Christianity, the social excitement, rolling on the ground, and speaking in tongues was to onlookers a kind of secondary encounter with God in alert consciousness. Why would people act like that if the Holy Spirit were not causing it? Some saw mysterious lights at these early meetings, and interpreted them as manifestations of the Holy Spirit. Jim Alosi witnessed such a light.

> When I was a kid the revival came down and I saw the Spirit work, but the Spirit didn't get me. In 1986 on the other side of the river from Siliam is a camp called Bagambil—Baraiab and Wuniod's camp. They made a big house for dancing there. One man was sick and was at this house. All the Spirit women went there to work spirit. About 8:00 in the evening I went outside my house at Siliam and sat on the verandah and saw a light shooting straight down on top to the roof and into the house—fire shot and came down. The flame of this light was very bright. Then I heard everybody call out loudly, "Yeah, Jesus" and cry loudly. Then I believed it was true—father God exists and sent the Holy Spirit down. That's the time I believed completely—I saw with my own two eyes. Then I forgot all the ancestral stories. They are all just lies, all these *wobuno* stories. This was the thing that changed my life. We started grade one at school in 1987. When I saw the light I was surprised, and I also called out, "Oh Lord, it's true, you exist, and you sent the Holy Spirit down!" and I prayed and cried. At the revival time I also believed, but the Spirit didn't work with me. This just strengthened my belief. Before 1986 I was Christian, but I doubted, but when I saw the fire of the Holy Spirit I lost all the old beliefs including this one. Now I don't smoke, chew betel nut, or drink beer anymore.

The emotional indicator of supernatural presence in alert consciousness also operates in Christian experience, but a positive affect is much more widely reported. In the traditional religion, even *wobuno* can be dangerous, so meetings with them are a cause for fear as well as interest. While alert meetings with supernatural beings in the indigenous idiom usually produced dread, encounters with Christian beings are joyful. Joyous emotion and a sense of escape from the dangers of witchcraft and capricious spirits characterize Christian religious experiences. People often interpret positive feelings and ideas that appear during prayer as evidence of God's presence. Isaguo, a Spirit woman, explained:

> I wasn't dreaming or anything, I was normal and just felt happy and felt I had to tell my people this, that they must leave these old beliefs, so I feel it was the Spirit of God causing this. I can't see the Spirit of God, but if he's in the belly

[the seat of the souls], you'll feel happy and have plenty of very good thoughts and feelings, and you will want to tell people to leave their bad ways. Then you know it's God's Holy Spirit doing it.

The Holy Spirit and angels, having replaced the functions of the *wobuno*, can appear as humans in dreams and as elusive cassowaries in waking life. Yalowad told me that the Holy Spirit, in cassowary form, crosses his path when he is hunting, playing with him by expertly dodging each and every arrow. The spirits, so easily visible in dreams, are elusive in waking life even for the Asabano, who believe in them so fervently.

The Range of Consciousness and Night Residues

The Asabano understand the supernatural to be a part of the experiential universe, knowable through dreams and trance as well as alert awareness. They are far from alone in holding this view, as the other chapters in this volume, for example, demonstrate. What is the relationship between dreaming and other forms of consciousness, and what does their relative phenomenology tell us about the nature of supernatural beliefs?

I suggest that we should model the forms of consciousness as ideal typical points on a continuum of possible forms of awareness, recognizing that memories of experiences characteristic of one form of consciousness transfer to and shape perceptions in the other states of awareness. Transfer of schemas among forms of consciousness lends characteristics of waking awareness to certain dreams, and dreamlike qualities to certain waking experiences. Bourguignon (1972:422) places dreams and various forms of trance on a continuum that connects the "altered" states of consciousness to one another, but leaves their relationship to "ordinary" consciousness unclear. Winkleman (2000:119) includes ordinary waking consciousness in his paradigm, and distinguishes emic "states" of consciousness from biological "modes" of consciousness. It makes sense to speak of a continuum of consciousness, within which people have variable ranges in the daily cycle and through special forays into extraordinary states of awareness. But what criteria should be used to define placement of different modes or states along that continuum?

One criterion by which one can distinguish dream, trance, and alert consciousness from one another is according to the relative balance between sensory and imaginary inputs to awareness. In dreams, one is relatively cut off from the senses and the imagination gains the upper hand. This allows Asabano to experience freedom of movement that they do not in fact have. Asabano do report occasionally seeing strange things like oddly behaving animals or apparitions when alert, but these can be explained as hallucinations or mistaken identity, sometimes provoked when a scene brings to mind a dream memory. In trance, there tends to be a more divided awareness, with both the imagination and the senses receiving conscious attention. Thus, the spirit worker is able to hear the words of the *wobuno* or Holy Spirit and also communicate with human companions.

While differentiating states of consciousness based on attention to imagination versus the senses is a partial and simplified model, it reveals two significant points about the relationship between the modes of consciousness. First, that dreams and trance are part of the normal range of consciousness. All people routinely experience both dreams and alert consciousness, and if not possession, other forms of trance like daydreaming are certainly universal. Dream and trance should be brought home from a status as "altered" states of consciousness, which implies abnormality, and placed squarely within the normal and complete range of consciousness. Just as we should be careful not to excessively exoticize the people we study, we should not think of dream and trance as more other than they are.

A second point that becomes clear in thinking of conscious states as a normal range is an extension of schema theory (see D'Andrade 1995:122–149). Schemas are mental models that guide perception and are changed by experiences. Experiences in alert, trance, or dream states create memories that are drawn upon to make sense of future perceptions in any mode of consciousness. This is illustrated by recalling that it is sometimes hard to determine if a remembered event happened in a dream or when awake. More importantly, our schemas are modified by dream experiences without our conscious knowledge.

In the dream narratives presented here, one can see that images and thoughts acquired in waking life find their way into dreams as Freudian "day residues" (1965 [1900]:309). In Jim Alosi's dream, these include the Old Woman, Jesus, and his anxiety about his religious identity and behavior. Images created by the mind in sleep also help shape schemas of expectation that make supernatural experiences more likely in waking life. One might call these images "night residues," and identify in them the contribution of dreams, with all their imaginative flights of fancy, to waking experience. One source of dreaming's distinctiveness is the imagination's greater freedom to portray scenes without contrary sensory information so easily interrupting the scenario's flow. In the Asabano narratives of supernatural encounters, the most richly imaginative scenarios usually came from dreams. It seems to me that this shows the general validity of Tylor's (1877 [1871] I:428) insight that dreaming and the human belief in a supernatural realm are intimately connected.

Conclusion

All people are capable of dreaming and daydreaming, and most people, based on their imaginative experiences, tend to assume that a spiritual realm of some kind exists. These points of commonality guide anthropological understanding of other imagined worlds.

My primary purpose in this chapter was to convey something of the world of spiritual experience inhabited by a small group in New Guinea. The Asabano are on the cusp of a massive change in their culture in response to missionary efforts and contacts with the West. The change from reliance on indigenous to Christian religious tradition is a metaphor of the change from one state of consciousness to another as people slip from alertness into trance, dream, and back again. Each promotes different ways of thinking and experiencing. Just as one's state of consciousness provides a venue for experience, so does one's cultural surround. Both set the scene and provide a backdrop of what is possible. Asabano traditional religion made possible encounters with spirits of variable and changing disposition. Only after the introduction of Christianity could all spirits be seen as manifestations of two great opposing beings of permanent disposition, God and Satan. While in waking life there are relatively few cases of direct spirit encounters, moving from trance to dream they become progressively more easy and realistic.

It is in dreams, the most unreal of experiential venues, that the spirit beings posited by religions become the most real in immediate experience. And the memories of these experiences shape expectations for waking life in the form of night residues, bringing the supernatural world more vividly into waking life as well. Perceived encounters with supernatural beings occur in all states of consciousness, but those of waking life are facilitated by the greater imaginative freedom of dreaming.

Acknowledgements

I thank the Asabano and all of the other wonderful people I met in Papua New Guinea. My fieldwork in 1994–95 was made possible by a Fulbright grant. Thanks to participants at the ASAO "Pacific Dreams" sessions in Hilo (1999) and Vancouver (2000) who helpfully commented on my paper, especially Elfriede Hermann, Doug Hollan, Wolfgang Kempf, Sylvie Poirier, and Bob Tonkinson.

References Cited

Bercovitch, Eytan
1989 Mortal Insights: Victim and Witch in the Nalumin Imagination. *In* The Religious Imagination in New Guinea. M. Stephen and G. Herdt, eds. Pp. 122–159. New Brunswick: Rutgers University Press.

Bourguignon, Erika
1972 Dreams and Altered States of Consciousness in Anthropological Research. *In* Psychological Anthropology. F. L. K. Hsu, ed. Pp. 403–434. Cambridge: Schenkman.

1973 Introduction: A Framework for the Comparative Study of Altered States of Consciousness. *In* Religion, Altered States of Consciousness, and Social Change. E. Bourguignon, ed. Pp. 3–38. Columbus: Ohio State University Press.

Craig, Barry, and David C. Hyndman, eds.
1990 Children of Afek: Tradition and Change among the Mountain-Ok of Central New Guinea. Sydney: University of Sydney.

Curley, Richard
1992 Private Dreams and Public Knowledge in a Camerounian Independent Church. *In* Dreaming, Religion and Society in Africa. M. C. Jedrej and R. Shaw, eds. Pp. 135–152. Leiden: E. J. Brill.

D'Andrade, Roy G.
1995 The Development of Cognitive Anthropology. Cambridge: Cambridge University Press.

Freud, Sigmund
1965 [1900] The Interpretation of Dreams. New York: Avon Books.

Lepowsky, Maria
1989 Soldiers and Spirits: The Impact of World War II on a Coral Sea Island. *In* The Pacific Theater: Island Representations of World War II. G. White and L. Lindstrom, eds. Pp. 205–230. Honolulu: University of Hawaii Press.

Lohmann, Roger Ivar
2000a Cultural Reception in the Contact and Conversion History of the Asabano of Papua New Guinea. Ph.D. dissertation, University of Wisconsin-Madison.
2000b The Role of Dreams in Religious Enculturation among the Asabano of Papua New Guinea. Ethos 28(1):75–102.
2001 Introduced Writing and Christianity: Differential Access to Religious Knowledge among the Asabano. Ethnology 40(2):93–111.
2003a Glass Men and Spirit Women in Papua New Guinea. *In* Shamanism and Survival, M. Winkelman, ed. Cultural Survival Quarterly (Special Issue) 27(2):52–54.
2003b The Supernatural is Everywhere: Defining Qualities of Religion in Melanesia and Beyond. *In* Perspectives on the Category 'Supernatural,' R. I. Lohmann, ed. Anthropological Forum (Special Issue) 13(2).
2003c Turning the Belly: Insights on Religious Conversion from New Guinea Gut Feelings. *In* The Anthropology of Religious Conversion, A. Buckser and S. Glazier, eds. Pp. 109–121. Boulder: Rowman and Littlefield.

Sered, Susan Starr
1994 Priestess, Mother, Sacred Sister: Religions Dominated by Women. Oxford: Oxford University Press.

Tuzin, Donald
1997 The Cassowary's Revenge: The Life and Death of Masculinity in a New Guinea Society. Berkeley: University of California Press.

Tylor, Edward B.
1877   [1871] Primitive Culture: Researches into the Development of Mythology, Philosophy, Religion, Language, Art and Custom. 2 vols. New York: Henry Holt and Company.
Wapnok, Diyos
1990   Diyos. *In* Daring to Believe: Personal Accounts of Life Changing Events in Papua New Guinea and Irian Jaya. N. Draper and S. Draper, eds. Pp. 154–160. Hawthorn: Australian Baptist Missionary Society.
Winkelman, Michael
2000   Shamanism: The Neural Ecology of Consciousness and Healing. Westport: Bergin & Garvey.

Chapter 11
Afterword

Beyond the Mythologies

A Shape of Dreaming

Waud Kracke

> *While we sleep here, we are awake elsewhere, and in this way every man is two men.*
>
> —Tlön aphorism.
> Jorge Luis Borges (1965 [1941]),
> "Tlön, Uqbar, Orbis Tertius"

It is often said, even by philosophers, that dreams are essentially different from other experiences in that we cannot share them: they are solely available to the individual who had them, not "interpersonally verifiable."

But are dreams unique in this? Is this not true, in fact, of *all* experience? Is not all of our inner experience unsharable? I cannot know what you see when you see "red," or "blue sky," or what you feel when you feel cold; I can only guess that it is something like my experience of red or blue sky or cold, but I can never get inside your head.

Dreams are not unique in this respect; they are only the most insistent challenge to our conventional assumption that we all experience the world in the same way. Our everyday life is constructed on the denial of this inescapable fact. We assume—American common sense assumes—that of course our experiences of "external reality" are identical. Only exceptionally do we have hints that this is not true—as when my wife calls the pants I see as gray "your beige pants," and insists that the pants I see as distinctly greenish tinged are pure gray. We recognize this impossibility more easily across cultures: "The ethnographer," Roger Lohmann observes in his introduction (Chapter 1:6), "cannot get inside the head of informants and directly observe or participate in the mental events in which we are interested." The truth that we avoid is that our experience is inaccessible to *any* other person, and theirs to us. Our lover, our spouse, our child—we never can directly know what they think, perceive, feel. Dreams remind us of that.

Dreams are the most obstinate stumbling block to our secure knowledge that we "know" the world around us, that we all share the same experience of it and of each other. Dreams are the one irreducible reminder that each of us is inescapably alone in our perceptions, that we can only know our *own* perceptions and nobody else's.[1]

This, I think, is one thing that makes dreams so disturbing to some people; it is why so many (e.g., Hobson 1988) would like to prove that dreams have no significance, why funding for dream research is so hard to come by. As Sylvie Poirier (this volume, Chapter 6) observes, anthropologists have neglected to study the cultural systems of dreaming even in Australian aboriginal cultures where dreaming is ontologically central to their cosmos and epistemologically central to their religious practice.[2] Dreams are worse than "insubstantial"; they are subversive to our whole scientific epistemology.

Poirier blames the depreciation of dreams, and the lack of attention to indigenous dream concepts, on Western rationalist epistemology that locates dreams as mental events within the thinking mind rather than as perceptions. She attributes this "privatization" of the dream to Descartes and Freud. I do not think such rationalist views of dreams can be laid at Freud's door. Far from furthering the assimilation of dreaming to the Cartesian self-bound mind, Freud radically challenged the Cartesian view by finding in dreaming a separate *subject who dreams*, a dreaming subject disconnected from, and alien to, the reflective subject who awakens from the dream and contemplates it (Freud 1953 [1900]:580n1, elaborated in Lacan 1988:135–6). Freud had a profound respect for folk wisdom, and took many of his ideas about dreams from folk beliefs, which he found far more perceptive than the "obscurantism of educated opinion." In assigning this dreaming subject to the "not-I"—the "it" or "that"—Freud redeems the popular perception of dreaming as a separate level of consciousness discontinuous with our waking perceptions—a "wandering soul" (or wandering dream-self) with its own awareness distinct from the waking self.[3]

As Poirier herself mentions on page 109, Freud also takes a very social view of dreams. Far from seeing dreams as "asocial" (this term of Freud's is quoted by Hunt from a passage in which Freud is characterizing the general view of dreams of his time), he saw dreams as inextricably enmeshed in the underlying patterns of the dreamer's language—"every tongue," he asserted, "has its own dream-language" (1953 [1900]:99n1)—and is intimately involved with the relationships of the patient's current and past life.[4]

Dreams and Religion

The chapters in this book are about dreaming in a group of cultures that *do* take their dreams seriously. People may not discuss their dreams equally in all of the cultures, but in all of them dreams play some very important role in social life. In addition, in all of these cultures, dreams play an important part in their *religious* life. The articles in this book, then, have a common focus: on the role of dreams in the religious life of Western Pacific cultures. In some, the religion in question may be the traditional religion of the group, in other cases it is recently introduced faiths that are to a greater or lesser degree syncretic, for the most part Protestant Evangelical Christianity; but in all these instances, dreams retain their key role in communication with supernatural beings.

Tylor's Theory: The Origin of the Soul in Dreams

This close relationship of dreaming and religious life brings to mind immediately the classic statement of Sir Edward B. Tylor on dreams and the concept of the soul, one of the first anthropological theories of the origin of religion, to which Roger Lohmann refers in Chapter 10. Tylor asks: "What, then, is this soul or life which . . . goes and comes in sleep, trance and death?"

> To the rude philosopher, the question seems to be answered by the very evidence of his senses. When the sleeper awakes from a dream, he believes he has really somehow been away, or that other people have come to him. As it is well known by experience that men's bodies do not go on these excursions, the natural explanation is that every man's living self or soul is his phantom or image, which can go out of his body and see and be seen itself in dreams. (Tylor 1970 [1881]:203)

This is a view of dreams that appears in all of the accounts in this volume, in each of the cultures described: that dreams are a journey of the soul, wandering as the body sleeps—the "dream travelers" of the title. Indeed, it is in part on descriptions from this part of the world that Tylor based his conjecture: "The Malays do not like to wake a sleeper," he tells us, "lest they should hurt him by disturbing his body while his soul is out" (1970 [1881]:203; see this volume, Tonkinson Chapter 5 on the Mardu).[5] Indeed, the reports of such a belief about dreams come from all over the world,[6] though I would argue that they are not universal in the sense of being shared by every culture, and I think that in the cultures that hold this belief it may be one among a set of alternative conceptualizations of the dream experience, and may not be held by all or even most members of the culture. Tonkinson (89) observes, for example, that "some SE Ambrymese seemed unsure about whether seeing themselves elsewhere in dreams indicated that part of them had traveled from their body during sleep." In addition, Michele Stephen's (1995:116) reflections on the translation of the Mekeo term *lalauga* provides a warning that we must not be too quick to translate terms referring to the dreaming subject, or to the experience of self in the dream, with the European concept of "soul." *Lalauga* may mean "soul" or "apparition," but may simply refer to an image, such as a drawing or (like the Ngaing term *asabeiyang*) a reflection—or a dream-image, including "the aspect of a person's self that acts in a dream."[7] Stephen opts for "dream self" or "dream image" as translations, depending on the exact referent of the term in context.

In a description that could be taken either way, but invites a reading like Stephen's, a Kukatja woman in the Australian Western Desert told Sylvie Poirier (this volume, Chapter 6:112), "When we are dreaming, we are thinking, we are feeling with our *tjurni* [abdomen, the seat of emotion], we look at our spirit going away, like in a picture [movie]," adding, "it is the spirit that goes on walkabout." The dream is like a projection from the *tjurni*—the abdominal area, the "guts." Describing a the dream experience from within, we might say that our dreaming self comes out at night and goes on a walkabout in a projected landscape.

In any case, the exact significance of the term translated "spirit" can be revealing of the significance of dreaming for the people in question. That the Kukatja term *kurunnpa* "relates to cognition, volition and to the expression of emotions," and that it is associated with the abdominal area which is the "seat of . . . *maparn* (medicine-man) power" tell us a great deal about what dreaming connotes for the Kukatja and their neighbors. (For the Parintintin with whom I work in Brazil, the *ra'úv* is associated with the liver, which is a seat of emotions, notably jealousy; and dreaming is central to shamanic power.)

The other side of Tylor's theory has to do with dreams of those who are absent or who have died. This aspect is developed in his *Researches into the Early History of Mankind* (1964 [1887]:5).

> The Belief that a man has a soul capable of existing apart from the body it belongs to, and continuing to live, for a time at least, after the body is dead and buried, fits perfectly in such a mind with the fact that the shadowy forms of men and women do appear to others, when the men and women themselves are at a distance, and after they are dead.

In one exposition of his theory, he goes on to derive spirits and demons from ghosts, noting that in some cultures spirits in general are not sharply distinguished from ghosts (1960 [1881]:210, 212ff).

An Alternate View: Making Spirits Real

The chapters in this volume give us an opportunity to return to Tylor's characterization of dreams as the origin of religious beliefs and rethink it. Tylor saw dreams as a source for the belief both in spirits (unidentified dream visitors) and in a soul that survives after death (and appears in the dreams of surviving kin). Of course, we have no basis for affirming or denying his conjectures on the origin of religious beliefs, plausible though they may be[8]— unless some of the speculations that Paleolithic cave paintings depict dreams or shamanic trance imagery can be shown to be convincing. But this group of essays, which offer many alternative ways of envisaging the relationship between dreams and belief, do provide considerable support for the *converse* of Tylor's conception: dreams are a way in which the adept, whether priest or lay person, can realize in his or her personal experience the presence of the beings that, according to the communal religion, inhabit the cosmos.

Most of these essays give examples of how individuals make spiritual entities real for themselves in their dreams. In the cultures which persist in traditional religious beliefs and practices, one of the frequent ways of interacting with spirits—"penetrating the screen and entering the world of souls" as Roy Wagner (1967:48) put it—is in dreams. Asabano dreams "often involve sightings or encounters with supernatural beings . . . [and] provide information about the spiritual causes of current problems and previews of the future" (this volume, Lohmann Chapter 10:192). Maria's dream, for example confirms her belief that witches kill old men. "For the New Guinea Highlanders," write Stewart and Strathern in this volume (Chapter 3:44), "all of whom have traditions of the continuing involvement of dead kin in their lives, dreams are the gates through which the shades of the dead . . . enter and mingle with the spirits and their living kin." In dreaming of the dead, they learn that the dead are still sentient and retain some feelings that the living have. This knowledge verifies with personal experience myths about an afterlife, and in turn is fed back into the myths that are told to the next generation.⁹

While dreaming appears to have a different role among the Australian Aboriginal groups described here, there are still ways in which dreaming plays an important part in making traditional beliefs real for the individual. Personal songs, or innovations in ritual, are revealed to the singer by ancestors in dreams, providing them with ancestral validation: "the process of dreaming," as Keen (this volume, Chapter 7:128) puts it, "*links* people to the ancestors," who alone are (conceptually) empowered to create. As Tonkinson (this volume, Chapter 5:94) comments, this establishes a "reinforcement through dream reporting of a dominant theme" of their religious belief. Tonkinson later stresses the trance state in which Mardu men dance ancestral ceremonies, in which they appear to "leave their earthly state and temporarily become one with that being" they depict in the dance.

> The great intensity of their movements and facial contortions often suggested to me a total absorption in the role, an almost trance-like state.... The dance is meant to be a transcendent experience, one that takes the actor into contact with the ultimate powers. (Tonkinson, Chapter 5:95)

Keen, too, observes how Yolngu men performing in ritual identify themselves with the ancestor they represent. Here is a clear instance of "night residue" as proposed by Lohmann (see below), in which a religious reality experienced in dream carries over to the waking state (here, to a trance state).

Where Protestant religions are establishing a new foothold in a community, dreams of God or other religious figures may play an important part in conversion. Even among the decidedly unspiritual Ambrymese, Robert Tonkinson (90) affirms that "[s]ince the adoption of Christianity, dreaming appears to have become the altered state of consciousness most often connected to encounters with, or revelations from, the Holy Spirit. For some people," he continues, such "particularly vivid dreams" are "the source of very powerful conversion or faith-renewal experiences."

Thus in these cultures, dreams serve to confirm or make vivid beliefs in spirits or deities which are already part of the person's "culturally constituted behavioral environment" (Hallowell 1955), whether as part of the traditional world view or nascent new religious beliefs to whom the person is being exposed: the converse of Tylor's view which attributed to dreams the *origin* of soul beliefs. Lohmann, closing Chapter 10 of this volume, adds one more codicil to this hypothesis: that the visions experienced in dreaming carry over into daytime reality as a source of images of the supernatural, making them a kind of "night residue" for daytime thinking.

Cultural Theories of Dreaming

Dreaming is a complex psychological phenomenon, most fully explored by Freud (1953 [1900]), by studies in dream laboratories (Cartwright 1977, Lavie 1993, Strauch and Meier 1996)—and most recently in neurological studies by Mark Solms (1997).[10] In cultures which take dreams seriously, correspondingly complex theories have developed to explain dreams and their variations—theories which have rarely been fully developed in ethnographic[11] accounts of dreaming and dream beliefs. These native theories address a range of questions concerning dreaming, and the articles in this collection deal with a number of them: What *are* dreams in native theory? How are they caused, and how is the mechanism of dreaming described? Then the question of typology: What are the significant differences among dreams—the different kinds of dreams? What are the causes of these different kinds of dreams, and what are their different mechanisms? Anthropologists may also raise questions about the place of dreams in the society they describe: How are dreams used in different societies? And, finally, the anthropologist may explore the personal meanings of dreams to the informants who tell their dreams to him or her, and ask the question: How do these personal meanings relate to the cultural ideas about dreams, and the cultural uses of dreams? I will comment on how these papers address each of these groups of questions, beginning with the cultural theories of dreaming.

That the soul in sleep communes with the souls of the dead and other spirits—or angels and God—are beliefs that are shared, in one form or another, in all the cultures discussed in this book, and in many others around the world. So is the concept of the soul's nocturnal dream journey, of which the dream itself is supposed to be either a direct experience or a "report." These are some of the beliefs with the most dramatic consequences for personal religious experience—personal confirmation either of one's traditional beliefs or of a new religion to which one is undergoing conversion. But they are not the only concepts held about dreams in these cultures. A number of other concepts of dreams emerge in these articles, some of them special to a culture or to a regional cultural formation, others concepts which can be found the world around.

Communication in Dreams

A belief that is entailed in, yet distinct from, the notion of spirit travel is the idea that one can communicate with others through dreams. Sylvie Poirier points to it in the Kukatja culture in Australia. This idea comes up in one form or another, implicitly or explicitly, in most of the cultures discussed—as it does in many cultures around the world. Indeed, the possibility of direct thought transmission—telepathy—in dreams, even with the Western prejudice against the possibility noted by Sylvie Poirier, has been taken seriously enough to be tested in sleep laboratory experiments (Cartwright 1977:3–4).[12]

Portents in Dreams

In Melanesian cultures, as in folk cultures around the world—and Europe is no exception in this—an important role of dreams is to foreshadow coming events or states. As Stewart and Strathern note in this volume, "Dreams are valued as omens" (Chapter 3:45). As another anthropologist has put it, referring to a different part of the world, dreams "reveal emergent possibilities or likelihoods, events that are developing but are not yet accomplished facts" (Brown 1992 [1987]:157). Much of the sharing of dreams in such cultures is in the service of discovering the dream's "meaning," that is the event or condition that it foreshadows—illness, success in hunting particular game, or in seeking political leadership. Dreams may either be taken as literal visions of what is to come, or as cryptic metaphoric allusions—"turned" (*ropel rorom*) in the Melpa phrase (Stewart and Strathern, Chapter 3). These predictions are a major part of the traditional interpretation of dreams. Stewart and Strathern mention a list of 31 such traditional interpretations collected by Vicedom among the Central Melpa. All but one of the eight dreams told to Hollan, as noted in this volume (Chapter 9) by one Toraja informant, were understood as coded prophecies.

In some cases such interpretation may be reassuring, as when a dream of uncontrolled vomiting was interpreted as predicting that the dreamer would become "an expert on traditional customs and a divider of meat at feasts" (this volume, Hollan Chapter 9:172). But in other cases it may turn an anxiety dream "all the more harrowing," as when a young Asabano woman was told by her grandmother that "If you see dead people in dreams, you will die soon" (this volume, Lohmann Chapter 10:194).

The interpretation of dreams as portents is rendered more difficult by the multiple possibilities. Any dream might be a straightforward anticipation of the future, or a disguised message, metaphorical or encoded in the traditional code of dream interpretations. It may contain multiple possible references, according to which elements are selected or highlighted, so that it "may require the assistance of a specialist to interpret it" (this volume, Stewart and Strathern Chapter 3:44). And beyond this, as Robbins (this volume, Chapter 2:25) observes for Urapmin, the dream may "go straight"—give a true prediction—or it may be deceptive. This additional complication, the possibility of deceptive dreams, seems to be especially marked in communities where fundamentalist Christian sects have taken root, as among the Urapmin or the Melpa, in which dream messages may come from God or from Satan—or from traditional spirits who have become equated with Satan.

The concept that dreaming is connected with the coming into being of future states and events is also important in Australian Aboriginal cultures. But since dreaming plays such a different part in Australian cultures from what it does in Melanesian ones—dreaming is so much more fundamental ontologically in the Australian cosmology—I would prefer to discuss the Australian cultures as a group, and will return to them later on.

Cultural Typologies of Dreams

These articles devote most attention to the categories of dream already discussed: dreams viewed as nocturnal travel; those in which communication with souls of the dead or other spirits, angels or deities take place; and dreams that are seen as portents—literally or through symbolic encryption. These may have different kinds of relations with each other. For example, dreams may be portents of the future considered as communications from dead ancestors, spirits, or from God (who may regularly appear in such dreams as messengers). Or, they may be a totally distinct type, read as an impersonal communication coded so that those who understand the code may read it—rather as a good hunter can read the signs that a certain species of game has passed by. Dreams of communication with spirits may "blend together" with dreams considered soul-journeys, as Levy comments (1973:374), or they may be contrasting ways of conceiving a dream.

But the systems of thinking about dreams in most cultures are much more complex than just these three categories of dream. Cultures categorize dreams into a number of types, and have variant ways of conceptualizing dreams, and some of these crop up in several of the chapters in this volume (Hollan Chapter 9, Lohmann Chapter 10, and Stewart and Strathern Chapter 3).[13]

Spirit Attacks

One type of dream that recurs in these accounts is the "ghost attack" or "spirit attack." Although Douglas Hollan's chapter focuses on the *tindo* (the prophetic or omen dream), the one dream he presents that was not of this type was a nightmare of spirit attack. Hollan distinguishes two types of anxiety dream or nightmare *(tauan):* In one, the dreamer "relives an unpleasant or disturbing experience" from the past, often the previous day (this volume, Chapter 9:175). The second type—the kind his informant told him—are nocturnal attacks by malicious spirits, accompanied by "a sense of motor and verbal paralysis . . . , suffocation, and an overwhelming sense of dread and anxiety."

The Tiwi suffer similar dream attacks by *mabidituwi*, ghosts, whom Goodale (this volume, Chapter 8) describes as having "long, claw-like nails" with which "at night they will clutch at the throat," leaving the dreamer "a little bit sick," as if with a sore throat. These resemble the ghost or demon attacks described in other cultures, in which the demon sits on the dreamer's chest or chokes the dreamer. The Parintintin with whom I work attribute intense nightmares to the proximity of a demon or ghost (*añang*) that chokes the dreamer. Tahitians attribute them to a *tupapa'u* spirit (Levy 1973:395–397). In Chaucer's time, the term "nightmare" (or the French *cauche-mar*) originally referred to a demon (*mare*) who sat on the sleeper, "producing a feeling of suffocation by its weight" (OED 1971:1926). These spirit-attack dreams are often described as accompanied by symptoms like those described by Hollan, which resemble the nocturnal anxiety attacks nowadays called "night terrors."

Spirit attacks may occur in dreams in a sexual form, too. Among the Tiwi, a woman may avert these dangers by spitting on the fire after being afflicted with the dream visitor (this volume, Goodale Chapter 8). A man may be afflicted by a female spirit who proposed marriage to him in his dream, again with dangerous consequences for his well being—recalling the Moroccan dream spirit *A'isha Qandisha* who similarly afflicted Moroccan men in their dreams (Crapanzano 1975, 1980). Sexual attacks by spirits in dreams is a danger in many cultures (e.g., Levy 1973:129, 154, 165; Stephen 1995:129 on "dreams of water spirit lovers"; Devereux 1961:139, 154–57, 160–61).

Dreams as Continuation of Daytime Thought

One more category of dreams seems to be a residual one for these cultures: dreams stimulated by recent events or thoughts. These dreams—dreams in which the day residue is evident—are considered by the Toraja (this volume, Hollan Chapter 9) and other cultures to be a mere continuation of daytime thoughts, "a form of nighttime thinking in which the mind continues to mull over the events and activities of the previous day," (this volume, Hollan Chapter 9:175). "Such dreams, which usually carry little or no affect, are not considered to be especially significant and are not given much thought" (Hollan 1989:168). The description of these dreams sounds rather like the un-dreamlike "nocturnal thinking" that dream laboratory researchers report as the most frequent mental activity in non-REM periods of sleep (Cartwright 1977:9; Cartwright and Lamberg 1992:57; Lavie 1993:69–70).[14] Alternatively, they could be dreams in which the day residues are especially clear and easily identifiable. Without examples of this kind of dream (or non-dream: in his earlier article Hollan (1989:168) suggested they are not considered dreams) it is hard to decide between these two possibilities.

In a Christianized culture, day residues are recognized to have a beneficial consequence in dreams: Asabano "pastors' descriptions of paradise . . . inspired visual dreams in which these wonderful places were actually seen," and Asabano drew on such dream visions for their waking "spirit work" (this volume, Lohmann Chapter 10:201).

Dreaming Central to Cosmology: Australian Aboriginal Dreams

Melanesian cultures, as more than one of the papers mentions, are marked by their diversity. The Aboriginal cultures of Australia, by contrast, seem to share a cultural nexus both of social organization (centered on the crosscutting matrilineal and patrilineal moieties resulting in a system of marriage sections, and matrilineal clans that are "owners" of specific territories) and of cosmology. A distinctive feature of their cosmology is the centrality of dreams, both in ontology and in epistemology. The entire region might be said to comprise a group of "dream cultures" such as the Mojave, Yuma and Chemehuevi who were so designated by Kroeber (1922:754–785, 782–3, 600). The three or four cultures included in this volume from that group share a distinctive complex of beliefs and practices related to dreams, especially concerned with the relationship with the ancestors and with the ancestral lands. The Tiwi, as Goodale (this volume, Chapter 8) makes clear, are in a peripheral relationship to this complex, sharing some features but in other features contrasting sharply both with the cultures of mainland Australia and with Melanesia.

Dreams are an essential avenue of contact with the ancestors in Australian Aboriginal societies. It was through dreams that ancestors conveyed their creative powers to the now living. All innovation, all creative processes, come to the artist or innovator from the ancestors through dreams. No new ritual, song or artistic theme can be introduced to ritual without coming from the ancestors in the form of a dream as a validation of the innovation, a confirmation that the new form was really rediscovered from the Dreamtime; Keen (this volume, Chapter 7) calls this a denial of creativity. The role of ancestral dreams in creativity was discussed eloquently by Nancy Munn (1973), writing about the creation of bark cloth designs by Walbiri (Warlpiri) women; and is confirmed by each of the writers about Australian societies in this volume.

Dreams are also critical in other aspects of the maintenance of life. Each person dreams of his or her clan land, and in so doing plays a part (as the very title of Poirier's chapter intimates) in maintaining its fertility and productivity—if only, as Poirier suggests, through cherishing it (this volume, Goodale Chapter 8). The conception of a child is also mediated by a dream which the child's father-to-be has from his clan land. The child is "'found' or 'dreamt' by the mother, the father" or another relative, in a dream which "validates" the spirit child's coming over from the ancestral realm. "It is in dreams that spirit-children announce their intentions to take on a human form" (this volume, Poirier Chapter 6:218).[15] The Tiwi share both of these beliefs.

Dreaming takes an essential part in the very coming into being of the present: every event, as Poirier describes, must be entailed in someone's dream. This is true even if the dream is not remembered—or, as often happens, if the significance of the dream as a part of coming-into-being was not appreciated by the dreamer at the time of the dream.

Dreams and Revitalization Movements

The uses to which dreams may be put are wide, and a range of the possible social uses of dreams is represented here. Melanesia is of course one of the foci for the religious use of dreams by the leaders of new cults and revitalization movements. The widespread occurrence earlier of revitalization movements with a "myth-dream" as the founding message (Burridge 1995 [1960]), and more recently of Christian charismatic cults in which dreams are privileged communications with the deity, make dreaming a favored mode of spiritual communication in Melanesia—or rather, as chapters here show, *continue* the importance of dreaming as a religious activity.

Revitalization movements instigated by dreams are hardly limited to Melanesia; they occur the world around. Wallace (1971) documented the Iroquois religious movement initiated by Handsome Lake's dream; Hong Xiuquan's dream of being Christ's younger brother engendered the Taiping Heavenly Kingdom and the Taiping Rebellion (Spence 1996); the Mormon church was founded on the dream vision of Joseph Smith, and the Salesian order sprang from the 1883 dream of Italian priest Don Bosco, which envisioned a promised land in the Brazilian Planalto where Brasília is today.

The Political Use of Dreams

The outright political use of a dream must also occur in any society in which dreaming is a valued mode of gaining knowledge of the future (can Brasília be partially attributed to Don Bosco's dream?), but this again comes out most clearly in New Guinea. Some years ago, Gilbert Herdt (1992 [1987]) called attention to the political use of dreams in a traditional highland New Guinea community, documenting the difference between a leader's public, oratorical version of a dream and his private account of it. The political use of a public dream account continues to be effective even after a society has converted to Christianity, as Robbins's account (this volume, Chapter 2) shows. He demonstrates beautifully how a well-timed recounting of a dream can have a powerful effect in sparking important political developments—moving intransigent leaders toward reconciliation, or curbing the charismatic pretensions of an overambitious political leader who aspires to add sacristal power to his temporal influence.[16]

Another political use of dreams is demonstrated further west, among the Toraja of Sulawesi, in northern Indonesia. Here, in a somewhat more overtly hierarchical society, dreams are used to validate leadership status. The first three of the nine dreams recounted to Hollan (this volume, Chapter 9) by an elderly man of high prestige were dreams he had when young which foretold, and thus validated, his later position as a widely respected leader and village headman. In Australian societies, the fact that any innovation must be validated by coming from the ancestors in a dream is, Keen (this volume, Chapter 7) points out, of the essence of Weber's "traditional" form of legitimacy of a political order.

The Personal Side

Dreaming, like Obeyesekere's "personal symbols," as Hollan points out, has two levels—two "poles," to use Victor Turner's (1967:28–9) metaphor. On the one hand, dreams are enmeshed in a network of cultural and linguistic systems of meaning, including the systems of cultural beliefs about dreams that we have been discussing. On the other hand, dreaming is an intimately personal experience which expresses with special sensitivity the feelings, attitudes and conflicting desires and aspirations each of us undergoes in our lives as we live them.[17]

Anthropology, of course, is primarily concerned with the cultural pole of dreaming, so that most of the articles give their main attention to the cultural systems of conceptualization of dreaming and their embeddedness in cultural cosmologies and in social processes. The chapters vary in the attention they give to the more personal side of dreaming, but a number of the dreams presented do give an opportunity to comment on what the dreamer may be expressing through them, and how he or she makes use of cultural forms, beliefs and systems of interpretation in doing so.

Emotion in Dreams

One personal aspect of dreams is the role of emotion in them. This role is recognized in the Australian Kukatja concept of dreams as activities of the *kurrunpa* (spirit) which "relates to cognition, volition and to the expression of emotions." The *kurrunpa* resides in the abdominal area, the seat of emotions (this volume, Poirier Chapter 6:111). Lohmann (this volume, Chapter 10:202) observes, "a shiver of fear, awe, or joy" marks the presence of a supernatural being in a dream or waking encounter. What activates the schema (in waking) of "supernatural being" may be a perception of incongruity such as odd behavior of an animal, but most likely it is also presaged or prepared by unconscious sources: a twinge of anxiety or guilt that mobilizes the activation of the schema. Thus Jim Alosi must have been feeling some twinge of anxiety or guilt when he interpreted a bird song as a cannibalistic witch; and Lonika was feeling some anxiety when she dreamed she was washing clothes with her mother and a stone spirit grabbed her by the neck and pulled her under (this volume, Lohmann Chapter 10:194). That the spirit was "like a baby" and the recurring image of "stone" (she struck the *stone spirit* with a *stone*) might be clues, for someone who knew her and her current situation, as to what the guilt or anxiety might have been. Without more context, one can only guess: perhaps anxieties over pregnancy, or issues of sibling rivalry.[18]

Stewart and Strathern (this volume, Chapter 3:45) also acknowledge the personal aspect of dreams and the importance of emotion in dreams. Discussing dreams about the dead, they comment that "dreams become one vehicle by means of which conflicts are actually expressed and dealt with, in particular those conflicts that involve aspects of relationships out of which emotions of jealousy, fear and anger are generated between people."

The intriguing dream reported at Hagen by L., that her mother's deceased co-wife "pressed her body down" on L's "in a suffocating manner" suggests a plethora of conflicting feelings, in addition to cultural significance in terms of her father's ritual relationship with the deceased spouse (this volume, Stewart and Strathern Chapter 3:50). This, and Y's dreams of pregnancy and, later, of angry frustration, cry out for understanding through fuller access to the context of their speech and of their lives.

Relationships: The Anthropologist and the Informant

Two of these papers discuss the dreams of a person, and the context of telling them, in especially rich detail. Wolfgang Kempf and Elfriede Hermann's descriptions of the circumstances in which a young Ngaing man told his dream to Kempf, and especially those in which a young woman told her dream to Hermann, enable one to see clearly the relationship that these dreams expressed to each of the anthropologists, and to bring out the significance of the dreams at a social level as well (this volume, Chapter 4). Douglas Hollan's chapter offers the only explicit discussion of the transference relationship between a Toraja dreamer and himself, achieving an understanding that cast a new light on the significance of the informants communications to Hollan and deepened the understanding of the ethnographic material (this volume, Chapter 9). Both of these papers contribute valuable insights into the dream as a personal communication, and into the articulation between the informant's personal life and the social context in which he or she lived.

Elfriede Hermann's very moving account communicates eloquently a young woman's experience of a traditional initiation, prolonged by the elders' wish to restore traditional forms and to please the anthropologists (this volume, Kempf and Hermann Chapter 4). Visiting Madubang every day in her menarche isolation, she establishes a warm rapport with the young woman, giving her support during a very trying confinement in a narrow, constricted hut. She gives a very astute interpretation to the young woman's dream (to which I will return). The dream Madubang recounts to her demonstrates vividly the girl's response to her support: Madubang's visit, in dream, to an Australian couple who (in dream) adopt her bespeak her affection for her friends, Wolfgang Kempf and Elfriede Hermann, revealing a warm, parental transference to the two of them; she regards herself as their daughter. (This could be so even if the Australian couple in the dream is a real couple of her acquaintance: do not dreams, as the Ambrymese perceive,[19] sometimes misidentify the people that they are about?) At the same time, the fact that her visit to Australia lands her in prison when she shows too much curiosity about the things that are set before her may be chiding Kempf and Hermann: their interest in the traditional puberty ceremony has led to prolonging her "imprisonment" in the seclusion hut. (It is interesting that the dream is more accurate than her waking estimate of the time she has spent in it: after 3 ½ weeks in the hut, she estimates that she has been there 5 ½ weeks, but dreams of 3 ½ weeks in jail.)

The dream that one of the male initiates reports to Wolfgang Kempf suggests similar feelings of solidarity. I have no doubt that Kempf's interpretation is correct; but in addition, Cliff's emphatic comment that the woman in his dream, and the men as well—ancestors—were white, adding "her skin was the same as yours," suggests similar intimate transference feelings to Wolfgang and Elfriede. The white ancestress, too, is a "Miss," he stresses: she is available. An erotic element is added to the significance of the dream.

I say "transference" in both cases because the feelings are not consciously expressed; they are expressed in a displaced form in dreams, probably without conscious awareness that the "Australian couple" and the ancestral woman and men in the dreams stand for the German couple that the dreamers feel warmly toward, as toward their own parents.

The other initiate's dream of driving to the city in a car, wearing socks, shoes and a wristwatch (in place of the *tambaran* dancing decorations that Jethro spoke of?) may have expressed an identification with Wolfgang.

On another level, the phenomenon that Wolfgang Kempf notes, the move of the initiates toward whiteness, associated with power—which Elfriede Hermann also picks up in her empathic interpretation to Madubang—points to just the kind of identification with the white colonizer that Franz Fanon demonstrates so poignantly in *Black Skin, White Masks* (1967). As Elfriede Hermann perceptively hints in her interpretation, Madubang's perception of her blackness as "dirty" also reflects the dynamics of self-diminishing that Fanon points out. The erotic attraction of the white woman (in Cliff's dream) is yet another theme that Fanon develops in the same book.

At yet a third level (and all of these levels may be condensed into the same dream symbols and ritual symbols), again implicit in Wolfgang Kempf's reading of the dreams and the ritual symbols, the white core (of the earth, of the *sariwat* palm tree) suggests the inner core of mother's milk—the feminine/maternal identity that the young men must repudiate, must "wean" themselves from—to be transformed into the black skin of masculinity that makes a tough outer shell, a transformation wrought by the ritual (cf. Herdt 1981). Interestingly, in the superincision ritual the color symbolism is reversed, or at least displaced: the black blood is the female blood, and the "pure male" blood stored in bamboo flasks is red.

The ritual level of meaning having to do with separation from the maternal, the social level of meaning at which whiteness means becoming one with the colonizer, and the expression of transference love toward a white couple taking a parental role in their lives, are woven together in these dreams. The transference to Kempf and Hermann as parent substitutes may be perhaps a kind of ritual parenthood such as occurs in many Brazilian Indian cultures, where a ritual parent substitute is a regular part of the initiation process (e.g., Da Matta 1973, 1982).

Douglas Hollan's contribution is the first to explicitly introduce the concept of transference. In previous work on dreams, Hollan has stressed the differences among Toraja individuals in the dream concepts they hold and in the way they use them to deal with their dreams. The dreams he discusses in this article are all of one informant, a leader who has achieved considerable respect and renown in the community. Yet there is a thread of anxiety that runs through them. Many of the dreams are anxious, either predictions of disaster, though with intimations he would survive it, or dreams of calamity—one ending in his own death—for which he managed to find an interpretation that gave it positive import. Two dreams he himself took as a prediction of his own death, which he averted in one case by taking appropriate action (fleeing the guerillas), in the other by ritual means. One dream was an outright nightmare of spirit attack. Many of the later dreams were responses to Hollan's solicitation of dreams of a certain type, but even the dreams volunteered at the beginning as omens of his success in leadership included at least one anxiety dream. And as he proceeded, they were more and more openly dreams of anxiety; the last three were an outright nightmare (of being throttled by a demon), a dream of ill portent, and a dream that he was killed which he turned positive by interpretation: it meant he would kill many buffalo for feasts.

These dreams, anxious dreams from (most of) which Nene'na Limbong draws a reassuring message, are suggestive of the "examination dreams" which Freud (1953 [1900]:307–310) sees as reassuring reminiscences when faced with a difficult task: one reassures oneself by recalling examinations which at the time seemed formidable, but which one passed successfully. As Hollan (this volume, Chapter 9:180) observes, "the dreams and their interpretations also assert, over and over again . . . that one can persevere and survive even in the face of . . . bodily assaults of all kinds. These," he concludes, "are important and reassuring lessons for a weakening, older man who has been challenged to review his life course and the direction in which it is heading." In this regard, the dream of being stabbed by guerillas is of special significance, for that was a period of great danger to his life, which he survived. Likewise, the dream of falling into the sea, which he interpreted in terms of illness and hospitalization—(and the interpretation must be treated as an integral part of the dream)—refers back to episodes of serious illness which he also survived. The source of the image of vomiting in the second dream is less clear; perhaps it also refers to an episode of illness.[20]

The intensity of the anxiety in the dreams is notable. Many of them involve violence directed at him—he is bombed, stabbed, ordered to jump into the sea, a nightmare of being attacked by a she-demon with long, unbound hair, and on one occasion visited by his father's ghost who wants to carry him off, presumably to *Puya*, the land of the dead. Many of these dreams are given reassuring interpretations as predictions of success, or at least that he would come through illness or the deaths of his parents without "going under," but this does not always succeed in containing the anxiety. The last dream he told was of having his throat cut and his body butchered and distributed like ox-meat. When he first recounted this dream in print, Hollan commented, "Although Nene'na Limbong awoke in horror when he had this dream and although his voice trembled as he recollected it, he was adamant that it was just another dream that accurately foretold his future fortune," representing "the many buffalo he would sacrifice at community feasts" (Hollan 1989:177).

Nene'na Limbong, at least as he presented himself in his interviews with Hollan, was a man driven by anxiety—in this not alone. "He complained to me, as did several other villagers, that he often lay awake at night worrying about how he would pay for both his ritual obligations and his children's education" (Hollan 1989:174). In this article, Hollan recognizes the expression of his anxiety in the transference as a competitive relationship with a vigorous, young and educated anthropologist, whose high status he envies, and from whom he fears disregard if not rejection. Hollan perceptively details the expression of this transference in assertions of his status and power, in actions such as missing an interview then showing up unexpectedly at another time complaining he was being neglected.

Without much longer and deeper interviews—such are the limits of anthropological fieldwork—we cannot come to the roots of this anxiety, this competitive drive, in his early life, or understand the intensity of the anxiety. But it is clear that it was manifested in his relationship with Hollan. Perhaps another element of the "cut or be cut" anxiety might lie in issues such as those raised by Wolfgang Kempf (this volume, Chapter 4): anxieties about the disprisal and condemnation by European or American missionaries—probably anglophone—of the traditional religion to which, it seems, his informant still adhered (could the dream of being ordered to jump in the ocean have reference to baptism?); or anxiety about his status as a colonized subject.

Understanding transference relationship with Nene'na Limbong casts his interviews in a different light, making clear what some of the issues are that are facing him at the stage of life in which he is confronting a young anthropologist, and how that influences how he presents himself and his culture to Hollan. This is an eloquent demonstration of the importance for anthropologists of understanding the dynamics of our relations with our informants: not just what they mean to us, but what we mean to them.

The Continuum of Consciousness: The Place of Dreams

I have left for the end the discussion of Roger Lohmann's theoretical model of the place of dreams in relation to other modes of perception, a proposed model which makes this book an important contribution to dream research as a whole. Lohmann's proposed continuum of modes of consciousness takes dreaming out of the artificial Tart (1969) pigeonhole categorizing of "regular" and "altered" states of consciousness, with dreaming set alongside "trance" and "drug-induced trips" as altered states. By putting "alert" at one extreme, (if we take "alert" to refer to the highly attentive state of a hunter waiting for prey, or an artist focused on the model or scene being painted,) Lohmann's model allows for the fact that daytime waking thought includes many different states of mind, including reverie, introspection, ordinary wakeful inattention, elated effervescence or depression, or that special state that psychoanalysts call "evenly hovering attention," which Freud recommended as the optimum state of mind for an analyst listening to a patient: the attention hovering between what the patient is saying (and *not* saying) and the fantasies that are stirred up in the analyst's own mind by what the patient says—as well as trance states.

Thinking about waking states of mind, it occurs to me that the actual focus of attention on an object out there is a rather small part of what occupies my attention at any waking moment. For the lamp I am seeing right now to have any continuity at all, part of my mind has to be occupied with remembering what it looked like a moment ago, or over the last few minutes, or—for comparison—what it looked like when I first caught sight of it. So, just to maintain a sense of continuity of experience, I must be constantly remembering the recent past: the present moment, then, is a construction built on memories. All this in addition to the schemas which, Lohmann mentions, must take part in my construction of the object as an object—schemas themselves built of memories (this lamp is like that lamp I saw yesterday, like or unlike the lamp I have in my living room or that was by my bed as I grew up).

And then there are the trains of thought that are constantly running through our minds all day (and night too, the sleep researchers tell us); we follow them, lose them, pick them up again, drop them for another . . . and incorporate into them what we see, hear, or sense during the day. Or pick up another train of thought stimulated by something seen or heard, or some event. As I was contemplating Lohmann's model as I was sitting at the table waking up one morning, it struck me that in that state of mind, waking though it may be, outside input of sensory stimuli is mere background for the musings going on in my mind. James Joyce's *Ulysses* is a good corrective for any philosopher of science or psychologist who thinks our waking attention is constantly focused on things in the world around us.

So if the thinking that we undergo during the day, and even our perceptions of things, are so thoroughly embedded in memory and in chains of thought, the disjunction between waking modes of perceiving and dream-perception is even less radical; the continuity between dreaming and waking thought which is emphasized in the dream-alert perception continuum is even greater. Dreams are based almost entirely on memories from the day, but even waking perceptions are constructed on memories.

Sleeping modes of awareness also vary through the night. As I have mentioned in connection with cultural classifications of dreams, mental activity during the night sometimes takes the form of visual/auditory dreams (of greater or lesser vividness), and sometimes comes in trains of thought expressed in words, like daytime trains of thought. Even visual dreams differ, with dreams toward midnight often more fragmentary, absurd and "dreamlike," dreams in the morning just before awakening often longer, more sequential and story-like—and often more connected with current daily life. (Perhaps this is why in many systems of dream interpretation, dreams just before waking are privileged as more accurately predictive than others.) Dream researchers like Rosalind Cartwright find that a train of thought can be traced through the night, expressed alternately in verbal thoughts and, during REM periods, expressed visually in dreams (Cartwright 1977:9, 26–31). Again, we find continuity between waking and sleeping thought.[21]

All this simply reinforces the point that Lohmann makes about dreams as experiences comparable to waking experience; and that intense dream experiences may provide convincing religious (or other) experiences that are "night residues" for daytime thinking. This is a suggestion to be taken seriously in the study of religion—and in other domains as well. In the end, is this so different from Kekulé's use of his dream of snakes biting their tails to come up with the idea of the Benzene ring?[22] Kekulé's Benzene ring can also be considered a night residue.

Notes

1. In the culture I work with in Amazonian Brazil, there is a certain acceptance of this individuality of thought and perception that we repudiate. If you ask a Parintintin what another person thinks about something or someone, even if the person is a close relative or friend, the Parintintin is likely to respond: "He is the one who knows that; ask him." Each person is privy to his own thoughts and perceptions; it is not for another person to pronounce on them.
2. Munn's (1973) work on the role of dreams in the creation of designs in Walbiri bark cloth art is a major exception.
3. Far from seeing dreams as taking part in a hermetically sealed, monadic individual psyche, Freud took seriously the possibility of thought transfer in dreams; see note 12, below.
4. In particular, a dream is a message to the person to whom the dreamer chooses to tell the dream.
5. Tylor (1871 [1924]:441) attributes this practice to the Tagals of Luzon.
6. (Hallowell 1955, 1967; Degarrod 1990; Dentan 1983:30; Gregor 1981; Levy 1973:374; Radcliffe-Brown 1964 [1922]:166–167).
7. The range of meanings of *lalauga* is similar to the range of meanings of *ra'úv* in Kagwahiv language (Kracke 1979:127; 1987:69). In translating a word that refers to the subject of dreaming in mystical terms—as "soul"—we risk overlooking a more direct subjective-descriptive reading of it, as "myself in my dream."
8. Levy (1973:374) comments that "The connection between dream and the deduction of soul and ghost has been anthropological common sense at least since Tylor's *Primitive Culture* in 1871."

9. Several of my Parintintin informants have entered the world of mythology in their dreams. One old man visited in his dream the home of Mbahira, the trickster/culture creator figure of Parintintin myth. A woman dreamed herself in the role of Kagwahivahi, the female protagonist of one of the very racy Parintintin stories (Kracke 1995:187–188). Her father in dream summoned from the sky, to cure his grandson, the sky-dwelling beings called *ikā'nā* (Kracke 1990:152).
10. In a work which will stand as the third major landmark in the psychological and neurological understanding of dreaming, Solms completely reorients the psychoneurological understanding of dreams, challenging the equation of dreaming with periods of rapid eye movement (REM) at night. Hobson (1988) argues that, since REM periods are initiated from the primitive brain stem, and do not involve higher cortical centers, REM—and therefore dreaming—cannot possibly involve higher levels of thinking such as symbolic representation: they cannot have meaning in any form.

    But Solms noted that his own patients with brain injuries that affected their dreaming all had injuries to higher cortical parts of the brain; and further, the neurological patients who had injuries to the brain stem did not stop dreaming. Through a thorough survey of published cases of patients with neurological injuries that stopped or affected their dreaming, he demonstrated that dreaming involves activation of higher brain centers involved in motivation and abstract thinking, completely reversing Hobson's simplistic "activation model" which excludes thinking from dreams.
11. Exceptions are Firth (2001), Meggitt (1962), Stephen (1995), Hollan (1989), and Dentan (1983). I have attempted to be as complete as possible in my description of Parintintin concepts of dreaming in Amazonian Brazil (Kracke 1979, 1999).
12. In papers and articles not widely assigned to analytic candidates in institutes, Freud entertained the possibility of telepathy taking place, and that dreams are an especially propitious medium for it. Though remaining skeptical of telepathy taking place over a great distance, he took seriously the possibility of "thought transfer" between two people near each other: "it may well be that telepathy [in this sense] really exists" (1953 [1925]:136). "The possibility cannot be dismissed of their reaching someone during sleep and coming to his knowledge in a dream" (1953 [1925]:138). In his first published work on the topic, he went so far as to say that "sleep creates favorable conditions for telepathy" (1953 [1922]:219) as "an activity of the unconscious mind" (though he concludes the article with a disclaimer). In the additional lectures he appended to the Introductory Lectures in 1933, he took the position that "it shows no great confidence in science if one does not think it capable of assimilating and working over whatever may perhaps turn out to be true in the assertions of occultists" (1964 [1933]:54–55). I stress this; however, to emphasize that Freud was not at all closed to views of the dream that are at odds with the rationalist tenets of positivist science. He is more in sympathy with Poirier that she thinks he is in her receptiveness to Australian views of the dream.

13. Tonkinson alludes to the differences between individuals in how they conceptualize dreaming—a topic which Hollan has addressed at length in an earlier publication (1989).
14. Though recent study shows that dream-like dreams do occur also in non-REM sleep (Strauch and Meier 1996:135–141).
15. Another parallel with the Parintintin, except that among this Amazonian group it is only shamans who announce their coming birth, and in the dream of a senior shaman.
16. Robbins's very interesting analysis of Urapmin political ethos can be compared with Clastres's (1974) analysis of Amazonian polities as resisting hierarchy, to which he alludes. Clastres saw Guaraní "messiahs" who led pilgrimages to find the "Land Without Evil" as subversive to this resistance. The Tupi were less successful than the Urapmin in neutralizing the hierarchical effects of such religious movements. Compare also Turnbull (1962, 1965) on the BaMbuti.
17. Dreaming in this respect is like all experience of life, but represents this polarity in a particularly vivid way.
18. To have an idea about what the dream means to her, we would need to know more about her life and experiences, about the context of her life at the time she told the dream, and about her relationship with the person to whom she told the dream. The exact verbal context of her telling the dream would also be revealing, including what she talked about before and after it and her own associations to the dream.
19. For SE Ambrymese, "not all dreams are held to be true. For example, the events depicted may be regarded as true but the *dramatis personae* involved as mistaken" (this volume, Tonkinson Chapter 5:89)—a perfect description of the mechanism of displacement!
20. It might also be a dream of feminine identification—a dream of pregnancy.
21. Though Cartwright considers this continuity incompatible with Freud's views on dreams, Freud did not consider dreaming discontinuous with daytime thinking at all. On the contrary, the material of which dreams are made is, in Freud's view, always essentially the thoughts, wishes, "unsolved problems, tormenting worries, overwhelming impressions," uncompleted trains of thought, etc., from the previous day (1953 [1900]:180–81, 554–6)—even if the unconscious wish by which these thoughts are transformed into dreams is an infantile one (1953 [1900]:551–554).
22. See Barrett (2001:86–87).

References Cited

Barrett, Deirdre
2001   The Committee of Sleep. New York: Crown.
Borges, Jorge Luis
1965   [1941] Tlön, Uqbar, Orbis Tertius. *In* Labyrinths. D. Yates and J. Irby, eds. New York: New Directions.

Brown, Michael
1992 [1987] Ropes of Sand: Order and Imagery in Aguaruna Dreams. *In* Dreaming: Anthropological and Psychological Interpretations. B. Tedlock, ed. Pp. 154–170. Santa Fe: School of American Research Press.

Burridge, Kenelm
1995 [1960] Mambu: A Melanesian Millennium. Princeton: Princeton University Press.

Cartwright, Rosalind D.
1977 Night Life: Explorations in Dreaming. Englewood Cliffs: Prentice-Hall.

Cartwright, Rosalind D. and Lynne Lamberg
1992 Crisis Dreaming. New York: Harper Collins.

Clastres, Pierre
1974 Society Against the State. New York: Urizen.

Crapanzano, Vincent
1975 Saints, *Jnun* and Dreams. Psychiatry 38:145–59.
1980 Tuhami: Portrait of a Moroccan. Chicago: University of Chicago Press.

Da Matta, Roberto
1973 A Reconsideration of Apinaje Social Morphology. *In* Peoples and Cultures of Native South America. D. Gross, ed. Pp. 277–293. New York: Doubleday, Natural History Press.
1982 A Divided World: Apinayé Social Structure. Cambridge: Harvard University Press.

Degarrod, Lydia Nakashima
1990 Punkurre and Punfuta, the Nocturnal Spouses: Nightmares and Night Terrors among the Mapuche Indians of Chile. *In* Forms and Uses of Dreams in Amerindian Societies. Symposium for the 46th International Congress of Americanists. M. Perrin, ed. Quito: Abya Editions.

Dentan, Robert Knox
1983 A Dream of Senoi. Special Studies Series, Council on International Studies, State University of New York. Amherst: State University of New York at Buffalo.

Devereux, George
1961 Mohave Ethnopsychiatry and Suicide. Bureau of American Ethnology Bulletin no. 175. Washington: United States Government Printing Office.

Fanon, Franz
1967 Black Skin, White Masks. New York: Grove Press.

Firth, Raymond
2001 Tikopia Dreams: Personal Images of Social Reality. The Journal of the Polynesian Society 110(1):7–29.

Freud, Sigmund
1953 [1900] The Interpretation of Dreams. The Standard Edition of the Complete Psychological Works of Sigmund Freud. Vols. 4–5. London: Hogarth.
1953 [1922] Dreams and Telepathy. International Journal of Psychoanalysis (3):283–305. The Standard Edition of the Complete Psychological Works of Sigmund Freud. Vol. 18:197–220. London: Hogarth.

1953 [1925] Some Additional Notes on Dream Interpretation as a Whole. The Standard Edition of the Complete Psychological Works of Sigmund Freud. Vol. 19:127–138. London: Hogarth.
1964 [1933] Dreams and Occultism. The Standard Edition of the Complete Psychological Works of Sigmund Freud. Vol. 22:31–56. London: Hogarth.

Gregor, Thomas
1981 "Far, Far Away my Shadow Wandered...": Dream Symbolism and Dream Theories of the Mehinaku Indians of Brazil. American Ethnologist (8)4:709–720.

Hallowell, A. Irving
1955 The Self in its Behavioral Environment. *In* Culture and Experience. Philadelphia: University of Pennsylvania Press
1966 The Role of Dreams in Ojibwa Culture. *In* The Dream and Human Societies, G. E. von Grunebaum & R. Caillois, eds. Pp. 267–292. Berkeley: University of California Press.

Herdt, Gilbert
1981 Guardians of the Flutes. New York: Columbia University Press.
1992 [1987] Selfhood and Discourse in Sambia Dream Sharing. *In* Dreaming: Anthropological and Psychological Interpretations. B. Tedlock, ed. Pp. 55–85. Santa Fe: School of American Research Press.

Hobson, J. Allan
1988 The Dreaming Brain. New York: Basic Books.

Hollan, Douglas
1989 The Personal Use of Dream Beliefs in the Toraja Highlands." Ethos 17(2):166–186.

Kracke, Waud
1979 Dreaming in Kagwahiv: Dream Beliefs and their Psychic Uses in an Amazonian Indian Culture. Psychoanalytic Study of Society (8):119–171.
1990 El sueño como vehiculo del poder shamanico. *In* Antropologia y Experiencias del Sueño, M. Perrin, ed. Pp. 145–157. Quito: Ediciones ABYA-YALA.
1995 The Construction of Woman in Parintintin Imaginative Life. Savoir: Revue de Psychanalyse et Analyse Culturelle 2:1–2, issue on La Fémininité, pp. 183–190.

Kroeber, A. L.
1976 [1925] Handbook of the Indians of California. Bureau of American Ethnology Bulletin no. 78. Mineola: Dover Press.

Lacan, Jacques
1988 The Seminar of Jacques Lacan, Book II: The Ego in Freud's Theory. J. Miller, ed. New York: Norton.

Lavie, Peretz
1993 The Enchanted World of Sleep. New Haven: Yale University Press.

Levy, Robert
1973 Tahitians: Mind and Experience in the Society Islands. Chicago: University of Chicago Press.

Meggitt, Mervyn J.
1962   Dream Interpretation among the Mae Enga of New Guinea. Southwestern Journal of Anthropology 18:216–229.
Munn, Nancy
1973   Walbiri Iconography. Chicago: University of Chicago Press.
OED
1971   Compact Edition of the Oxford English Dictionary, Oxford: Oxford University Press, Vol. 1.
Radcliffe-Brown, A. R.
1964   [1922] The Andaman Islanders. New York: Free Press.
Solms, Mark
1997   The Neuropsychology of Dreams. Mahwah: Lawrence Erlbaum Associates.
Spence, Jonathan
1996   God's Chinese Son. New York: Norton.
Stephen, Michele
1995   A'aisa's Gifts: A Study of Magic and the Self. Berkeley: University of California Press.
Strauch, Inge and Barbara Meier
1996   In Search of Dreams: Results of Experimental Dream Research. Albany: State University of New York Press.
Tart, Charles T., ed.
1969   Altered States of Consciousness: A Book of Readings. New York: Wiley.
Turnbull, Colin
1962   The Forest People. Garden City: Doubleday.
1967   Wayward Servants: The Two Worlds of the African Pygmies. Garden City: Natural History Press.
Turner, Victor
1967   Symbols in Ndembu Ritual. Pp. 19–47 *In* The Forest of Symbols. Ithaca: Cornell University Press.
Tylor, E. B.
1924   [1871] Primitive Culture. New York: Brentano's.
1960   [1881] Anthropology. Ann Arbor: University of Michigan Press.
1964   [1878] Researches into the Early History of Mankind. Chicago: University of Chicago Press.
Wagner, Roy
1967   The Curse of Souw. Chicago: University of Chicago Press.
Wallace, Anthony F. C.
1971   Handsome Lake and the Decline of the Iroquois Matriarchate. *In* Kinship and Culture. F. L. K. Hsu, ed. Pp. 367–376. Chicago: Aldine.

About the Contributors

JANE C. GOODALE is Professor Emerita of Anthropology at Bryn Mawr College. Her many publications on the Tiwi include *Tiwi Wives: A Study of the Women of Melville Island, North Australia* (1971). She has also conducted fieldwork among the Kaulong of New Britain. Her publications on the Kaulong include *To Sing with Pigs is Human: The Concept of Person in Papua New Guinea* (1995).

ELFRIEDE HERMANN is Research Fellow the Institute of Ethnology, University of Göttingen. She has done extensive fieldwork on emotions, historicity, and gender among the Ngaing in Papua New Guinea. Her recent fieldwork is among the Banabans of Fiji. Her publications include "'Kastom' Versus 'Cargo Cult': Emotional Discourse on the Yali Movement in Madang Province, Papua New Guinea," in *Cultural Dynamics of Religious Change in Oceania,* edited by T. Otto and A. Borsboom (1997).

DOUGLAS HOLLAN is Professor of Anthropology and Luckman Distinguished Teacher at the University of California, Los Angeles and senior instructor at the Southern California Psychoanalytic Institute. He is the author of numerous articles that explore the relations among psychological and cultural processes. He is also co-author, with Jane Wellenkamp, of *Contentment and Suffering: Culture and Experience in Toraja* (1994) and *The Thread of Life: Toraja Reflections on the Life Cycle* (1996).

IAN KEEN is Reader in the Department of Archaeology and Anthropology at the Australian National University. He has carried out research on kinship, the control of religious knowledge, and relations to country in the context of Aboriginal land claims, among Yolngu of northeast Arnhem Land, in other parts of the Northern Territory of Australia, and in Gippsland, Victoria. His publications include *Being Black* (1988), *Knowledge and Secrecy in an Aboriginal Religion* (1994, 1997), and many articles in journals and edited books.

WOLFGANG KEMPF is Research Fellow at the Institute of Ethnology, University of Göttingen. He has taught at the Universities of Tübingen, Heidelberg, and Göttingen. He has conducted extensive fieldwork on male ritual and religious change among the Ngaing of Papua New Guinea. Most recently he conducted fieldwork among the Banabans of Fiji. His numerous publications include *Das Innere des Äusseren: Ritual, Macht und historische Praxis bei den Ngaing in Papua Neuguinea* (1996).

WAUD KRACKE is Professor of Anthropology at the University of Illinois-Chicago. He specializes in the ethnography of Amazonia and has conducted fieldwork over many years among the Kagwahiv of Brazil. An early interest in leadership has been supplemented by an ongoing focus on dreaming from a psychoanalytic perspective. He is the author of many articles on dreams and *Force and Persuasion: Leadership in an Amazonian Society* (1978).

ROGER IVAR LOHMANN is Assistant Professor of Anthropology at Trent University, having also taught at the University of Wisconsin, Western Oregon University, the College of Wooster, and the University of Toronto. His fieldwork among the Asabano centered on spiritual experiences and changing beliefs. He is the editor of "Perspectives on the Category 'Supernatural,'" a special issue of *Anthropological Forum* 13(2) 2003. His publications include "The Role of Dreams in Religious Enculturation among the Asabano of Papua New Guinea" (*Ethos*, 2000), reprinted in *Dreams: A Reader on Religious, Cultural, and Psychological Dimensions of Dreaming*, edited by K. Bulkeley (2001).

SYLVIE POIRIER is Associate Professor of Social Anthropology at Université Laval. She has carried out fieldwork in Aboriginal communities of the Australian Western Desert and North Central Quebec, comparing their changing relationships to land. She maintains a long-term interest in the anthropology of dreaming. Her writings include *Les jardins du nomade* (1996) and articles on the politics of rituals, ancestrality, and relations to land among contemporary hunters and gatherers.

JOEL ROBBINS is Associate Professor of Anthropology at the University of California, San Diego. He has published on Christianity and changing attitudes toward the environment and development among the Urapmin. He is the author of *Sins Between Cultures: Christianity, Cultural Change, and Moral Torment in a Papua New Guinea Society* (2003).

PAMELA J. STEWART is Research Associate in the Departments of Anthropology and Religious Studies at the University of Pittsburgh. She has been a senior visiting fellow at the International Institute for Asian Studies, Leiden University, and a visiting researcher at the National Museum of Ethnology, Osaka. Her interests include gender studies, political and religious change, and medical anthropology. She conducts research in Papua New Guinea and Europe. Her co-authored books with Andrew J. Strathern include *Humors and Substances: Ideas of the Body in New Guinea* (2001).

ANDREW J. STRATHERN is Mellon Professor of Anthropology at the University of Pittsburgh. His interests are in political and legal anthropology and historical change. The author of many articles, his books include *The Rope of Moka: Big Men and Ceremonial Exchange in Mount Hagen, New Guinea* (1971) and *Voices of Conflict* (1993). His co-authored books with Pamela J. Stewart include *Arrow Talk: Transaction, Transition, and Contradiction in New Guinea Highlands History* (2000). His ongoing research is in Lowland Scotland and Papua New Guinea.

ROBERT TONKINSON is Professor Emeritus of Anthropology at the University of Western Australia, having also taught at the University of Oregon and Australian National University. He has done extensive fieldwork in the Western Desert of Western Australia and in Vanuatu. The author of numerous articles, his books include *The Jigalong Mob* (1974) and *The Mardu Aborigines* (1978, 1991). His interests span social organization, religion (including sorcery), change, gender relations, migration, identity, and the politics of tradition. Recently he has conducted land claim research on behalf of the Aborigines with whom he worked.

Index

afterlife, 2, 64, 157, 215, 216
agency, 127, 133, 138, 141–143
Ambrym, 88–89
ancestors, 45–47, 62, 69–70, 78, 91, 95, 120, 127–134, 139–143, 150–151, 163–164, 174, 194, 216, 219, 221, 223, 225
anthropology of dreaming, 2–6, 108; methods of, 5–6, 109, 171–2, 217
Asabano, 5, 38n2, 88, 190–192, 215, 218, 221
Australia, 83n8, 93, 95, 128, 132, 141, 149, 150, 162, 221; Aborigines, 88, 93, 98, 109–113, 128, 129, 140, 143, 221
authority, 22–23, 27, 35–36, 127, 184; big man vs. great man, 36–37; charismatic *see* charisma; legitimate, 22–23, 35, 95; traditional, and the denial of creativity, 139–142; utilitarian, 35; *see also* dream narratives, political uses

Barrett, D., 232n22
Barth, F., 25
Basso, E. B., 4
Bauman, R., 109
Bercovitch, E., 203
Berndt, R. M., 88, 123n13, 130, 131, 135
Biesele, M., 117, 123n12
Bird-David, N., 110, 114, 121
Blackwood, P., 91
Bloch, M., 127, 139–141
body/mind division, 109
Bos, R., 130–132
Bourguignon, E., 2, 23, 198, 206
brain-mind, 5–6
Brazil, 11, 214, 222, 226, 230n1
Brightman, R., 5
Brown, M. F., 4, 122, 218
Bulkeley, K., 2, 5
Burridge, K., 20, 87–88, 99, 101, 222

Callois, R., 1
cargo cults, 20–21, 23
Cartwright, R., 217–218, 221, 230, 232n21
Cawte, John, 131, 132
charisma, 20–24, 28, 139, 222; defeat of, 33, 35, 223; fleeting, 32–33; limits of, 38
Charsley, S., 4
Chowning, A., x, 98, 102 n9
Christianity, 27, 45–46, 63, 66, 88–91, 130, 189, 195–199, 205, 213, 216, 223
churches, 26, 29–34, 45, 57, 89–91, 108, 130, 132, 151, 192, 197, 199, 201, 222
Christie, M., 127, 135–137, 142, 144n8
Clastres, P., 39, 232 n16
Clunies, R., 138, 144n6
Codrington, R. H., 2, 101 n3
colonialism, 38, 62, 66–67, 226, 228
conception theory, dream, 118, 222; *see also* spirit-children
consciousness, 189–191, 213; alert, 202–206; altered states, 206, 216; attention in, 228–230; range of, 206–207, 228–230; *see also* dreaming; spirit possession; trance
cosmology, 80, 88–89, 93, 97–99, 107, 113, 128–129, 143, 192, 212, 221–222
Crapanzano, V., 183, 220
creativity, 102n8, 127, 142, 143; denial of, 95, 133–138, 221
curing, 26, 88, 92, 111–114, 214, 131, 163–164, 198, 201; *see also* shamanism
Curley, R. T., 5, 192

dance, 34, 69, 89, 94–96, 120, 135, 138, 150, 153, 159–161, 165n9, n12, 194
D'Andrade, R. G., 2, 207
dead, the, 2–3, 25, 43–57, 78, 90, 96, 113, 131, 141–142, 179, 192–195, 202, 204–205, 216–217, 219 224, 227

death, 48, 55, 89, 118–119, 131, 152–154, 178–180, 184, 194, 213, 226, 227
De Certeau, M., 67, 82n3
Degarrod, L. N., 230n6
Dentan, R. K., 230n6, 231n11
desires, 2, 20, 88, 169–170, 223
Devereux, G., 183, 220
displacement, 232n19
divination, 9, 49, 88, 90–93, 97–99
Domhoff, G. W., 4
Dougherty, J., 83
dream, ix, 1; bizarreness, acceptance of, 2; categories, 25–28, 115, 219, 220; enculturation, 109–110, 116, 200, 202; incubation, 53, 65, 131
dream interpretation, 2, 4, 5, 25, 43–44, 53–55, 62, 77–79, 121, 176, 180, 218, 225, 230; as precursor to events, 65–66, 71, 110, 116–118; as prophetic, 26, 45, 89, 172; opposite meaning, 65, 177, 226–227; specialists, 44, 52, 174, 176, 197
dream narratives, 4, 6, 43, 62–63, 79, 80, 109–110, 218; as entertainment, 110, 115–116; influences on, 81, 121, 185, 207; political uses, 34, 96; preoccupations in, 170; religious uses, 18, 26, 94, 112; willingness to share, 114–116, 192
dream self, 64–65, 214; identified with others, 95–96
dream-spirit, 9, 92–96, 133
dream traveling, ix, 11, 51, 77, 80–81, 93, 112, 113, 214; sense of motion in, 1; "bad," 92; bodily, 129; flight, 4, 92, 192; in groups, 93; to "increase sites," 93; walking, 112; walking on water, 192
dreaming, 2–6; aesthetics, 110; art, 116, 230n2; biology, 1, 5; to connect with the world, 124; and cultural change, 66; and death, 2, 118–119, 131, 173, 174, 178, 180, 194, 213, 215, 226; cultural inputs, 1, 3, 6, 44, 78, 87–88, 169, 186n6, 189, 208, 221, 223; danger, 46, 49, 96, 163, 195, 220; discourse, 63, 108, 114, 120; history and, 45, 62; information from, 5, 24–27, 47, 91, 94, 96, 192–93, 215; and the lifecycle, 62, 180; and reflections, 53; lucid, 6; and music: 65, 94, 113, 119, 135; power acquired in, 3–4, 23–24, 28, 62, 79, 88, 90, 111, 221; private or not, 3–4, 26, 87, 108–109, 113, 212; religious uses, 2–3, 5, 8, 33–34, 51, 73, 88, 94, 97, 129–132, 171, 190, 193, 197, 212; safety in, 46, 93, 96, 190, 192, 195; scenario shifts in, 1, 207; similarity to waking, 57, 206–207, 228–230; as social process, 110; theories of, ix-x, 2, 3, 5, 8, 25, 44, 107–109, 111–114, 213–219; value of, 3, 45, 98–99, 109–112, 116, 120, 185, 195, 222
dreamings, 158–162
dreams; anthropologists', 6; anxiety, 55, 96, 178, 207, 218–220, 224, 226–227; children's, 193–194, 224; of cities, 70–73, 75, 77–78, 226; as commodities, 99; dangerous, 49, 64, 92–93, 96, 163, 174, 195, 220; of the dead, 2–3, 23, 44, 49, 50, 78, 113, 129, 142, 168, 192, 194–195, 215–216, 219, 227; eating in, 65, 71, 131; as evidence, 2, 90, 196, 213; experience of, 3, 44–46, 53, 63–65, 88–89, 94–95, 99, 113, 119, 129, 142, 175, 192, 194, 206–208, 211–214, 223; and generation, 98; "good," 46, 115, 173; hearing in, 4, 45, 56, 113, 196; hunting, 26, 119, 151, 156, 193, 195–196, 218; lying about, 89; as objects, 110; as omens, 27–28, 45, 88, 117, 155, 171, 176, 185n1, 219; of places, 1–2, 26, 52, 113, 115, 156, 201; as "real," 2, 5, 8, 89, 92, 101n2, 117, 163, 175–176, 191–194, 208, 215–216; seeing in, 2, 8, 25, 26, 44, 53, 65, 89, 116, 120, 175, 190, 195, 213; sexual, 129, 155, 220; telepathy in, 112, 231n12; transformation, 2, 78–79, 232n21; wish fulfillment, 3, 5, 54, 77, 169–170, 232; witches in, 49, 190, 194–195
dreamscapes, 62, 79–82, 196, 231n9, 214
Dreamtime, The, 92–99, 107, 110–111, 119, 129, 150–153, 164, 221
Duna, 47–49
Dussart, F., 102, 123n13

education, 73, 137–138, 185, 228
Eggan, D., 3
Elkin, A. P., 102n7
emotions, 2, 45, 90, 111–114, 135, 141, 175–176, 181, 202, 205, 214, 223–224
epistemologies, 28, 108–110, 121–122, 129, 212, 221
Epstein, A. L., 5

ethnography, 53, 55
Europeans, 5, 62, 72, 78–81, 88, 143, 162, 195, 197, 202. 214, 228
Evans-Pritchard, E. E., 141
Ewing, K., 122n3, 183
exchange, 4, 21, 36–37, 57, 82, 98, 109, 119, 141
experience, 5–6, 45–46, 69, 71, 87, 94, 108, 120, 122 n1, 136–138, 163, 170, 186n6, 189, 206; others' unobservable, 212–213; out-of-body, ix, 89, 201

Fabre, D., 108
Firth, R., 2, 231 n11
Fortes, M., 47, 141
Foucault, M., 79–80
Frater, M., 89, 91
Freud, S., 3, 108–109, 207, 212–213, 217, 227, 228–229, 230n3, 231n12, 232n21

gender, 43, 74, 79, 144, 185, 190, 200–201
genital operations, 67–68
George, M., 6
ghosts, 47–53, 91, 131, 141, 148, 154–156, 161, 191, 204, 215, 219–220, 227, 230n8
Gillen, F. J., 128
global-local conflation, 63
glossolalia, 97, 191, 205
Glowczewski, B., 123n13
Godelier, M., x, 36
Goodale, J. C., ix, x, 5, 10, 46, 128, 133, 143, 148, 149, 153–160, 162, 164, 165, 220–222, 237
Goulet, J.-G., 6
Graham, L. R., 108
Grau, A., 152
Gregor, T. A., 5, 230

Hagen, 43–46, 50–55, 224
Hallowell, A. I., 216, 230n6
Hamilton, A., 93
Harris, S., 137–138, 144
Hart, C. W. M., 149, 152
Hastrup, K., 62
Hayashi, I., 44
hegemony, 62, 81
Herdt, G., 5, 43, 63, 81, 110, 122n5, 222–223, 226
Hermann, E., x, 9, 44, 60, 61, 64–66, 73, 78, 88, 130, 183, 202, 208, 224–226, 237

Herr, B., 5
heterotopias, 80
Hiatt, L. R., 138, 144n6
Hobson, J. A., 1, 5, 212, 231n10
Hollan, D., ix, x, 5, 10, 62, 81, 87, 90, 94, 168–171, 178–180, 186, 195, 208, 218–228, 231n11, 232n13, 237
Howard, A., 5
Hughes, C. C., 175
Hunt, H. T., 109, 213
hypercognition, 186n6
hypocognition, 178, 186

imagination, 2, 5, 47, 76, 82, 83n9, 108, 143, 181, 189, 191, 206–208
individualism, 109, 230n1
Indonesia, 1, 170–171, 173, 178, 223
Ingold, T., 110, 113, 122n6
innovation, 67, 88, 99, 101, 120, 123n13
intentionality, 135–138
intersubjective context, 180–183
Irwin, L., 2

Jackson, M., 43
Jedrej, M. C., 1, 2, 62, 63
Jigalong, 92, 113
Jorgensen, D., 25, 36, 37

Kagwahiv, 11, 230n7, 231n9
Keen, I., ix, x, 10, 65, 92, 95, 101, 120, 126, 127, 130, 133, 134, 138, 141, 143n3, 144, 150, 162, 216, 221, 223, 237
Keesing, R., 82, 122n5
Kempf, W., x, 9, 44, 61, 66, 67, 70, 71, 82n2, 83n4, n9, 88, 130, 183, 202, 208, 224, 225–226, 228, 238
Kennedy, J. G., 2, 170
Kilborne, B., 2
kinship, 3, 29, 37, 44–45, 78, 99, 141–142, 152, 165n9, 179, 185n2, 194, 202, 215
Knopoff, S., 135
knowledge, 3, 25, 45, 62, 88, 111, 163, 192, 202, 212; control of, 34, 120–122
Kohn, T., 5
Kracke, W., x, 3–5, 11, 183–184, 211, 230n7, 231n9, n10, 238
Kroeber, A. L., 221
Kulick, D., 83

Lacan, J., 212

land, 114, 130, 156, 158, 196, 221; cared for by dreaming, 93, 113; consubstantiality with person, 113
Langness, L. L., 2, 170
Larcom, J., 91
Lattas, A., 4, 5, 80
Lavie, P., 217, 221
law, ancestral, 107, 110, 127, 139–142
Lawrence, P., 20, 23, 61, 65, 78, 82n2, 83n9, 98
Leavitt, S. C., 5
Le Goff, J., 108
Lepowsky, M., x, 195
LeVine, S., 5, 183
Levy, R. L., 5, 178, 186n6, 219, 220, 230n6, n8
Liep, J., 36
Lincoln, J. S., 3
Lindstrom, L., 88, 94
linguistics, 4, 45, 63, 90, 111, 122n8, 135–138, 149, 186n6, 192, 213, 223, 230n7
Lohmann, R. I., ix, x, 1–7, 19, 23, 38, 46, 63–65, 82, 83, 88, 90, 91, 122, 123, 129, 130, 136, 143, n1, 176, 185, 188–190, 194, 195, 201, 202, 212, 213, 215, 216, 218, 219, 221, 224, 228–230, 238
Luhrmann, T. M., 6
Lutkehaus, N. C., 82

MacKnight, C. C., 135
Maddock, K., 92
Mageo, J. M., ix, 5
magic, 4, 68, 86, 91, 92, 96, 113, 197
Malinowski, B., 3, 4
Mannheim, B., 5
Mardu, 87, 92–96, 100, 113, 135, 214, 216
Marxism, 20–21
Mauss, M., 55, 57
medicine, 67, 75, 78–80, 91–92
medieval Europe, 108
Meggitt, M. J., 43, 88, 93, 231n11
Meier, B., 217, 232n14
Meigs, A. S., 43
Melanesia, 2–3, 8, 9, 19–24, 35–36, 62, 82n1, 87–94, 97, 98–99, 101n1, n2, n3, 102n9, 110, 122n4, 123n9, 139, 163, 164, 195, 218, 219, 221, 222

memory, 28, 91, 136–137, 144, 150, 180, 191, 197, 229; of dreams, 65, 109, 118, 172, 176, 180, 184–185, 207, 222
menstruation, 62, 73,–74, 225
Merrill, W. L., 5, 192
millenarianism, 24–27, 34, 88, 94, 97
mind, 5, 6, 87, 108–111, 135–138, 162, 175, 180, 207, 212, 215, 229, 231n12
missionaries, 5, 9, 62–66, 73, 92, 111, 123, 128, 151, 191, 208, 228
morality, 31, 46, 53, 66, 80, 99
Morphy, H., 92, 127, 128, 130, 135, 138, 141
Munn, N. D., 95–96, 102n8, 123n11, n13, 127, 128, 140, 143, 221, 230n2
Myers, F. R., 114, 129, 133, 137
myth-dream, 88, 222
myths, 65, 68–70, 88–91, 115, 128–130, 150, 189–192, 196–197, 200, 216, 231n9

Ngaing, 61–63
nightmares, 28, 50, 101n4, 115, 131, 174–175, 177, 194, 227; see also night terrors
"night residues," 11, 189, 206–208, 216, 217, 230
night terrors, 175, 219–220

Obeyesekere, G., 169, 223
offerings, 176, 194, 196, 201, 204; dreams connected with, 193
O'Flaherty, W., 122n3
old age, 62, 179–180
Olwig, K. F., 62
"ontology of dwelling," 110, 122n6
"openness," 111–112

Papua New Guinea, 3, 6, 20, 43, 73, 164
Parman, S., 43
Patterson, M., 89, 91
Paul, R. A., 3
Peile, A. R., 111
perception, 4, 25, 43, 90, 138, 190, 206, 207, 212–213, 224, 226, 228–229, 230n1
person, 43, 63–64, 108–110, 114, 121, 122n4, 127, 136–138, 142
phenomenology, 43, 45–46, 206
Pilling, A., 149, 152, 164n2
Poirier, S., ix, x, 4, 9–10, 64, 92, 94, 106, 107, 113, 114, 116, 120, 122, 128, 129,

143, 150, 162, 185, 208, 212–214, 217–218, 222, 224, 231n12, 238
politics, *see* authority
Povinelli, E. A., 112
prayer, 26–28, 32, 50, 57, 90, 131–132, 191–201, 205; and dreams, 193
psychoanalysis, 5, 11, 108, 228
psychology, 3, 43, 108, 169, 178, 217, 229, 231n10

race, 5, 67–75, 78–80, 143, 163, 181, 195, 225–226; ancestors associated with whites, 78, 195
Radcliffe-Brown, A. R., 230 n6
Reid, J., 102n7
relationships, 3, 5, 26, 45, 50, 57, 110, 121, 137, 150, 191, 200–201; anthropologists and subjects, 81, 170, 181–183; dreamers and dream-characters, 115, 197, 224; transference, 224–228
religion, 2, 3, 5, 8, 23, 46, 64, 88, 91, 127, 130, 171, 189, 213
religious; conversion and dreams, 90; "revival," 24, 131, 132, 191
revelations in dreams, 90, 94, 120, 133; access to, 99; evidence supporting, 56, 94; ownership of, 91

revitalization movements, 222
Riches, D., 43
ritual, 27, 61, 93, 99, 135, 139–142, 148, 161, 201; initiation, 66–68, 73–74, 226; originating in dreams, 94–95, 99, 102n8, 112, 120, 123n13, 216, 221
Rivers. W. H. R., 3
Robbins, J., ix, x, 8, 18, 19, 24–26, 29, 34, 37, 39 n3, 65, 82, 88, 94, 98, 101, 123 n9, 129, 139, 163, 176, 191, 192, 218, 223, 232n16, 238
Robinson, G., 159
Róheim, G., 5, 94–95
Roscoe, P. B., 82

sacra, 133, 138, 142, 144n6
sacrifice, 45–50, 55–57, 178, 227
schemas, 207, 224
Schieffelin, E. L., 23
Schluchter, W., 35
secrecy, 4, 56, 66–69, 72, 82n2, 83n6, 91, 93, 95, 102n8, 113, 190, 192, 203

secularity, 89
self, 1, 43, 44, 63–64, 78–79, 96, 113, 122, 136, 212–214; *see also* dream self
Seligman, C. G., 3
Sered, S. S., 200
Seremetakis, C. N., 6
shamanism, 2–3, 5, 36, 37, 198, 200–201, 202, 214, 215, 232n15; *see also* curing
Shaw, R., 1, 2, 5, 62, 63
Shulman, D., 1
Simons, R. C., 175
sleep, 1, 32, 49, 64, 90, 111, 153, 156, 174, 190, 207, 211–214, 218, 221, 229, 230, 232n14; places of, influence on dreams, 55, 62, 90, 113–114, 157
Slotte, I., 130–132
social freedom vs. constraint, 99
sociology, 22
Solms, Mark, 217, 231 n10
songs, 42, 47, 49, 89, 94, 113, 115, 129–131, 134–135, 140–142, 153, 159–161
sorcery, 4, 86–91, 97, 101n2, 116, 163
souls, 4, 5, 38–39n2, 52, 175, 190, 198, 204, 214, 216–217, 230n7; loci of, 47, 90, 111, 196, 206, 215; mobility of, 2–3, 53, 64, 108, 176, 192, 200–201, 213
space, 44, 61–63, 69, 75–80, 113, 193
Spence, J., 222
Spencer, B., 128
spirit-children, 96–97, 152; in dreams, 118, 156, 222
spirit-familiars, 90, 92
spirit possession, 5, 34, 95, 101, 198, 199, 207; gender differences in, 200–201; by spirit-children, 96–97
spirits, 2–3, 5, 25–26, 42–49, 62–65, 82n2, 90–93, 111–114, 153–154, 159, 175–176, 189–208, 214–217, 219–220, 224
Stanner, W. E. H., 88, 92, 99
status, 22, 35, 81, 88, 98, 139, 170, 171, 177–178, 182–183, 228; legitimacy from dreams, 23, 99, 186n5, 223
Stephen, M., 2, 4, 5, 19, 23–24, 43, 62–65, 83, 88, 90, 92, 98, 99, 101n2, 214, 220, 231n11
Stewart, C., 2
Stewart, Pamela J., ix, x, 5, 8, 25, 42–47, 49, 51, 65, 194, 215, 218, 219, 224, 238–239

Strathern, A. J., ix, x, 5, 8, 22, 23, 25, 35–37, 42–47, 49, 51, 65, 194, 215, 218, 219, 224, 239
Strathern, M., 114, 122n4
Strauch, I., 217, 232n14
Strauss, H., 44, 53, 55, 57
Stroumsa, G. G., 1
supernatural beings, 23, 217; encounters with, 23, 25, 141, 189–192, 198, 202, 213, 215, 224; loci, 3, 47, 190, 206–208
symbolism, 127, 140, 143, 163, 169, 223, 226, 231n10; blood, 54, 67–68, 226; in dreams, manipulation of, 5, 19, 65, 66, 109, 142, 176, 192–193; inside/outside, 70–72, 226; light/dark, 66, 78
syncretism, 53, 213

taboos, 44, 65, 72, 74, 91, 154, 161, 190
Tamisari, F., 130, 141
Tart, C. T., 228
Tedlock, B., 1, 2, 4, 6, 43, 62, 63, 65, 81, 108, 170
Tikopia, 2
Tischner, H., 44, 53–55, 57
Tiwi, 10, 133, 143, 149, 152, 220–222
Toner, P., 135
Tonkinson, M., 102 n7
Tonkinson, R., ix, x, 5, 9, 23, 64, 65, 86, 87, 89–94, 97, 98, 100, 101–102n6, 102n7, n9, 113, 128, 133, 135, 150, 163, 195, 208, 214, 216, 232n13, n19, 239
Toraja, 10–11, 169, 171, 218, 221, 223, 225, 226
tradition/custom, 23, 45–46, 66–68, 73–74, 115, 139, 158, 191, 208
trance, 5, 65, 69–70, 73, 80, 83, 97, 189–191, 206–208, 213, 215, 216, 228–229; causes of, 83 n6, 95, 197–199, 201
tricksters, 101n5, 118, 165n4, 231n9
Trobriand Islands, 4
Trompf, G. W., 45, 102 n9

Turner, V., 223
Tuzin, D., 2, 5, 43, 202
Tylor, E. B., 2, 108, 207, 213–216, 230n5, n8

Urapmin, 8, 18, 19, 24, 94, 191, 218–219, 232n16

Van de Castle, R. L., 43
Vanuatu, 2, 87, 90–92
Venbrux, E., 152, 157, 164
Vicedom, G. F., 53–55, 218
visions, 24–28, 34, 45, 55, 97, 130–135, 143n4, 191, 198, 199, 216, 218, 221, 222
volition, 111, 202, 214, 224
Volkman, T., 171
von Grunebaum, G. E., 1

Wagner, R., 43, 88, 94, 215
waking, 1–5, 32, 47, 53, 57, 63–65, 69, 77, 79, 96, 111, 116, 133, 155, 175, 176, 189, 191, 194–197, 201–208, 213, 216, 221, 224, 225, 228, 229, 230
Wallace, A. F. C., 4, 222
Warner, W. L., 130, 131, 135
Weber, M., 20–24, 35, 127, 139, 142, 223
Weiner, J., 5
Wellenkamp, J. C., 170, 178–181, 186
West, the, 62, 73, 80, 108–109, 127, 208, 212, 218
Williams, F. E., 3
Wilson, B., 21–22, 35–36, 38
Winkelman, M., 198
Wirrimanu, 111–113, 118, 122, 122n7, 123n9
witchcraft, 45, 49, 201, 205
Wolowitz, H., 5
worldviews, 8, 102; cosmocentric vs. anthropocentric, 109
Worsley, P., 20–22

Yali movement, 66, 77–78
Yolngu, 10, 95, 127–128, 143n2, 162, 216